Preventing Suicide

Preventing Suicide

The Solution Focused Approach

John Henden

BA (Hons), RMN, Dip Couns (Univ of Bristol), MBACP

John Wiley & Sons, Ltd

Chichester • New York • Weinheim • Brisbane • Singapore • Toronto

Other Wiley Editorial Offices

John Wiley & Sons Inc., 111 River Street, Hoboken, NJ 07030, USA

Jossey-Bass, 989 Market Street, San Francisco, CA 94103-1741, USA

Wiley-VCH Verlag GmbH, Boschstr. 12, D-69469 Weinheim, Germany

John Wiley & Sons Australia Ltd, 42 McDougall Street, Milton, Queensland 4064, Australia

John Wiley & Sons (Asia) Pte Ltd, 2 Clementi Loop #02-01, Jin Xing Distripark, Singapore 129809

John Wiley & Sons Canada Ltd, 6045 Freemont Blvd, Mississauga, ONT L5R 4J3, Canada

Wiley also publishes its books in a variety of electronic formats. Some content that appears in print may
not be available in electronic books.

Library of Congress Cataloging-in-Publication Data

Henden, John.
   Preventing suicide: the solution focused approach/John Henden.
      p. cm.
   Includes bibliographical references and index.
   ISBN 978-0-470-51808-3 (cloth) – ISBN 978-0-470-51809-0 (pbk.: alk. paper)
   1. Suicide–Prevention. I. Title.
   HV6545.H373 2008
   362.28'7–dc22

                                                                        2008009592

British Library Cataloguing in Publication Data

A catalogue record for this book is available from the British Library

ISBN 978-0-470-51808-3 (hbk) 978-0-470-51809-0 (pbk)

Typeset in 11/13pt Times Roman by Thomson Digital.

Printed and Bound in Singapore by Markono Print Media Pte Ltd

This book is printed on acid-free paper

To all my clients over the past 33 years, from whom I have learnt so much about how to be helpful and useful to people in distress.

Contents

About the Author   ix

Foreword   xi

Acknowledgments   xiii

1 How to Use This Book   1

2 The Book's Style and Purpose   5

3 Defining Suicide and Self-Harm   23

4 Current Service Provision: Risk Assessment,
   Management and Medication   31

5 Other Approaches to Helping the Suicidal   47

6 What is Solution Focused Brief Therapy?   67

7 Suicide Encounters: The Crucial First Ten Minutes   109

8 The Solution Focused Approach in Working with
   the Suicidal   121

9 Case Study: Reg and 'The Demons Calling from the Deep'   151

10 Some More Case Vignettes   177

11 Where Do We Go From Here?   189

Appendix 1   Flow Diagram for an Episode of Treatment   **199**

Appendix 2   Training Workshops   **203**

References   **205**

Author Index   **218**

Index   **223**

About the Author

John Henden is an internationally known and well-respected workshop presenter and trainer, who has a special interest in various challenging applications of the solution focused approach to psychological problems. The subject of suicide is one such interest.

John, having gained a first degree in psychology, worked in UK mental hospitals, along with many hundreds of other psychology graduates in the 1970s, to bring about positive change. During his NHS career, he had two papers published on the changing language of mental health and presented an early paper on this subject at a mental health promotion conference.

After 22 years in the UK National Health Service as both a practitioner and a manager, John set up a training, counselling and consultancy partnership providing a wide range of products and services to both public and private sectors.

John Henden is a counsellor and psychotherapist and over time has specialised in couples work, drug and alcohol dependency, and working with abuse and trauma.

It is his specialised approach to suicide prevention which has gained most public attention over the last few years. He has presented workshops at conferences; run training courses in several countries; and has had numerous suicidal clients on which to field-test the radical tools and techniques he outlines. Suicide rates within mental health services have been reduced significantly in areas where this new approach has been applied.

John has a personal interest in the subject, as he had strong suicidal thoughts as a child; lost a cousin to suicide; and witnessed an exceptionally high number of suicides within formal mental health services.

As a trainer and workshop presenter, John Henden has an energising and inspirational teaching style which incorporates a high level of humour, despite the seriousness of the subject.

As a solution focused practitioner, John never ceases to be amazed at how its effective and well-structured approach lends itself to the widest possible range of difficulties with which practitioners are presented.

John Henden is among one of the leading innovators within his field, having developed some interesting ideas and techniques of his own: 'leapfrogging' the problem; 'the five o'clock rule'; 'the solution focused feelings tank'; and, 'beating the "if only …" monster'.

Having had various articles and papers published over his long career, he has at last been persuaded to get all his ideas on suicide prevention out in book form.

Foreword

This book reminds me of a story that touched me deeply. It was told by Heather Fiske, a wise and soulful family therapist. Heather heard this story (Fiske, 2008) from a young Canadian aboriginal man in the context of his speaking about suicide deaths in his community and family, and describing his personal struggle to find reasons to carry on.

In the story, a young man is confiding to his grandfather about feelings of despair. He tells Grandfather that he has next to nothing in his life – no job, no marketable skills for getting a job, and that he has been recently rejected by the girl he loves. He tells Grandfather that half of the young people with whom he grew up are now already dead by suicide and that most of the rest are feeling hopeless like he is, and it is hard for them to find reasons to go on. Instead they sit around and get stoned or drunk. Many nights he has joined them. Why should he not?

His grandfather listens thoughtfully for a long time. Finally he tells his grandson: "Your despair is a wolf. This wolf is very powerful. This wolf will kill you, and it will eat your soul. But hope is also a wolf, just as powerful, and it will fight the wolf of despair for you." And then he stops.

Naturally the grandson wants more of an answer and so he protests: "Grandfather, please tell me—I NEED to know! Which wolf wins the fight? Which wolf survives?" And his grandfather answers: "The one that you feed."

I am confident that reading this book will help therapists and other care givers discover further ways to help their clients nourish (feed) hope.

Yvonne Dolan, Director

The Instititute for Solution-focused Therapy, Highland, IN. U.S.A.
Fiske, Heather (2008). *Hope in Action: Solution-focused Conversations About Suicide.* Philadelphia, PA: The Haworth Press/ Taylor-Francis Group.

Acknowledgments

First and foremost I would like to thank the three unnamed past attendees of my training workshops who, quite independently, urged me to write this book.

The work became 'an ongoing project' for over four years. Over this time I have consulted various friends and colleagues about how best to present my thoughts and ideas.

I am grateful to members of the Bristol Solutions Group: Kate Hart, Mark McKergow, Jenny Clarke, Alasdair Macdonald and Harry Procter, for their various comments and suggestions about how both to select and present the material.

My thanks go out to my AMED Learning Set colleagues: Hazel Valentine, Esther Cameron, Colin Heyman, Gerald Conyngham, Ginny Brink, Anita Hayne and Di Aldrich, who have been very understanding, each time I have raised particular points about the project's impact on me; my 'day-job'; and the possible implications it may have within the field. Their well-targeted interventions have been appreciated.

I am grateful to my wife, Lynn, particularly, who has listened to my ideas on the subject from the outset. At each twist and turn, she has been support-ive and continued to encourage me – especially during the intensive research and writing spells, when I have gone away to one of the several retreats, for peace, quiet, inspiration and study. I am grateful, too, for her forbearance when chapters of the book and various papers have spilled out from the study into many other parts of our home.

I am especially grateful to Ginny Brink, over the past three years. She was helpful in the early days with her advice on the overall structure of the work and specifically with regard to some chapters. I have appreciated her willing-ness to be sounded out on particular points during the middle part. She has been of great help, too, in the latter stages, in both coaching and encouraging me at various 'low' points.

My thanks go out to Chuffy Jenkins, who has a particular way of inspiring and encouraging people – both in her job and amongst her friends. I have felt the benefit of this quality when, at various times, we have discussed the project. I am grateful, also, for the use of her home during the research stage.

I am thankful to Kate Hart, who has been a great help to me during both the research and writing stage. Her 'little shed by the sea' with its tranquillity and views across the Severn Estuary was the location for much of the note-taking and writing over some two and a half years.

The helpful suggestions and peer advice I received during the early part of 2007 from Harry Procter was invaluable in both ensuring my overzealousness was curbed and that the work was positioned better within the specific academic field. Without his help on the original proposal, the book might not have reached a wider audience. My thanks go out latterly to Harry for reading and commenting on various chapters prior to submission to the publishers.

I am grateful to another BSG member particularly – Alasdair Macdonald, who has been able either to provide me with references and research findings off-the-cuff, or has pointed me in the right direction. Alasdair has not only saved me a great deal of time, but has also been an encouragement in my pulling together of the project during the final months.

I reserve particular thanks to my secretary, Alison Wright, who has persevered long into the afternoons to word-process the whole book from a handful of mini-cassette tapes! Some chapters and sections have undergone many revisions and I am thankful for her patience with the process. Another "thank you" to Dawn Wesley for finding some creative moments during her busy schedule, to construct the diagrams.

My final thanks go to John Wiley & Sons and particularly to Nicole Burnett and Sarah Tilley who have encouraged me with their emails and have shown much patience ahead of the manuscript's delivery.

1

How to Use This Book

Whether you are a healthcare professional, an academic, advice-line volunteer, or someone who is feeling suicidal at the present time, you will find this book helpful.

If you are a healthcare professional (general practitioner, psychiatrist, psychologist, counsellor, therapist, mental health nurse, social worker, or another member of either a primary care team or a specialist mental health team); and, have already a basic grounding in solution focused brief therapy, then you might find it most helpful or useful to go straight to Chapter 8. Here you will find out about the specialised solution focused tools and techniques and see how they are applied to the suicidal service user.

If you have no previous knowledge about solution focused brief therapy and want to learn about it in a nutshell, then you might like to begin at Chapter 6, before picking up on the specialised techniques in Chapter 8.

You might be inquisitive as to how the solution focused approach to preventing suicide sits alongside other approaches and models of working. You might be from an established tradition (e.g. biomedical, cognitive behavioural, person-centred, etc.) and are curious as to how solution focused compares and contrasts with your own way of working. A number of other models are set out in Chapter 4. The author is respectful of other ways of working: all have validity.

If your interest in the subject is purely academic and you are on a journey of discovery within the wider subject of 'suicidology', then you might like to begin at the first chapter, 'The Book's Style and Purpose'.

You may be a tutor running a counselling or psychotherapy course, either wanting to understand the solution focused approach a little more and/or wanting to see how you might teach the tools and techniques herein to your students. You will find the book easy to follow and understand, and will find the many examples and sections of counsellor-client dialogue helpful in learning about which techniques to apply and when. Also, you will appreciate, I hope, that the solution focused approach is not simply 'techniquey', but is a relational process between worker and client that flows. Also, you will discover that the approach produces long-lasting results, despite the relatively few number of sessions required.

You might be a reader who has made an attempt on your life already or are thinking of doing so. I hope you will find the book both interesting and helpful to you in your current state of thinking. If you are such a reader, I would suggest you go straight to the *'worst case (graveside) scenario'* in Chapter 8 and spend about 10–15 minutes answering it as carefully and honestly as you can, before reading other chapters in the book. You might like to read either *Suicide: The Forever Decision: For those thinking about suicide, and for those who know, love or counsel them,* by Paul G. Quinnett, or *How I stayed alive when my brain was trying to kill me: One person's guide to suicide prevention,* by Susan Blauner. (See section at the back of the book for full reference details.)

You might be a solution focused practitioner who is interested in finding out about yet another specialist area which has been given the solution focused treatment or had solution focused principles applied to it. In the spirit of generosity, which is a fundamental part of the solution focused tradition, this is my offering. Please feel free to use any of the exercises in your work for the benefit of others. All I ask is that you acknowledge the source. Throughout the book, apart from a little within Chapters 4 and 5, I have avoided using the jargon of the study of suicide. The main reason for this is to keep the book simple and understandable for the widest possible readership. As first and foremost a practitioner and trainer, my overall aim is both to save lives and to help others to save lives too. My 'academic hat' is very much secondary. This whole area of research, education and practice has been given the title 'suicidology'. For those readers wishing to know what the jargon of suicidology is comprised of, and for serious academics who may wish to study aspects of the subject further, I would suggest you enter this term into your preferred internet search engines, along with other terms such as, 'suicidal ideation', 'completed suicide', and 'postvention'. Many of the references at the back of the book will be helpful too.

Throughout the book, you will find many different titles for 'practitioner' and for 'client'. I have used a maximum of interchangeability with the many terms that refer to these two titles, in order to ensure the book is of widest appeal across the healthcare, helping, social care and welfare sectors, where suicidal people are encountered. So for 'practitioners' the following alternative terms will appear: 'health professional', 'worker', 'therapist', 'helper', 'clinician' and 'counsellor'. For 'client' the following titles will be used: 'patient', 'service user', 'person' and 'helpee'. Also, I have used the male and female pronoun interchangeably from time to time.

2

The Book's Style and Purpose

"It is the quality of the personal encounters which, in the end, are the essential factors in creating positive change."

John Eldrid

"Before people kill themselves, many have had recent contact with a helping agency. Two-thirds of those who contact their family doctor have received medication, which about half use to poison themselves."

David Aldridge (1998)

" The death toll from suicide . . . with 25 mentally ill people a week taking their lives. Some 1300 mental health patients a year commit suicide."

J. Slack, *The Daily Mail*, 4 December 2006

THE BOOK — IN A NUTSHELL

For decades, health professionals and policy makers have resorted to head-scratching, chest-beating and hand-wringing over high suicide rates. Questions were, and are still asked today, such as:

Could we have asked the right question?

Shouldn't we have recognised the signs?

Wasn't there a clue somewhere in what he/she said?

(Aldridge, 1998)

The issue of resolving the problem of suicide has taxed intelligent minds across many disciplines for a very long time. Camus (1942) in referring to it said, "There is but one truly serious philosophical problem and that is suicide".

In spite of the vast increase in research into the problem, nearly two-thirds of a century later it seems, worldwide, we are little further forward. Another main purpose of this book is to shed new light and make in-roads such that Simon's (2002) statement ("There are two kinds of psychiatrist: those who have had patients commit suicide and those who will"), can be revised to something like: "There are two kinds of mental health care-givers: those who used to have clients commit suicide and those who do not".

Much has been written about the subject of suicide, but little on the specific 'how-to-do' or 'what works' in the 1:1 relationship between worker and suicidal person.

This book concentrates on how lives are saved; what workers do and say that is effective; and, what clients have said they found helpful.

THE BOOK'S STYLE

I have aimed to make the style of this book clear, easy to read and jargon-free, wherever possible. The principle of 'Occam's Razor' is applied: that is, if more straightforward words or stories can be used to describe something, then it is those which will be chosen.

REASONS FOR WRITING

AN APPROACH WHICH IS EFFECTIVE

The many tools and techniques outlined in later chapters have been field-tested over some 15 years or so. They have been demonstrated to work both efficiently and effectively. Students of training workshops have reported similar success rates over the past six years or so. There is a growing body of practice-based evidence which shows significant reductions in suicide rates both in individual caseloads and within teams.

A SHORTAGE IN THE LITERATURE OF EFFECTIVE BRIEF THERAPY TREATMENTS FOR SUICIDAL CLIENTS

From my extensive literature review, it seems the vast majority of research, review and discussion material on the subject of suicide, is concerned with matters other than the matter of central concern: *the verbal and non-verbal communication that occurs in a 1:1 relationship with a suicidal person.*

Instead, writers become lost in national suicide trends and statistics, methods used in completed suicide, community attitudes and beliefs towards suicidal behaviour, etc. There are numerous research and discussion topics on suicide and these are dealt with more than adequately elsewhere. Should readers be interested in following up any of these, there are various avenues of inquiry. My concern is to emphasise the crucial matter of how to manage the one-to-one encounter with someone experiencing strong suicidal urges and there is evidence that how this is conducted in the first 10 minutes can make a significant difference to the outcome (see Chapter 7). This is the central focus of the book.

PERSONAL INVOLVEMENT IN THE TERRITORY

My personal interest in this subject can be traced back to my early childhood years when I tried suffocating myself on many occasions, under the bed covers, in order to escape severe and enduring emotional abuse and neglect. On other occasions I prayed to God that he would take me away in my sleep. I am pleased to realise now that He had other plans! It is only in recent years, while talking to my brother, two years my junior, that I learned he hoped to die too, as a way out.

No doubt another source of my interest is that my cousin, John Neil Henden, took his life by carbon monoxide poisoning some 15 years ago, as a result of various personal and employment difficulties. (He had been diagnosed earlier as being clinically depressed.) His death impacted on me both in that I lost a cousin, but also the less-than-satisfactory treatment he received when asking for help. Both my personal experience of suicidal thinking and the experience of close family members, has given me a heightened empathy towards suicidal people.

The connections I have had with helping agencies, both statutory and voluntary, over the past 30 years or so, have opened my eyes to what works; what helps a little; and, what patently fails those whose problems and difficulties are such that they experience recurrent suicidal thoughts and ideas.

During the course of my life, to date, I have taken various calculated risks to achieve personal objectives. On some occasions these did not work out. At those times, I considered the suicide option, albeit briefly. I know now that this type of thinking is quite normal. At a time in the mid 1990s, I found myself in a changed job situation, where job satisfaction was deteriorating by the week. I began to have regular thoughts about how I might be able to set up an elaborate suicide in the cellars of the building in which I worked, and not be found for some time. I mentioned this to a very non-directive person-centred counsellor friend of mine, who responded in no uncertain terms by saying, "John, you must leave as soon as possible!" My career; my contributions to the wider mental health field; and, my job satisfaction have progressed immeasurably since.

A HOW-TO-DO BOOK

PRACTICAL GUIDE

As you navigate through this book, you will get a clearer understanding of what is important to bring to the therapeutic encounter with a suicidal person, whether that be for 10 minutes in an Accident & Emergency (A & E) Department or for a more extensive counselling session.

It is about how-to-**be** with the suicidal person. Much is taught about risk assessment and management: spotting the signs, applying various protocols and ensuring a rigid care programme is often set in place, but little mention is made about how to get alongside the person and their pain. This book is about just that.

All professionals undergo comprehensive training courses but, sadly, many graduates feel ill-equipped to deal with overt expressions of suicidal thinking or intent. Trimble, Jackson and Harvey (2000) found that the majority of psychologists working with clients who are suicidal, questioned the adequacy of their training in this area. This book addresses the shortfall of many courses, when it comes to working with the suicidal. A central aim is to increase confidence when working with such clients and also, to increase workers' sense of their own competence.

Help with 'The Jitters'

In addition to feeling that their training has been inadequate in terms of what questions to ask and how to conduct themselves, etc., workers can feel jittery or uncertain in a variety of ways. Richards (2000) when interviewing psychotherapists working with suicidal clients, found them to be deeply affected, both personally and professionally, by accompanying feelings of hopelessness and helplessness, and a sense of failure. I, and close colleagues, have found that this can result from particular lines of questioning — particularly those which go into excessive problem or despair-delving. This book enables workers to replace hopelessness and helplessness with hopefulness and a sense of feeling equipped.

Milton (2001), in an American study, reviewed several articles which addressed assessment and response to suicidal risk in clinical practice. He found many reasons why working with suicidal clients is particularly stressful. These included the fact that, as humans, we all experience a certain amount of anxiety about death, but there are also issues related to the levels of responsibility felt by therapists, should the worst happen, and the client take their own life. We must remember here that, when suicidal clients meet with either a professional or lay worker, their 'radar' is up, in that they have a heightened sensitivity towards, and awareness of the worker. Milton highlighted the danger in cases where the level of stress or distress experienced by the worker compromises their ability to be effective. Suicidal clients will pick this up as easily as a boxer sensing their opponent is feeling intimidated. Clearly, worker stress or distress is not helpful to client, therapist or therapy. It is, he suggests, critically important for the therapist to attend to the suicidal thinking and ideas with as much respect as they would to anything else the client might present with. The key is not to panic. Once a therapist comes to understand the meaning and function of the suicidal thinking, they can work with it in a constructive way.

Reeves and Mintz (2001) used semi-structured interviews with counsellors to study their behavioural, cognitive and emotional responses to suicidal expression: both on a personal and professional level. They found that the counsellors studied, experienced a range of responses including fear, anxiety, anger and professional impotence. Self-doubt about professional competence was also prevalent.

Another concern amongst counsellors was the threat of litigation for negligent practice, should anything go wrong.

This book aims to replace the negative feelings mentioned above with calmness of approach; confidence in a way of working which works; and, a combined sense of challenge, hope and optimism, thus removing or minimising any jittery feelings.

Relationship is Key

Many suicidal clients will have made their minds up about the potential of the professional worker to help within the first few minutes of the encounter. It is crucial, therefore, that the worker gets it right in terms of what is important in establishing good rapport. (This aspect is dealt with more fully in Chapter 7.)

Carl Rogers (1951), in his *Client-Centred Therapy*, stressed that what is important is the trust that the therapist must have genuinely in the client: an attitude that trusts the client's capacity to change at every level. This quality is, of course, communicated to the client by the therapist's *genuineness* (authenticity; self-congruence), *unconditional positive regard* (non-posses-sive warmth; acceptance) and *empathetic understanding*. If this essential triad of qualities (or core conditions) for effective counselling is not in place, rapport will not occur and so no effective working relationship will be developed. I have come to the view that to some extent, these qualities can be developed on training courses.

Returning to genuineness in the therapeutic relationship, there is no real alternative to this. Clients' radar will pick up the slightest lack of it, as Truax and Carkhuff (1967) found. Even if the worker were a skilled, polished actor they suggest, it is doubtful that a therapist could hide his/her true feelings from the client. They go on to say, in this important study, that when the ther-apist pretends to care, pretends to respect, or pretends to understand, he is fooling himself only. The client may not know why the therapist is 'phoney' but he just knows. Clients can distinguish easily true warmth from phoney or insincere professional warmth. What can sometimes get in the way of pro-fessionals when working with clients is that either they have undue concerns about status or they want to masquerade as a more genuine person. This hinges on the personality of the counsellor, rather than on their qualification and can, therefore, relate to both professional and lay therapists. There may be other factors as well which can hamper effective working with clients.

It is important to say some more about unconditional positive regard. Hurding (1985, p. 31), in referring to it as "non-possessive warmth", claims that the effective helper needs not only to be respectful and concerned to-wards the client, but also should be able to show that 'positive regard', both verbally (by words used) and non-verbally (through eye contact, facial ex-pression, gestures and silences). This warmth needs to be communicated, as people in difficulties are often desperate for someone *who really cares*. With this non-possessive warmth, it is helpful, Hurding suggests, if the counsellor is also at ease in the world of feelings and emotions — both his/her own and those of the client.

Accurate empathy (or empathic understanding) is the third core condition, which must be in place if rapport is to occur. Empathy may be defined as "the power of projecting one's personality into, and so fully understanding, the object of contemplation" (Oxford English Dictionary). This sounds rather matter-of-fact, when applied to suicidal clients. A softer way of putting it might be to imagine being in the other person's shoes as if they were your own, but maintaining the 'as if' quality.

So, to summarise, genuineness, unconditional positive regard and accurate empathy must be in place for rapport to occur. The beginnings of a work-ing relationship will then develop. Amazingly, all the above happens ideally within the first 10–15 minutes of the first interview!

THE SEARCH FOR AN APPROACH THAT WORKS

Reviews of the extensive literature show many cases where both academics and practitioners feel absolutely stumped as to what to do about high suicide rates among various sections of the population, despite their best efforts to bring about reductions. Heard (2000, p. 503) reviewed psychotherapeutic approaches to suicidal behaviours which have been well developed and been subject to randomised controlled trials. He looked at cognitive-behavioural therapies, which included problem-solving therapies and cognitive therapies, and at outreach and intensive therapies (therapies that had outreach components to, or intensified, standard psychotherapies). Heard considered firstly, whether the field had actually developed effective psychotherapies for suicidal behaviour. He found that, although a substantial amount of literature on psychotherapy existed for suicidal patients, a review of this literature revealed the absence of solid empirical data, particularly in the form of controlled treatment trials. With regard to the present solution focused approach, this is called for within this book. (See Chapter 11.)

PREVENTION IN THE FORM OF HEALTH PROMOTION

Much has been written about the many and various strategies in targeting at-risk groups, providing better awareness, education and signposting for when they feel at risk. This aspect of suicide prevention is a science all of its own and is outside the remit of this book.

PREVENTION IN THE FORM OF EFFECTIVE INTERVENTIONS

Which treatments are effective?

Hawton and Van Heeringen (2000), in their comprehensive study of suicide and attempted suicide, reviewed many different treatment strategies for suicide attempters. They suggested, of relevance to the primary care physician, is the fact that to date no form of treatment has been shown to be clearly effective in reducing the risk of repetition. How damning an indictment is this? Hawton and van Heeringen went on to say that continuity of care is a problem. A good question to ask here is: 'Was the therapeutic relationship established sufficiently well for the client to want to come back?' (see below and in Chapter 7).

Michel (2000, p. 668) said, "There can hardly be any doubt that a trusting and consistent relationship with a health professional is of eminent importance".

Gunnell (1994), in examining the evidence on the available interventions and points of access to the population at risk (i.e. suicidal clients), concluded that "No single intervention has been shown in a well conducted, randomised, well controlled trial to reduce suicide".

Gunnell called for more research into various interventions, and before the effectiveness of any intervention is accepted, controlled research is needed. The Gotland Study (Rutz, von Knorring & Walider, 1989, p. 22–23) was a programme targeting general practitioners (GPs) on an island off the coast of Sweden. Ten of the eighteen GPs on the island of Gotland were given a two-day training course encouraging the early diagnosis and treatment of depression amongst the island's population. Following the programme, significant reductions in the suicide rate were noticed, and a reduction in the sickness rate for inpatient care for depressive disorders and the prescribing of tranquillisers was also achieved. Two years after the programme, both suicide rates & inpatient care for depression rates increased to the levels prior to the educational programme. Methodologically, the Gotland Study has received a degree of criticism. However, Macdonald (1993), by using a 5-year moving average, after referring to a follow-up study, showed that the suicide rate had been on a downward trend for some years anyway, before the intervention. By making this point, I am not putting forward a case against better GP training in the area of depression identification and suicide detection: the more training, the better.

Silverman and Maris (1995) said "It still remains an open question whether the development and implementation of successful preventive interventions will lead eventually to a refinement of development of a set of specific interventions for those already expressing self-destructive intentions". As will be seen in later chapters, the good news is that there are some very successful preventive interventions outlined for immediate application by both professional and lay practitioners. Randomised controlled trials, as called for by Gunnell (1994a), will be needed before these can be accepted as mainstream. The practice-based evidence, however, is building. Scott and Armson (2000, p. 710) have come nearest in support of the approach described in this book. In one section towards the end of their comprehensive review, when discussing potential developments in treatment they stated: "It is essential that pragmatic brief therapies suitable for a sizeable proportion of suicide attempters, be developed". Solution Focused Brief Therapy is one such brief therapy and is a promising development.

FINANCIAL CONSIDERATIONS

Another reason for this book is that the approach presented, is a cost-effective way of working with suicidal people. Allowing people with suicidal thinking to become psychiatric patients is a costly business, especially if they are admitted to an inpatient unit and receive lengthy aftercare.

In 2006, the UK National Health Service (NHS) was some £80m in deficit; so any ways in which scarce resources can be spread further to help the greatest number, must be welcomed. Heard (2000, p. 503) stated: "In view of the limited resources for healthcare, those developing and delivering psychotherapies must now also concern themselves with the financial cost, as well as the clinical success of their therapeutic approach".

Resources for working in the field of mental health have never been and will never be sufficient. Within the NHS over recent years, they have been stretched further as more money has gone into areas of healthcare provision seen as more glamorous; and towards projects which have achieved waiting list reduction for investigations and operations. Recent pay increases and the rising costs of drugs have also stretched resources vastly.

Many mental healthcare trusts have been encouraged to work only with 'serious mental illness' (SMI), turning away others whose degree of distress symptoms have been thought to be treatable within primary care. How many suicidal clients have not had the opportunity to be seen by specialists in secondary care, if they needed such an appointment? Waiting lists for outpatient appointments can be long in some districts.

A trend began in the 1980s towards GP practice counsellors. These counsellors, who generally, can offer around six sessions for GP referrals, again have long waiting lists in some urban areas especially.

The employee assistance programme (EAP) sector has grown rapidly since the 1990s with many more organisations — both public and private sector — having enabled their workforces to access what is a truly confidential service. The downside recently has been that this sector has become more competitive with both the number of sessions available to employees being reduced, and the hourly fee for counsellors being frozen at a low level.

Within the burgeoning private sector for counselling and therapy provision, there is a wide range of session fees charged, putting an increasing burden on clients who often have limited financial resources.

Solution focused brief therapy (SFBT) has provided an optimum level of service to both public and private sector organisations for well over 15 years now. The solution focused approach to mental health aims to be respectful, effective, empowering and long lasting: it is cost-effective in terms of time and financial resources. Above all other considerations, these two factors have made the solution focused approach attractive to managers. After training their workforce in SFBT or recruiting staff with solution focused skills, it does not take long to notice increases in caseload turnover, client goals achieved more quickly, fewer sessions needed, increased worker morale and higher staff retention rates. (See European Brief Therapy Association website: www.ebta.nu)

This approach is applicable in wider services than just the mental healthcare sector. It is being taken up in education (Department of Education &

Skills, 2003), social work and probation (Milner & O'Byrne, 1998; Milner & Myers, 2007), the Prison Service and Youth Service; and, more recently, the business sector (Leuger & Korn, 2006), which have all embraced solution focused ideas, with effective results being obtained.

Within the mental healthcare sector over recent years, we have seen cost-effective applications of solution focused ideas to alcohol abuse (Berg & Miller, 1992); eating disorders (Jacob, 2001); sexual abuse (Dolan, 1991); abuse and trauma survival (Dolan, 1998); and speech and language difficulties (Burns, 2005). Within all of these specialist areas, not only is there greater client satisfaction, but clients are held on caseloads for less time, with enormous savings resulting. Some of the longer term savings are hard to calculate when consideration is given to the lower incidence of future physical problems; fewer re-referrals and other social and welfare services which are no longer needed as clients have built their own unique solutions and sorted their lives out. This is not to claim that this is true in every case, but the gathering body of evidence all points in this direction. There is scope here for some future research with a rigorous methodology using double-blind trials. I will refer to this again later. Maybe, also, some retrospective research could be useful, looking at large populations who have been exposed to different treatment approaches.

The subject of this book — the solution focused approach to suicide prevention (Henden, 2005) — is now another specialist area which could have the cost-effectiveness spotlight cast upon it. Hospital admissions, long-term outpatient follow-ups, community mental health workers' time and long courses of psychotropic drugs, all add up to considerable expense. Many service users who are served by this route, also end up losing their job, spouse, and home; with other financial, personal and social costs resulting.

Four to five sessions of SFBT from a healthcare professional trained in a particular range of specialised tools and techniques for working with suicide, adds up to a fraction of the cost.

UK HEALTH OF NATION AND OUR HEALTHIER NATION TARGETS

Currently, the proposed target as outlined in the UK Government's White Paper, *Saving Lives: Our Healthier Nation* (Department of Health, 1999), for a reduction of 20% by 2010 looks unrealistic. It is not based on proven effective interventions. This is a bold target that the government has set itself. The question many have been asking is how will it be achieved?

The White Paper acknowledges that suicidal thoughts in the wider population are quite common, but are rarely acted upon. To support this, I am sure many can recall times in life when they have been under severe strain for whatever reason and at these times may have had a suicidal thought come to mind, albeit fleetingly.

Figures show that suicide rates within the UK are reasonably similar in England, Wales and Northern Ireland, but Scotland's rate is slightly higher. It is noted, however, in the White Paper that suicide rates for the UK as a whole are one of the lowest across Europe.

Quite rightly, *Saving Lives: Our Healthier Nation* puts an emphasis on better mental health promotion as being a mainstay in reducing both the incidence of mental illness and the suicide rate. The first of two new National Service Frameworks has mental health as its subject. National standards have been set and service models defined for mental health promotion, suicide prevention, assessment, diagnosis, treatment, rehabilitation and care. The Frameworks are to be used to ensure that professional staff in these areas have the skills to detect early signs of mental illness and to assess suicide risk. Another valid question to be asked is: 'Have all these professional staff now obtained the necessary skills, not only to assess suicide risk, but to treat effectively the suicidal people whom they have assessed?' And if they have not had this training themselves, have the specialists they are referring onto had this professional training? What treatment models are being used and how much is their practice evidence-based? There is a real opportunity here, with appropriate and well-funded training, to reduce the suicide rate significantly. Past research (Appleby, 1992; Appleby et al., 1999) has shown a high rate of completed suicides in people who are already in contact with mental health services. This indicates a need for ongoing professional development training for staff currently working in the field.

The UK Government White Paper sets out to put in place a range of actions to reduce suicide. This would be achieved not only within the National Health Service (NHS) and its partner agencies, but in the media too. There would be others (e.g. pharmacies) who could be encouraged to reduce access to the methods of suicide. I believe that by setting a maximum number of paracetamol tablets to be purchased at any one time, the number of deaths by this method has been reduced.

Saving Lives: Our Healthier Nation has a nine-step plan to reduce suicide. This plan covers important issues such as better follow-up of suicide attempters, improved helpline services, and good practice guidelines for looking after suicidal people in both primary and secondary care.

The National Service Framework for Mental Health, in setting standards and service models in accordance with *Saving Lives* recommendations, has a clear drive towards implementation and delivery. This is seen as a key element in reducing the suicide rate by a fifth by 2010, as it addresses the whole range of mental health service provision from primary care settings to formalised, secondary healthcare — the specialist mental health services.

In attempting to ensure that all this works, the UK Government has set up a high level Task Force, accountable to the Chief Medical Officer. It is the Task Force's job to ensure that all the essential groundwork is in place to set the course of achieving the target for so many more lives saved (up to 4000), which would be lost otherwise to suicide.

In an earlier work (Henden, 2005), I called for research into specialised solution focused interventions for those practitioners working with the suicidal population. In the meantime, the more practitioners — both professional and lay — that apply the principles, tools and techniques outlined, the greater the body of evidence that can be gathered. My hope is that a wider application of this ground-breaking approach will make a significant contribution towards reducing suicide rates both across the UK and worldwide in the years to come.

THE WORLD HEALTH ORGANIZATION (WHO)

For many years, WHO has been concerned about the global mortality rate resulting from suicide. "The rising trend in suicide and attempted suicide continues to give cause for concern" (Diekstra 1989; WHO, 1996). In the year 2000, it was estimated that 1 million people died through suicide, which approximated to one death every 40 seconds.

WHO states that suicide, which has increased by 60% worldwide over the last 45 years (WHO, 2000), is now amongst the three leading causes of death in the 15–44 years age group. The figures for suicide do not include attempted suicide, which is up to 20 times more frequent than completed suicides. In countries with market economies and the former communist bloc economies, suicide is estimated to represent 2.4% of the global burden of disease by 2020.

Mental health problems, particularly depression and substance abuse, are connected in some way with more than 90% of all cases of completed suicide.

WHO is concerned about effective interventions and is aware of both the challenges and obstacles to any strategy to reduce the suicide rate. It points to the restriction of access to the common methods of suicide as being effective in reducing suicide rates. It calls for more crisis centres and states that there is compelling evidence for reducing suicide rates, resulting from the inadequate prevention and treatment of depression, alcohol and substance abuse. With regard to reducing youth suicide, WHO points to school-based intervention programmes which involve self-esteem enhancement, crisis management, the development of coping skills and healthy decision-making strategies.

One of WHO's specific objectives (WHO, 2000) was to raise general awareness about suicide and provide psycho-social support to people with suicidal thoughts or experiences of attempted suicide. If the contents of this book can help WHO with this objective, again much will have been achieved.

WHO made some helpful recommendations during the 1980s and a few countries (especially Canada, the USA and the Netherlands) established national task forces, which were charged with devising all-encompassing national programmes for the reduction and prevention of suicidal behaviour (Diekstra, 1989). The main recommendations of these task forces, based on the WHO recommendations, were:

1. Scientifically sound information on the causation of suicide behaviour, the efficacy of intervention and prevention schemes, and effective methods for implementing such schemes in a variety of cultural and socio-economic contexts should be assembled;
2. Services dealing with suicidal persons or persons at high risk for suicidal behaviour should be expanded and improved;
3. Effective information and training should be provided for relevant organisations and the general public; and,
4. Special services should be provided for high risk groups.

The WHO European Ministerial Conference on Mental Health in January 2005 called for an Action Plan for Europe. Two actions to consider were: (a) to establish self-help groups, telephone helplines, and websites to reduce suicide rates; and, (b) to target particular high-risk groups.

CONTACT WITH HEALTH PROFESSIONALS

Many who take their lives have been/or are currently in contact with health professionals. It says something about our services, when those in the midst of despair and hopelessness do the right thing by going for help, only to be let down in some way or another by the practitioners they are seen by. Questions have been asked and are still being asked about what happens in these cases:

How have they been let down?
What did the distressed person not find in the practitioner?

In what ways were they not helped?

What could the practitioner have done differently to have been more helpful?

Did the person feel they were taken seriously enough and, if not, how not?

Almost all suicidal persons who contact physicians want to live (Tabatchnik, 1970). Barraclough et al. (1974) found that two-thirds of successful suicides had contacted their family doctor in the month before their death; 40% within the previous week. Similar figures have been reported by Murphy (1975); Morgan (1979); Michel (1986); Aldridge (1988); Gunnell (1994b); and, Pirkis & Burgess (1998). Also, regarding secondary care by specialists, Barraclough et al. found that over a quarter were seeing a psychiatrist, and 80% of these were receiving psychotropic drugs. The issue of drug therapy for people who are suicidal has been a contentious one for some time. Morgan (1979) suggested that "over half of all suicides are under medical or psychiatric treatment at the time they kill themselves and are receiving some kind of psychotropic drug" (p. 79). As self-poisoning with prescribed drugs is a large problem, he recommended practitioners question the efficacy of drug treatments, by asking themselves: "Is this the correct dose; and should anything be prescribed at all?" Stenger and Jensen (1994), in discovering that many people had contacted some kind of help agency before killing themselves, found that two-thirds of those who contacted their GP had received medication. About half of these had used the medication to poison themselves.

Morgan (1979) found with regard to potentially suicidal patients, that although they made contact, many were "not regularly recognised as being at risk of suicide" (p. 75). With regard to how the practitioner reacts, he found that "a suicidal individual is more likely to declare his problems and actively turn for help if he thinks that a positive response will be obtained". Maybe this is a statement about potentially suicidal people making a judgment on the ability of the practitioner to be accepting, genuine and empathic, as described above and looked at more closely in Chapter 7. For those who take their lives shortly after seeing a practitioner, clearly something is going wrong in that interview. What did the client not feel from the worker? Retrospective studies are of course not possible with the deceased; the results might help inform our training programmes for key groups of health workers. An interesting piece of research, which might shed some light on this area, would be to question serious suicide attempters who failed, due to circumstances outside their control. Morgan (1979) calls for medical staff to be trained in developing better skills in the area of relating well to suicidal individuals:

> We often forget the utmost importance of the basic ingredients of the helping process . . .
>
> Our ability to empathise, and our non-judgmental acceptance of the patient and his problems.
>
> Morgan, (1979, p. 64)

Others have considered the need for better training generally, in this area (Maris et al., 1973; Bongar, Lomax & Harmatz, 1992).

Vassilas and Morgan (1993), in reviewing case studies, found that approximately 40% have had contact with a healthcare professional in the month before death, and 25% in the week before. Of those who successfully commit suicide, 50% were found to have been under psychiatric care at some stage in their life and 25% were currently, or were recently under such care. Appleby et al. (1999) support these last figures. More recently, a UK Department of Health (10 May 2005) Press Release stated that one in four suicides are among people in contact with specialist mental health services, in the year before their death. Conwell (1994), in referring to studies of older adults, found that many who commit suicide had visited a primary care physician very close to the time of the suicide: 20% on the same day; 40% within a week; and, 70% within one month of the suicide.

These findings raise more interesting questions: Firstly, what was the quality of the care and treatment from the professionals first seen?; and secondly, what was the type and quality of the treatment intervention such that a person decides eventually to take the last resort option?

Diekstra (1992) pointed out that no studies control for the effect of treatment history on subsequent attempts. Many suicidal people, including first attempters, have been in contact with helping agents and/or healthcare professionals and their experience in this respect may have been negative, rather than positive. With regard to future help, therefore, they may have negative expectations. This would go a long way in explaining low compliance with treatment services which is reported in most studies. So, it is this emphasis on the importance of the *relationship* that I want to cover in this book.

FEELINGS OF ISOLATION AND BEING IGNORED

Whether someone has made a serious attempt and failed, or has made a cry-for-help, it is interesting to hear what survivors have said about how they were treated. Research in A & E Departments of general hospitals, has found that many people are treated less-than-satisfactorily by staff (Repper, 1999). The message communicated, often non-verbally, is 'This is something you have inflicted upon yourself. You are taking up a cubicle/bed which could be used for a real patient'. It should be added that A & E Departments have been addressing this problem for some time and there are some examples where improvements are being made (Wilstrand et al., 2007).

Whitfield and Southern (1996) found that following an attempt, many individuals felt isolated or ignored by health professionals. This was found to be the case in an earlier paper by McGaughey et al. (1995). Whitfield and Southern urged health professionals to identify and treat underlying illness such as depression; help provide remedies for social and problem-solving deficits; and, provide help with family psychosocial education and conflict resolution, as outlined in Brent (1993).

INADEQUATE ASSESSMENTS

Another reason for this current work is to highlight the often inadequate assessment process for service users who are suicidal. Suffice it to say at this point, that it is my view that practitioners often adhere too rigidly to the process of assessment, thereby missing some important content cues. There is little point in producing exemplary assessment documentation on a service user, if they are dead within the following month — or in many cases — by the next day.

Most models and approaches to helping have some sort of assessment procedure. Some of these are very simple and straightforward, others are lengthy and tiresome to complete — both for the service user and the practitioner. I have devoted a large section (Chapter 7) to this aspect of engaging and assessing suicidal people, so my purpose here is simply to flag it up as an important issue. Other research, Bridges and Goldberg (1987) and Freeling et al. (1985), found that only 50% of cases of major depression that present in primary care are recognised by GPs. One would hope the detection rates nowadays are much higher.

Again, returning to secondary inpatient care, Morgan (1993) found that in three out of four of a series of suicide and expected deaths of current or recent inpatients, the seriousness of risk was not recognised. Morgan and Priest (1991), in carrying out a multidisciplinary audit of those presenting to psychiatrists and GPs prior to suicide, found that the seriousness of risk was not fully appreciated in 75% of inpatient and recent inpatient suicides. Again, this says something about the nature of training both for recognition and interventions for mental health specialists within secondary care. Staying with secondary care (specialist mental health services), and considering the whole multi-professional team, an American study (Domino & Swain, 1985–6), explored the relationship between knowledge about suicidal lethality and attitudes in a sample of 280 mental health professionals representing eight groups. The findings were that psychiatrists, psychologists and crisis interventionists showed significantly greater degrees of knowledge than their fellow mental health team colleagues. Specifically, they recognised a greater number of signs of suicide and tended to view suicide as acceptable and as an understandable reaction to external stresses.

In terms of suicide victims communicating intent to clinicians, Isometsa et al. (1995) reported that in a large number of completed suicides, clinicians are caught unaware of patients' suicidal intent. Across all treatment settings, they reported that about 22% of victims communicate intent. They found the problem to be worst in primary care, where the rate is lower. In Finland, a psychological autopsy study was conducted of *all* suicide victims over a 12-month period, whose last appointment occurred 28 days before suicide. From healthcare professionals' interviews, research has found that 39% and 30% of patients, respectively, communicated their intent to outpatient and inpatient mental healthcare providers. In a related study (Isometsa et al., 1994), the same investigators found that 59% of suicide victims with depression communicated their intent to psychiatrists, compared with 19% to medical providers. It is worth mentioning that none of these studies indicated whether clients were asked explicitly about suicide intent by their clinician, or whether they reported intent spontaneously. It should be remembered that the fact remains that suicidal intent is not communicated in a sizeable portion of all patients, regardless of treatment setting.

In considering the shortcomings outlined above, what might lead us to improving services? Certainly, questions around intent need to be asked. Also, verbal and non-verbal cues need paying attention to. I will deal with this more fully in Chapter 7.

Another issue for workers to be aware of is that, as some clients are thinking seriously about death, they may be asking spiritual or existential questions. Many workers are able to field this sort of question well. If not, they need to be aware of colleagues, some who may be ministers of religion, to whom they can refer.

So, to conclude this chapter, I have outlined the main reasons for writing. Others include a desire to commit to paper all the best practice ideas I have developed over several years; and, the fact that so many colleagues and former trainees have, in recent years, urged me to present it in book form, for reading by all those who are interested in making a difference in their work with the suicidal.

3

Defining Suicide and Self-harm

DEFINITIONS AND CLARIFICATION OF TERMS

Before embarking on a description of this innovative approach to suicide prevention, it will be helpful to both you the reader, and me the author, if the basic terms used are defined.

FIRSTLY, WHAT DO WE MEAN BY SUICIDE?

Durkheim (1897) defines suicide as, "the termination of an individual's life, resulting directly from a negative or positive act of the victim himself, which he knows will produce this fatal result". In a coroner's court, the verdict of 'suicide' can only be given when the evidence is clear, as outlined in Durkheim's definition. If there is any doubt at all, then an 'open' or 'accidental' verdict will be recorded.

Davis (1968) defined suicide as, "the intentional act of self-destruction committed by someone knowing what he/she is doing and knowing the probable consequences of his/her action".

A further definition is that found in Encyclopaedia Britannica (1994–1997): "the act of voluntarily or intentionally taking one's own life". Encarta 1998 (1993–1997) says of suicide: ". . . intentional, self-inflicted death. A uniquely human act, suicide occurs in all cultures. People who attempt or complete suicide, usually suffer from extreme emotional pain and distress . . .".

Leenaars (2004) prefers the definition of suicide as outlined by Schneidman (1993): "the human act of self-inflicted, self-intentional cessation".

Vanda Scott of Befrienders International and Simon Armson of the Samaritans said that suicide "is frequently regarded as the ultimate expression of distress. That is the point when there is no vision of a future, when it seems that every aspect of life has become so futile or overwhelming, that there is no possibility of coping, and the only option is of complete and final destruction" (Hawton & van Heeringen, 2000, p. 702).

I have mentioned elsewhere within the introduction to this book, that wherever possible, I will avoid the use of jargon. I hesitate therefore, before using the terms 'suicidality' and 'suicidology.' As defined by Milton and Crompton (2001), suicidality describes suicidal behaviour which includes both suicidal thoughts as well as actions. Suicidology, on the other hand, (Milton, 2001; Schneidman, 1999c), refers to the wider study of suicidal behaviour.

Nowadays, suicide is not regarded as some form of extreme madness or something other-worldly. Research has shown that during their lifetime many people, quite normally, consider occasionally the suicide option to their distress or extreme difficulty. It is regarded more often now, as 'a normal response by normal people to an abnormal set of circumstances'. McLaughlin (1994) suggested that in the UK, for example, one person every minute thinks about suicide.

Chiles and Strosahl (1995) made the point that any person has the potential to become suicidal when confronted with life situations that produce emotional pain, especially when this pain feels intolerable and is believed to be interminable and inescapable.

I have spoken much of suicide as the completed act where death has been the outcome. There is, however, a distinction between 'completed suicide' and 'attempted suicide'. For the purpose of this book, I am defining attempted suicide as a serious attempt to end one's life which has been unsuccessful for whatever reason. I put much emphasis on the word *serious* to distinguish it from other self-harming behaviours which I will discuss below.

I mentioned earlier, in one of the definitions, the idea of pain playing an important part in suicidal thinking and behaviour. Schneidman (1993) was very interested in this aspect, describing unbearable mental pain as "psychache". For the suicidal person, then, the cessation of consciousness is a reasonable solution to the ongoing unbearable mental condition that they find themselves in. Moving towards a definition, according to Schneidman: "the suicidal act should primarily be understood as an act aimed at obtaining relief from an unbearable mental state" (Michel, 2000, p. 666).

To summarise at this point then, so far we have definitions for suicide, attempted suicide, and unbearable mental pain.

Much has been written about the link between clinical depression and suicide, suggesting that the majority of people who commit suicide are depressed at the time (Isometsa et al., 1994; Reinecke, 2000).

What about a definition of 'clinical depression'? Whitfield and Southern (1996) defined it as: "the persistent and sustained feelings that the self is worthless, the world meaningless, and the future hopeless" (p. 296). Clinical depression is distinguishable from simply feeling miserable, sad, or having an off-day or few days. It is the persistent and enduring nature of the negative feeling which is key.

Seligman (1978) said of depression, that it is the "common cold" of psychopathology, but that the depression can kill. He emphasised that between 70–80% of all people who kill themselves are suffering from depression.

Others adopt a less pathological attitude towards depression. In conversations with colleagues in recent years, where depression has been construed more loosely and less clinically, I have heard depression being defined as "the absence of hope"; "the result of unexpressed emotion"; or, "the effect produced in the mind as a result of suppressed mental conflict".

Treatment, therefore, could then be formulated around restoring hope and encouraging the person to express the shut-off negative feelings about a situation or situations that they are holding deep within. Those who subscribe to this view suggest that there is no need to mystify depression as some complicated psychobiological condition that requires a complicated medico-scientific approach in order to understand and treat it.

HOW SHOULD WE DEFINE TREATMENT?

The Concise Oxford Dictionary (Fowler & Fowler, 1964) defines treatment as, "(Made of), dealing with or behaving towards a person or thing".

Silverman and Maris (1995) defined treatment as, "the evolution of techniques and technologies to effectively and efficiently treat individuals demonstrating early (and sometimes late) signs or symptoms of distress or disorder".

This book is essentially about suicide treatment, so how come the title talks of 'prevention'?

Felner et al. (1983) defined prevention as, "a co-ordinated and comprehensive set of specific interventions that are strategically linked to target populations at risk for the development of specific disorders and dysfunctions". However, the use of the term 'prevention' in this case, refers to mental health promotion in the wider sense. 'Intervention' in their definition relates to actions which could be taken to support such health promotion programmes *but*, the subject of this book is about suicide prevention by using appropriate treatment 'interventions'. I would suggest this can all seem very confusing, but please stay with it. It is no wonder that Maris and Silverman (1995) called for a classification and clarification of the existing terms in this area of study.

In various parts of the literature, distinctions have been made between *primary* prevention and *secondary* prevention, and *tertiary* prevention, when referring to the prevention of illness. I find these three classifications helpful and clear for the purpose of this book. Primary prevention refers to all that might fall under the heading of wider health promotion within society at large, mentioned above. Calling this category simply, prevention, in applying it to suicide, Diekstra (1992), said it ". . . implies measures adopted by, or applied to people who currently, are not feeling or displaying any sign or symptom of suicidal tendencies, intended to decrease the risk that such a tendency will afflict them in the future" (p. 73). Education programmes in schools, healthy work—life balance training in the workplace, and adult education programmes promoting suicide awareness, would all come within this category of primary prevention.

Secondary prevention takes several forms and refers to various treatment interventions. This sort of work can take place in crisis intervention centres, telephone helplines (e.g. the Samaritans), community mental health centres, and the many and varied counselling and therapy services, both statutory and private, and voluntary. Secondary prevention services can involve a wide range of treatment interventions. These may be psychological or social in nature, or may be of a medical nature involving some form of psychotropic medication. Whichever form of therapy is involved within secondary prevention, the main focus is to help the client alleviate the problem and/or circumstances which led to the crisis and distress that they find themselves in. Currently, there is a lot of talk about biopsychosocial approaches to care and treatment under this heading of secondary prevention, which combines various treatment approaches to helping suicidal people (for separate models and approaches to suicide prevention, see Chapter 5).

The third category, *tertiary* prevention (or "*post-vention*" as Diekstra, 1992 calls it), is concerned with 'after the fact prevention', once a person has completed suicide. Within this category is included help with coping for surviving relatives and friends. *Tertiary* prevention research might look at particular methods used, occupation of victims, psychological profiling, etc.

The present work, then, although called 'preventing suicide', is about *preventing suicide at the secondary prevention level by the use of effective treatments.* One might ask why not call it 'treating suicide'? The reason for this, in my view, is that the word 'treatment' does not link to outcomes in a powerful enough way. Treatment may or may not be successful. Prevention is about stopping things happening. As the work outlined in this book has helped reduce significantly the suicide rates across both practitioners' and teams' caseloads to date, the word 'prevention' is I think, a stronger and more appropriate term to use. (I will refer to this gathering body of practise-based evidence in Chapter 11.)

DELIBERATE SELF-HARM

As part of this chapter, I think it is important to add something about self-harm which does not result in suicide and is very unlikely to do so.

Currently, there is something of a fashion among the young in some Western countries, to make token displays of self-harm, usually in the form of cutting. This can range from a mild scratch with a pin across the wrist, to a moderate cut with a razor blade perhaps somewhere along the arm or on the thigh. Once one or two teenagers have done this to themselves, others follow for a variety of reasons. It may be simply that they are keeping in with the fashion; or, as a result of other psychological issues, feel it is a form of self-expression in which they can follow suit. In the vast majority of cases, this behaviour is short-lived and is not at all life-threatening. This subject will not be dealt with in this present work.

There is, however, a more sizeable and more seriously-inclined deliberate self-harming population amongst teenagers and those in their early 20s. These are often survivors of child abuse (usually child sexual abuse), who find a great sense of relief from cutting or self-mutilation of some sort or another. Usually, this is not life-threatening behaviour and can provide survivors with a sense of relief from a build-up of tension. Another aspect of this type of self-harm is that it is a way for the client to be and feel in complete control over their body. Control is an important factor amongst abuse survivors and something they felt out of, while being abused or during the period of their abuse. Typical statements from 'cutters or other self-harmers' in this category are as follows:

- "Thank goodness for cutting: it saved my life!"
- "As I cut my wrist and watch the blood flow, I feel I am being purged or cleansed from what happened to me."
- "When I do this (deliberate self-harm), I feel I am in complete control of my life."

This is an interesting subject and a challenging rewarding client group with which to work. The need is great but the workers, currently, are few. Again, this is not an area which will be dealt with in this book.

Another category of deliberate self-harmers is that in which people, often youngsters, take small overdoses; put ligatures around their necks; inflict a small wound; or, behave in other mildly life-threatening ways. This 'show' or 'expression' is a way of communicating hurt to others close to them that makes the point in a very strong, albeit non-verbal way, without being too risky. In a small proportion of cases, mistakes are made and death results. In many cases, once the behaviour has been noted, felt or reacted to by the other party/parties, the self-harmer moves on and resumes their life, however dysfunctional or haphazard that may be. They may move on significantly in their life after such an event. Again, this is not a group this book will consider.

The main thrust of this present work is concerned with people, who as a result of severe distress, depression, worry or deep concern, feel that the suicide option is the answer to their difficulties. This group can be divided into those who have a clear plan; those who have regularly occurring thoughts; and, those who have made a serious attempt which has failed.

POLITICAL SUICIDE AND SUICIDE TERRORISM

POLITICAL SUICIDE

This form of suicide seems to be characterised by social pressure and/or conformity. Another feature is a restriction on any possible influences which the wider society might want to exert.

During the Second World War, the Allied Forces were astounded and alarmed by the dedication of Japanese kamikaze pilots, who single-mindedly flew their planes, laden with explosives, at top speed towards Allied war ships and other key military targets. Strong loyalty to the Emperor coupled with intense control and conformity within an elite military unit, was probably the most likely explanation for this form of suicide. Given what has been experienced in the first few years of the 21st century, were these Japanese pilots an earlier form of suicide bomber?

The Jonestown Mass Suicide in the United States in 1978 seemed to have occurred as a result of both high conformity to the group's norms, coupled with intense control by the commune leaders. Extra-societal influences were virtually nil in the Jonestown suicide, as the leaders went to great lengths to ensure they were completely sanitised from the world outside.

A more recent case of political suicide is to be found in the United Kingdom. This occurred in 1981 at the Maze Prison in Northern Ireland when 10

IRA and INLA prisoners starved to death in sequence. Their demand was that they should be regarded as political prisoners rather than common criminals. It has been suggested that the main explanation for this sequence of suicides, apart from the personal convictions of the individuals concerned, was the influence of the group on each other. This certainly seems to have been one factor in acute mental health units and the former psychiatric hospitals, when a spate of suicides has occurred over a relatively short period. Also in this example it could be argued that, as with Jonestown, wider societal influences against their actions were restricted. It might be suggested that micro-societal influences amongst their friends and political supporters was also a contributory factor.

SUICIDE BOMBERS

Definition: "A suicide terrorist attack is an assault intended to achieve a political objective, performed outside the context of a conventional war, in which assailants intentionally kill themselves while killing others" (Yufit & Lester, 2005).

Suicide terrorism is both a political and strategic problem. It can often catch whole nations or particular groups completely by surprise. One such example was the attack against both American and French forces and their diplomatic missions in Lebanon in 1963.

Israeli (1997) looked at the Islamic frame of mind, suggesting that personality factors also play a role in the making of a suicide terrorist. He speculated three common characteristics of suicide bombers, suggesting they are:

a. Young and have few life responsibilities,
b. Unsuccessful or are shunned by their family and society, such that they feel isolated;
c. Of low self-esteem.

Israeli thought too, that they may have a propensity towards depression, thus seeking easy solutions. He wondered also whether they may be both unsuccessful and self-despising. Maybe suicide bombers would find solace in becoming martyrs as a result. By their suicide, they would transform frustration into glory; failure into victory; and self-depreciation into public adoration. Personal profiles of some more recent suicide bombers indicates a rather different story. I will refer to these below.

I mentioned earlier about suicide terrorism catching whole nations by surprise. Nothing had a more devastating effect in this regard than the New York 9/11 (Twin Towers) attack by suicide bombers using high-jacked passenger aircraft in 2001. The July 11th bombings on the London Underground System and the London Transport bus in 2005 had a similar effect.

This sort of suicide terrorism which is directed often quite randomly against populations attracts much public interest and concern. After the shock stage, it is surrounded by a great deal of mystery and fear. It has been suggested (Phillips, 2006), that the mystery aspect of this and the public's wish to find out the reasons behind it has not been helped by some politicians and establishment figures and sections of the media who have sought to explain it away by suggesting it is because the bombers were poor or marginalised. Phillips adds that attempts have been made to translate 'aggressor' into 'victim' as part of the explanation for the bombers' actions. She makes the case that mostly they are dedicated Muslim extremists who essentially have a loyalty to a worldwide community of Muslims (the 'unmah'); want to see the imposition of Sharia law; and, see the re-creation of the mediaeval worldwide Muslim caliphate.

The suggestion of "poor and marginalised" has been refuted somewhat by other attacks since 9/11, especially the Glasgow Airport suicide terror attack in July 2007, in which a vehicle loaded with explosives was driven into the airport terminal building. Later, five medical doctors, several of whom had worked in the UK National Health Service, were sought for questioning about the attack.

Returning to the characteristics of political suicides referred to at the beginning of this section, many would argue that there is a degree of social pressure and/or conformity operating in the case of suicide bombers. It has been found that many were originally influenced and indoctrinated by extremist clerics in mosques and Islamic centres, once they had been recruited (Phillips, 2006), before they went on to become suicide bombers. Once they had become immersed into this 'jihad' world of Islamic terrorism, it is not difficult to appreciate how any possible influences that the outside world might want to exert – even moderate Muslim thought – would be restricted greatly.

4

Current Service Provision: Risk Assessment, Management and Medication

The risk of clients harming themselves in the course of treatment, can debilitate the therapist from acting creatively and collaboratively and make their actions defensive, focused solely on risk assessment rather than therapeutic change.

Sharry, Darmody & Madden (2002)

INTRODUCTION

Professionals and lay workers alike are in the risk business when dealing with people who are working through psychological difficulties. This is the nature of the territory.

It is the duty of every practitioner to assess the degree of risk whichever psychological issue is the presenting problem. It is of the utmost importance to assess risk when working with people who are deeply depressed and/or suicidal.

The question is, how do we do this in ways which are helpful and not harmful to the client? The traditional risk assessment and management and medication approach has, in the view of many, let suicidal people down over many years, with thousands of deaths since the 1960s of people under its care.

Testing questions in the minds of care-givers when assessing people who might be having suicidal thoughts are:

- Is this person simply depressed and not at all suicidal?
- Is this person both very depressed and suicidal?
- Is this person not depressed at all but simply feeling so overwhelmed by the enormity of their problems that they are seeing suicide as a logical way out?

RISK ASSESSMENT

How is the degree of risk assessed within this approach to suicidal service users? Usually there is a clear process documented within agreed laid-down procedures, with an emphasis on improving the efficiency of these procedures. Clinicians are encouraged to try and interpret the meaning of various symptoms reported and may well have, as part of the suicide risk assessment procedure, a questionnaire in printed or remembered form. As mentioned earlier, the UK Government White Paper, *Saving Lives — Our Healthier Nation* (HM Government, 1999), listed one of the recommended steps towards further suicide rate reduction as "continued professional training about assessment of suicide risk".

With regard to the assessment of suicide risk, Williams (2007) urges healthcare providers to show compassion in the asking of questions, ensuring maximum eye contact and genuineness of caring displayed. Dr Williams recommends asking direct questions, in a matter-of-fact manner, thus ensuring normality in the situation. Sample questions are:

"Do you want to kill yourself?"
"Have you thought about killing yourself?"
"How would you kill yourself if you thought about it?"
"What kind of plan do you have?"

Dr Williams, in relation to the last of these questions, points out that the type of plan can give a reasonably accurate picture of how dangerous it is. It is important for the healthcare worker to be aware of this. In relation to the lethality of the plan, other questions (he suggests) might be:

"Have you ever had these thoughts before?"
"Have you ever tried it before; and how did you?"
"What stops you from doing it?"
"What stops you from going ahead and killing yourself?"
"How would you do it if you had the chance to kill yourself?"

With regard to performing assessments for suicide risk, Dr Williams concludes this web page with: "If I find a high risk of lethality, then we have a direct admission to save the individual's life".

Other factors (Healthopedia, 2006) are risk assessed in patients who are suicidal before deciding which section should be recommended for treatment. These are: the method the person plans to use; the person's social support networks; and, how far the person has control over his/her judgment of actions. The author of this website page recommends hospitalisation if the person has the following factors in place:

- A suicidal plan
- The means of carrying out the plan
- Poor ability to control his/her actions
- Poor judgment
- Lack of social support.

Clearly there is a percentage of suicidal clients who may both want and need admission to a secure place if they score on all of these five factors. Indeed, during my many years of clinical practice, especially when working in acute inpatient settings, I can recall a few. The question to be asked, though, of all hospital 'suicide' admissions, is how large (or small) is the percentage that really need admission? The more experienced staff become, the fewer need to be admitted (Taylor et al., 2006).

Whitfield and Southern (1996) have some helpful contributions to make regarding risk assessment. They state that "every person showing evidence of depression should be given the chance to talk about suicidal thoughts" (p. 296). Their view is that all depressed persons should be considered potentially suicidal, therefore it is important for the subject to be raised. The authors present us with a helpful continuum of suicidal ideation:

Non-specific ideation (Life is not worth living)		Specific ideation (suicidal ideas with intent to die, or with suicidal plan)		Action (deliberate self-harm or suicide)
	_____		_____	

In order to determine where a person sits on this continuum, seven clarifying questions were recommended:

1. "Have you ever thought that life was not worth living?"
2. "Have you ever wished you were dead?"
3. "Have you ever thought about hurting yourself?"
4. "Do you intend to hurt yourself?"
5. "Do you have a plan to hurt yourself?"
6. "Have you ever attempted suicide?"
7. "How do you see your future?"

It is unfortunate that apart from number seven, all of the above are closed questions, which might bring into question the accuracy of placing a person on the continuum. In their article, Whitfield and Southern dispel the myth that suicide talk with a person can push them closer to it. "It is important to note that you will never cause a depressed person to be suicidal, however bluntly you put the question" (p. 296). With their suggested lines of questioning, they point out that the process can be stopped at any time, should it become clear that suicidal intent is absent.

Whilst separate from the medical model, but with reference to risk assessment, the idea of hard-hitting questions about suicidal thinking and behaviour formed a key part in a paper written by Aldridge and Rossiter (1983). The form of questioning they used, not only determined seriousness of intent, but also caused people to think hard about the effects on the family system they would leave behind. As strategic family therapists, within the brief therapy tradition, the similarities between the solution focused approaches are not surprising. An abbreviated form of the very practical questions they asked is:

- "Have you made arrangements for the funeral? Do you know what sort of flowers, which friends, burial or cremation, hymn or songs?" (From Whittaker, 1973)
- "What will happen to your clothes, your personal effects, or your children?"
- "Have you made a will, who will benefit, and are you insured?"
- "Who will this death affect the most?"
- "How would you like the news broken to your spouse/partner?"

It is important of course, that such questions are asked within a very caring and empathic stance toward the client. On many occasions, when asking these questions, the authors were corrected by the client who would point out that they had got it wrong and they had no intention of dying.

Aldridge and Rossiter's method was, indeed, a novel therapeutic procedure. Their approach was that suicidal behaviour is regarded as a "benevolent, although misguided attempt to solve a systemic problem" (p. 59). One Ericksonian (see Haley, 1973) intervention, used on occasions, was: "Have you thought about a final fling?" (Rossi, 1980). This is one small aspect of a complex piece of work by Milton Erickson that consisted of 13 sessions over 3 months. This intervention was found to be beneficial, especially when clients persistently made veiled threats and/or dismissed repeatedly any suggestions made by the workers. Clients would be asked to postpone any suicidal plans for the time being, enabling them to enjoy the few months they have left. This worked paradoxically, of course, (Frankl,

1960). Paradoxical Intention is a tool which has been adopted by solution focused practitioners, as will be seen in Chapter 6.

Jobes (2006) provides a manual which offers a flexible and common sense model for clinical practice. It offers a range of essential tools and guidance for therapists of any orientation. The book's primary purpose is towards a step-by-step outpatient assessment and treatment plan. Jobes speaks of the 'Collaborative Assessment and Management of Suicidality' (CAMS); reviews of the 'suicide status form' and the need for an early identification of risk. In order to protect workers from litigation should untoward events follow, the need for 'co-authoring' of the outpatient treatment plan is highlighted.

With a more specific focus on risk assessment in the prevention of suicide: Appleby (2000) said that if mental health services are to improve, three clear steps should be taken:

1. High risk groups, identified by high risk factors, should be the main target;
2. Services should increase intensity of their activities at high-risk periods, such as the first three months following discharge;
3. Key aspects of services should be strengthened, e.g. good risk assessment to be based on training and measures taken to improve compliance.

It is widely accepted that depression is a risk factor in suicide but how does the practitioner decide whether someone is simply depressed and not suicidal? This question is a difficult one to answer for many newcomers to the field of mental health and was one of three challenging questions posed at the beginning of this chapter. Some avoid taking the risk and treat the patient as if they are seriously at risk; others miss suicidal ideation and intent completely; and, others respond to a 'hunch' they have that their patient may be at risk. For further guidance on this important issue and for important signs and signals to be on the lookout for, please refer to Chapter 7.

RISK FACTORS

It is not the purpose of this book to dwell overly on risk factors, as there is an extensive body of research already. (See Hawton & van Heeringen, 2000.) It is necessary, however, for workers to be aware of the most common factors. Some of these are: a previous attempt; being young & male; recent bereavement of spouse; life-threatening illness; a parent who has completed suicide; a recent serious attempt; and, a sense of meaninglessness in old age. Some workers become jittery and render themselves ineffective when they realise the person sat before them has two or three factors which make them high risk.

It is not, however, simply an awareness of the main risk factors which is helpful, but also about an understanding of the uniqueness of the person presenting. As Michel (2000) concludes with respect to primary care physicians: ". . . [they] need a thorough knowledge of the main risk factors and the skills to understand the patient as an individual human being. Only the integration of both aspects will allow the physician to decide on the adequate management of the individual patient" (p. 661).

There is a strong school of thought which suggests that treating the underlying depression can reduce suicide risk. This is supported in the literature. However, prescribing medication can be a risk in itself. The use of psychotropic drug treatment for the prevention of suicide is based on the principle that successful drug therapy of an underlying psychiatric disorder (usually depression) will decrease the risk of suicidal thinking and behaviour (Buzan & Weissberg, 1992). Currently, there is also evidence (Verkes & Cowan, 2000, p. 487), suggesting that drug treatment for recurrent and chronic mental health problems can make a useful contribution towards reducing suicide rates. A number of studies have demonstrated this in Hawton and van Heeringen (2000). It is important, however, to bear in mind that it is possible that those who seek help are less likely to consider completing the suicidal act anyway; and, that the lower rates of suicide amongst those who are receiving drug therapy may not be due to the specific effects of drug therapy. It could be that therapeutic relationships formed with key workers within the mental health system are more significant factors.

Some antidepressant drug treatment (e.g. Prozac) has been claimed to increase suicidal thoughts and feelings, so practitioners who prescribe them, and their mental health team colleagues, should consider this a valid risk factor.

ASSESSING THE LEVEL OF INTENT

Clinicians and other mental health practitioners can be caught out by the level of intent within service users they are assessing. In many cases it is either a case of the service user not saying or the clinician not asking, or both. As was mentioned earlier, it has been found (by Isometsa et al., 1995) that across all treatment settings, only about 22% of suicide victims communicate their intent. In primary care, the rate is much lower. In an earlier related study by the same investigators, 59% of suicide victims with depression had told psychiatrists of their intent, compared to only 19% to medical care providers (Isometsa et al., 1994).

It is to be expected that psychiatrists, being mental health treatment specialists, would be more aware of communication of suicidal attempt, and other clinicians would be less so. This was borne out by a study by Murphy (1975) who found the percentages of suicidal communication awareness were 87% and 17%, respectively. It should be pointed out that in none of these studies was it made clear whether service users were asked explicitly about suicidal intent.

A distinction needs to be made here about communicated intent and the seriousness of that intent. It is mentioned elsewhere in this work that it is normal for people in extreme and/or abnormal situations to have thoughts and feelings about suicide. However, practitioners need to assess seriousness as part of their assessment procedures. Shocks and surprises occur where this is less than satisfactory. In the multi-disciplinary audit of both GPs and psychiatrists (Morgan & Priest, 1991) who had seen service users prior to their committing suicide, it was discovered that the seriousness of suicide risk had not been fully appreciated in as many as 75% collectively, of inpatient and recent inpatient suicides.

Within the wider literature, questions have been raised about how well equipped practitioners are in assessing the level of intent. "How well trained are practitioners for this task?" was one of these questions. As outlined in Chapter 2, Trimble et al. (2000) found that the majority of psychiatrists working with suicidal clients questioned the adequacy of their training in this area. The Department of Health publication, *The Prevention of Suicide* (Jenkins et al., 1994), concluded that training in risk assessment and management by the range of professionals who meet people at high risk of suicide can and should improve their skills. An earlier study looked at the relationship between knowledge about suicide risk and attitudes towards suicide across eight professional groups within mental health teams. They found that psychiatrists, psychologists and crisis interventionists showed a significantly greater degree of knowledge compared to mental health practitioners in the other groups. They recognised a greater number of signs of suicide and tended to hold the view that considering suicide is a natural reaction to external stressors (Domino & Swain, 1986).

RISK MANAGEMENT

Once service users have been assessed as moderate to high risk, what should happen next? The outcome of such an assessment can depend on a number of factors: mental health/welfare services' protocols; practitioner knowledge and experience; and, the level of support available to a service user, to list a few. Some practitioners feel a sense of urgency to act swiftly in ways which can be overwhelming and frightening to the service user: "Patients who are suicidal, are medical emergencies. Once it has been established that the patient is high risk for suicide, he must be protected at all costs. Admission to a psychiatric hospital on 1:1 watch is crucial, making sure there are no implements in the room, electrical cords, etc. that an individual can use. When individuals are suicidal, they may become very creative in their desperation, and it is very important to be aware of this" (Williams, 2007).

Hospital admission is often indicated for people who are diagnosed as suicidal, within the medical model. Part of the prescribed treatment for such a diagnosis is hospital admission: firstly for the person's safety and the preservation of life; and secondly, so that medication can be prescribed and its effects monitored. Other aspects of the treatment will include allocation to a key worker who may themselves talk through some of the causal factors with the patient, or they may simply co-ordinate the activities of mental health team colleagues. These treatment activities might include occupational therapy, art therapy and various forms of group therapy. Depending on the assessed level of risk, the patient will be recommended for 'close' or 'special' observation, or another similar procedure to ensure the patient comes to no harm, whilst such an order is in place.

Increasingly, the hospital (or inpatient facility) admission option is being questioned as to its overall effectiveness for working with suicidal people. The NHS-funded National Electronic Library for Health — Mental Health (NeLMH, 2006) provided evidence-based treatment summaries for seven treatment modes. For hospital admission, they concluded that there is ". . . no good evidence to . . . suggest that it reduces the risk of completed suicide". The side effects of this option were highlighted as raised dependency, stigmatisation and the difficulties for patients to maintain employment and keep up their social activities.

Other outcomes are available instead of immediate hospitalisation. Aldridge and Rossiter (1983), in adopting a brief therapy approach, assessed suicidal behaviour strategically as a systemic phenomenon. They combined the brief therapy principles of Weakland et al. (1974) and the neutral approach of the Milan Associates (Palazzoli, 1980). Aldridge and Rossiter, in acknowledging with the patient their right to die, if that is what they chose, had a serious conversation as referred to above about both dying and the usefulness of a hospital admission, which probably, would change nothing. Part of 'hospitalisation talk' involves making it clear to the patient that hospitals can be strange and dangerous places with lots of pills around, knives in drawers and large panes of glass in the windows. This destroys the myth of safety in hospitals. They recognised that hospital admission was often more about the need for workers to protect themselves in law; and, to reduce worker anxiety, rather than a useful therapeutic intervention. If hospitalisation becomes an option, then the work would continue alongside that provided by inpatient mental health team colleagues, and may well continue post-discharge.

Jenkins and colleagues (Jenkins et al., 1994) outlined certain principles of treatment for those assessed as moderate or high risk. The main principle is that "suicide prevention is likely to follow from sound clinical assessment and management procedures" (Jenkins et al., Chapter 7). It was important too, that the care plan should be based on active collaboration with the patient, rather than something which is 'done unto'. The further guiding principle, and one which addresses the sometimes-perceived unfeeling approach of mental health systems, is ". . . an increase in the knowledge and sensitivity of all persons who come into contact with a patient at risk, are the essentials of both therapy and prevention" (also Chapter 7). Another key principle addresses the importance of all staff concerned working together, combined with an alliance in treatment and care between patient and staff. This involves an effective code of clinical practice, combined with clear levels of supportive observation and a regular monitoring of the degree of risk. Other risks than the suicidal thoughts in response to the person's original difficulties were identified within the management plan. These included: failure to gain hospital admission when the patient needed or wanted it; shift changes; weekends and bank holidays; premature discharge; and, the immediate follow-up period.

Culverhay Community Mental Health Centre (CMHC) in South Devon, one of the earlier pioneering CMHCs in the late 1970s/1980s, developed a suicidal prevention policy based on Morgan's principles. This policy was written by the team's psychiatrist at the time, Rose Jones. Each client's individual policy was created, in collaboration between key worker and patient. Working in this outpatient setting, each suicide prevention plan had the following key points:

- It is a critical aspect of helping people to form a good working relationship;
- Agreement to daily contact — either call in to the CMHC or be visited at home;
- The name of a contact person and how to make contact in times of crisis;
- A clear plan for the patient over the following 24 hours;
- Some problem-solving difficulties addressed, e.g. practical things the patient can do; and, where to get help;
- Including others in the plan from amongst family and friends;
- A specific strategy such as a temporary 'no-suicide' contract, with mention of a 'ritual tearing-up' at some point.

The advantages of the Culverhay community-based suicidal prevention policy — (a form of risk assessment?) — was that the patient was empowered to use their own coping skills to deal with identified stressors; there was reduced stigmatisation; and, reduced impact on self-esteem. Other advantages of this approach, and one which addressed directly the tendency of suicidal people to withdraw from social networks, was to encourage the patient to maintain contact with family and friends. Patients remained 'people' as they retained their sense of autonomy and sense of responsibility. With such a care plan/suicide prevention policy in place, work on the person's emotional difficulties and the various precipitating factors was made more comfortable for all concerned.

With regard to the training issue I mentioned earlier, it was ensured that mental health practitioners across all disciplines involved, had adequate skills training and experience in assessment and working with acute mental ill-health.

MEDICATION

The prescribing of antidepressants and other psychotropic medication for suicidal patients, in both primary and secondary care, is an issue which attracts both support and controversy. Verkes and Cowan (2000) as referred to earlier, support the view that antidepressant medication can treat successfully the underlying depression in suicidal patients; thereby reducing suicide risk (p. 487). In support of the argument against medication, they suggest that some antidepressant drugs can increase suicidal risk. Benzodiazipines (e.g. Valium and Librium) they suggest, can increase suicidal risk, too.

Diekstra (1992) suggested it is impossible to state anything definite with respect to the effects of various treatments on the frequency of suicidal behaviour. As far as antidepressant drug therapy is concerned, he suggests that if it is used properly, it may have an effect on both suicidal ideation and suicidal behaviour. *But*, he adds, it is a risk factor in itself as it can make people feel worse and many take their lives by overdosing on prescriptions provided (Diekstra, 1989). There is an additional point to be made here and that is the implication that they are 'ill' and need a means external to themselves. I am amazed at the range of side effects reported by clients who have been prescribed antidepressants in my own clinical practice and their descriptions of how debilitating these side effects can be. It is not necessary to list the side effects here as these are more than adequately listed on the appropriate pages within the British National Formulary (BNF), but the following are among the most commonly made statements concerning debilitation: "I feel I am in an all-encompassing fog and not able to make clear decisions"; "I feel my vital 'life spark' has been snuffed out by the drugs"; "On this medication I seem not to care much anymore"; "With these pills, all my feelings are numbed. I don't cry now, but neither do I feel happy. I used to enjoy a laugh"; "I can't seem to get going in the mornings, like I used to"; "Since taking these tablets, I just stare at my plans, but the motivation to do anything about them has just vanished".

A former colleague illegal of mine in the 1970s (personal communication) set himself the (illegal) task of trying out all the antidepressant and anti-psychotic medication available to his patients on an inpatient facility where he worked. He described an interesting range of unreal and unpleasant feelings as a result. At the end of his trial (of the medication and not any sort of ensuing legal process!), he concluded that all medical practitioners should sample the widest possible range of psychotropic medication, as part of their training. They would then have a greater appreciation of what their patients sometimes have to experience, and might think twice about either the dose or the brand they prescribe.

Baldessarini and Battegay (2003) found that generally the therapeutic benefits of psychiatric treatments, including the reduction of suicidal risk, is remarkably limited and poorly studied. They found an exception, though, in the growing evidence for suicide risk reduction with long-term lithium carbonate maintenance therapy in depression.

The UK NHS's National Electronic Library for Health — Mental Health (NeLMH), considers a range of evidence-based treatment summaries. In the case of antidepressants, they indicate that SSRIs (Selective Serotonin Reuptake Inhibitors) and TCAs (Tricyclic Antidepressants) can create a 50–60% improvement in depression. This is backed up by the website Mental Health America (formerly known as the national Mental Health Association) in the United States, which claims that research strongly supports the use of medication to treat the underlying depression (www.mentalhealthamerica.net).

Let us reflect for a moment here, though.

If depression can be defined simply as 'unresolved inner conflicts'; 'unexpressed emotion'; or, 'the absence of hope' rather than as some sinister underlying biochemical pathology in the brain, surely then, is it not better to encourage the person to talk things out and express their thoughts and feelings as soon as possible within the context of some goal-directed talking treatment? If medication becomes the option of first choice, will it not cloud their mind further and hamper their healing process? Can the medication sometimes simply get in the way?

In cases where I have found clients to be over reliant on medication, rather than on their own creativity and solution-building efforts, I have used successfully either or both of the following questions:

1. "When do you think you will be ready to have a conversation with your doctor about reducing this antidepressant medication?"; and,
2. "When you are no longer taking this medication, what side effects will you notice are no longer there?"

Both of these questions can loosen the person's construing around their reliance on medication; are empowering; and, have a subtle presuppositional quality.

From my own experience and from discussion with colleagues, it is never the case that the antidepressants are solely responsible for all the improvement. One way of illustrating this to patients on medication is to use the analogy of Bronze Age track-ways across peat marshes. The tracks were comprised of wooden slats, laid cross-ways through the marsh, from one area of firm ground to another. The travellers, although getting their feet wet as they trudged along the track, did not sink in, due to the wooden slats under foot. Although the wooden slats helped, the travellers still had to make their journey to the firm ground ahead. Medication can be a bit like the wooden slats: the emphasis being on the patient making the effort to travel in the right direction.

Antidepressants can increase suicide risk and attempted suicide amongst those it has been prescribed for (HCEU, 1994). A retrospective cohort study by Rubino et al. (2006), found that Venlafaxine use was consistently associated with higher risk of suicide, compared with Citalopram, Fluoxetine and Dothiepin. They did point out, however, that Venlafaxine users had a higher burden of suicide risk factors and "adjustment for measured confounders substantially reduced the excess risks". They used the cohort of nearly 200 000 people aged 18–89 years who were prescribed the above between 1995–2005.

There are many more studies in the literature on medication and suicide. Space does not allow further discussion here, so I would suggest further literature searches for readers who are interested in particular aspects of this. A good starting point might be Modestin and Schwarzenbach (1992); and, Verkes et al. (1998).

THE MEDICAL MODEL

The 'medical model' is the term cited by R D Laing for the set of procedures in which all doctors are trained (see Siegler et al., 1972). The full set of procedures is comprised of complaint, history, examination, ancillary tests if needed, diagnosis, treatment and prognosis. The medical model is the dominant approach to illness in Western civilization. It aims to find medical treatments for diagnosed symptoms and syndromes and then seeks to treat the human body as a complex organism.

The medical model has attracted many academic articles, both among supporters and critics alike. The model has dominated healthcare generally for well over a century now and attempts to explain many forms of illness. It assumes a causal relationship between disease and illness; illness being the perceived condition of poor health experienced by the patient. For example, a patient who has eaten suspect chicken wings from the fridge feels ill a few hours later. The causal relationship is then one of ingesting bacteria within the chicken wings, leading to feeling unwell.

For physical illnesses, clearly the procedures of the medical model can be useful. Many disease-based illnesses are well suited to the medical model. It has great intuitive appeal and a wealth of biological findings lend support. For example, a young boy falls off his bicycle and complains about a severely painful left ankle. On presenting in the A & E Department of his local hospital, the casualty officer takes a history from the boy of what happened. This is followed by a physical examination, which may involve mild finger pressure at various points on the suspect ankle. The doctor, in our example, decides that an ancillary test of an X-ray is required. This confirms a fracture within two bones of the ankle. The doctor then concludes his diagnosis of 'a fractured left ankle'. He prescribes the following treatment: pain-killing medication, a plaster cast for the lower left leg and foot; and, to give the ankle plenty of rest by keeping it raised for long periods. With regard to the prognosis, he tells his patient that it may take several months to heal completely, but that the plaster cast may be removed after a number of weeks.

We could cite similar procedures to the above example using heart disease or lung cancer.

All, however, is not so straightforward with mental ill-health. Let us look at how the medical model is applied.

One of the main components of the standard diagnostic procedure for a mental ill-health is the 'intake' or 'initial assessment interview'. So, applying the set of procedures outlined above, the presenting client feels unwell (the 'complaint'). He is then interviewed by (say) a young doctor, who may well be a GP trainee employed as a senior house officer within the psychiatric specialty. A significant part of this interview is comprised of history taking.

With a few cases of mental ill-health, the medical model may be helpful. Take, for example, the case of a young professional woman who has been feeling overwhelmed at work for some months, by added work being delegated to her by an insensitive line manager. She has been complaining of poor sleep, generalised worry and anxiety, and her eating pattern has changed markedly. A psychiatrist takes a full history, and indeed, does discover that all was well a few months previously when she was managing her workload well, was enjoying work, and feeling that life was good. Further questioning revealed that latterly, she was not feeling so well and he discovered a long list of symptoms. On physical examination, the psychiatrist noted also recent weight loss and a fine tremor in both hands. He noticed also that his patient was perspiring a lot and that her eyes had a wild look. Additionally, they were flickering continuously and were sensitive to bright light. He was able to diagnose 'severe stress' and prescribed a week off work, to be followed by her arranging an urgent meeting with her line manager to discuss workload and work patterns.

However, all is not so straightforward with a whole range of other presentations of mental ill-health. In fact, it could be argued that, in the above example, there were wider systemic and personality factors which were ignored.

One of the major difficulties is that the clinician relies too much on what the patient tells them. Mental health practitioners deal with human personality and behaviour, which, of course, vary from person to person. Further, the underlying mechanisms which may be operating are not well understood.

At the intake or assessment interview is where most practical issues arise when the medical model of 'mental illness' is adopted. Firstly, the patient is invited to self-report on their symptoms. Several dynamics can operate here. The patient may know a little already about certain 'mental illnesses' and the stigma attached, so may under-report on some of the more alarming symptoms that they may be experiencing. The patient may want help because they have been feeling unwell, but will do their best to avoid being diagnosed as having 'a mental disorder' on account of (say) 'auditory hallucinations' and 'ideas of reference'. Sensitive information then, may be withheld or minimised.

Another issue may be one of embarrassment about certain symptoms, in the presence of a complete stranger at this initial assessment interview. Again, under-reporting may occur.

Interpersonal factors may be operating in the interview, in that the person may get a sense of what they think the interviewer wants to hear, especially if they ask leading questions or seem to be more interested in some answers than others.

Then there is the problem of the person's attention and memory. They may have got so used to some symptoms, they forget to report them. Additionally, clinician and patient may have different understandings or definitions of the language used in the interview, such that any possible diagnosis might be skewed.

To summarise this section, there are many flaws in the information gathering process, with degrees of under-reporting or over-reporting, which can result in inaccurate symptom lists. How then, can this lead to an accurate diagnosis, if a degree of oversimplification or misrepresentation has occurred with their actual mental health profile and experiences?

Furthermore, what clinicians do with the information they have gathered can vary. This can be a very subjective process; some clinicians choosing to leave out information which does not fit the diagnosis they have been favouring. Also, they may be comparing and contrasting the list of symptoms gathered with other patients they have currently or have known previously.

This process does not answer questions around how symptoms may come, go, simply fade gradually, or grow in intensity, from time to time.

Once the medical model clinician has reached a diagnosis, which may be a little shaky given the foregoing, they then move on to the treatment stage, within the set of procedures. They may treat the disorder and not the client by, for example, focusing too much on the 'typical symptoms' of the condition, rather than other issues which comprise the whole person of the client. This can result in either inappropriate medication being prescribed or the wrong dose. In many cases, there is little or no mention of when the dose should be reviewed or the medication stopped completely.

Within the medical model, as applied to mental illness, medication is not the only treatment. Others may involve short-term admission to an acute inpatient facility, community mental health centre appointments, and/or outpatient appointments to monitor treatment. Physical treatments such as electro-convulsive therapy are rarely used nowadays. Pre-frontal leuco-coagulation (formerly leucotomy) is even rarer.

While a great deal of progress has been made in recent years to reduce the stigma around mental health problems, there is still much to be done. Generally, greater percentages of the population feel more comfortable about saying they "feel a bit stressed at the moment"; or, "I've been a bit depressed lately". However, other diagnostic categories still have high stigma value. For instance, a declaration: "My paranoid schizophrenia has been troubling me greatly of late", is many years away from being an acceptable remark in polite society.

People's fears about stigma are not unfounded. A comprehensive survey (Pescosolido & Joseph, 1996) confirmed the existence of a persistent and strong set of negative attitudes towards those experiencing mental ill-health. A significant number of respondents associated psychiatric illness with mental deficiency, violent or socially deviant behaviour, poor life skills and bad character. The same survey found that people carrying a psychiatric diagnostic label shared these negative attitudes with a subsequent consequence on their self-image. There was also a greater tendency to experience social stigma and marginalisation.

In addition to people with mental health problems seeking to avoid stigma, there can also be their wish to avoid institutionalisation, which might result, should they declare a full range of symptoms and co-operate with the full rigours of the medical model. Although most of the old mental hospitals are now shut, many of the community mental health facilities have become 'mini-institutions'. Some of these facilities feed into a ghetto-ised array of community care centres, sheltered housing, or social/rehabilitation centres. Many service users say it is hard to break free from this new type of community institution, once they have been integrated fully into it. Being in receipt of disability benefit can compound their difficulties.

Another limitation of the medical model is that it locates the 'problem' or 'pathology' inside the individual, thereby underestimating the importance of *relational* issues in the person's life, which are nearly always central.

Recently, there have been two interesting developments regarding the medical model as applied to mental ill-health. On the one hand, there is a growing trend in support of it, as pharmacological treatments and research seek greater evidence and understandings into the biological underpinnings of mental ill-health. However, on the other hand, there is a growing appreciation amongst mental health practitioners of the negative consequences and limitations of the medical model. This is matched by a willingness to consider other approaches towards diagnosis and to acknowledge the value of talking treatments and complementary therapies in helping individuals regain their mental health.

5

Other Approaches to Helping the Suicidal

INTRODUCTION

This chapter is intended specifically for those readers who would like to gain an appreciation of what is on offer already to help suicidal people, within 'the field of psychotherapy'. It is also intended to provide a context for and an enrichment of the SFBT approach.

There are countless models and approaches, sub-models and sub-approaches, and generally, they fit within the three main groups: psycho-dynamic; person-centred; and, cognitive behavioural. All have validity and within this chapter, I will consider some six or so different models, which generally are considered as safe, simply describing the core principles outlining the approach they offer to people who are feeling suicidal. Many references to the literature are provided, to allow the reader to investigate one or several in more depth. You will notice some overlap here and there and you may wish to compare and contrast one with another and/or compare one or other with the solution focused approach. There has been much movement towards evidence-based practice over recent years and I will make a start at reviewing the evidence base within some of these models. With regard to the medical model, with its reliance on risk assessment and management, and medication, I have dealt with this in Chapter 4.

Before examining briefly the following models, which are applied to working with the suicidal, I am going to make an apology. I am apologising for lapsing into jargon and possible over-complication, something I set out to avoid at the outset. However, I believe it is important to do the models justice, by using their own particular terminology and ways of explaining things. As I do so, I will compare and contrast from time to time with the solution focused approach. If you wish to skip this chapter or just skim through it, please do so.

THE MODELS

It has been suggested that there are between 250 and 400 different models and approaches to helping people with difficulties, worries and concerns (Karasu, 1986). For the purpose of this book, I will consider just six of the main ones as follows:

- Person-centred
- Cognitive behavioural
- Rational emotive behaviour therapy
- Psychoanalytic
- Transactional analysis
- Existential therapy.

PERSON-CENTRED COUNSELLING

The principle contributor to the body of knowledge of person-centred counselling (or humanistic approaches, as it is sometimes referred to), was Carl Rogers (1959), who laid much emphasis on the importance of establishing a good therapeutic relationship. Rogers' core conditions of acceptance, genuineness and empathy are essential in establishing rapport, trust and then a good working relationship, as discussed already in Chapter 2. (I will refer again to the key part played by Rogers' core conditions in Chapters 7 and 8.)

For many years, person-centred counselling (or therapy) has been the basis for crisis counselling with suicidal clients (Hamelinck, 1990; Kalafat, 2002). There has been a trend over recent years, however, for many psychotherapists to consider that this approach on its own is insufficient.

Antoon Leenaars (2004), being essentially a person-centred practitioner with a multi-modal approach, suggested that "No psychotherapy with suicidal people can be isolated; intervention may require medication, hospitalisation, and direct environmental controls . . . Psychotherapy with suicidal people must use a multi-component (multi-modal) approach (i.e. medication, hospitaliza-tion, etc.)" (p. 196). Leenaars speaks in terms of 'highly lethal individuals' when referring to the suicidal and favours a variety of measures to be helpful. In addition to the above-mentioned, these might include support, behavioural techniques and psychodynamic interpretation. Also, ". . . the involvement of others to whom the patient was (and is) attached, but also 'social agencies' — teachers, priests, elders, the Chief, doctors, social workers, anyone — all of whom serve, directly or indirectly, to mollify the pain" (p. 207). This contrasts with the solution focused approach, which could be described as largely uni-modal, as it emphasises the client-therapist relationship as being key in bring-ing about recovery.

Leenaars describes the phenomenon of 'cognitive constriction' in suicidal people, where they narrow their vision, as if through blinkers, to make a choice between suicide or not. In his approach to suicidal people, he makes suggestions of alternatives to 'widen the blinkers', such that they consider more than "A or not-A" (p. 217). Leenaars provides a useful and hopefully, a life-saving response in his recent work (2004), saying he is indebted to the work of Edwin Schneidman, whose best comments on psychotherapy can be found in the following references: Schneidman (1999a, 1999b). Leenaars quotes Schneidman in what can be considered a very person-centred approach to the suicidal person: "Suicide prevention is not an efficiency operation, it is a human exchange" (Leenaars, 2004, p. 211).

Leenaars believes, too, that the relationship is of great importance. Sui-cide prevention, he adds, should be based on a humanitarian approach to life and the psychotherapy. It has been established over a long period that those who persevere with and benefit from psychotherapy are those who have de-veloped a good working relationship (Dyck, Joyce & Azim, 1984; Luborski et al., 1985). It is the sense that such people feel heard and understood, that is important.

Like Rogers, Leenaars in suggesting that psychotherapy must be person-centred — not this or that disorder-centred — urges practitioners to keep in mind that they are essentially treating the person. He talks about the person's feeling of trauma, that is, "driving up the patient's sense of perturbation" (p. 223). According to Leenaars, the practitioner's goal, via the multi-dimensional approach, which is essentially person-centred, is to reduce that sense of trauma.

The person-centred therapist asks the person questions such as: 'What is going on?'; 'Where do you hurt?'; and, 'What would you like to have hap-pen?' as a way of connecting with the suicidal person. It is well known that suicide is a way of stopping painful tension and thus providing relief from the psychological pain which the person is finding intolerable. Questions such as these, built on a basis of Rogerian core conditions, can be another way of helping reduce tension and thus providing relief from psychological pain. One should also be realistic in this process. Leenaars again: "One should not attempt to establish an impossibly perfect situation. Indeed, one needs the hopelessness to psychologically move the person. Yet one should provide initially, some transfusion of sound hope, self-help, and not feeling boxed in" (p. 216).

In believing strongly that it is important always to understand the person fully if they are to be treated effectively, Leenaars suggests that psychotherapists working with the suicidal must constantly adapt their approach to each unique individual.

Egan (1998) developed a problem-management approach to helping, which is essentially client-centred. He states that there are two goals of helping. The first of these relates to clients managing their lives more effectively; and, the second relates to clients' general ability to manage problems and develop opportunities. In referring to the many and various helping models, Egan concluded that, "ultimately, all models converge around the principle client-centred goal of managing problems in living more effectively and developing opportunities more fully" (p. 13).

Egan's Helping Model is a collaborative model between client and helper and seeks to clarify the *current scenario,* the *preferred scenario,* and the *strategy for getting there.* It is a dynamic model which involves action at various stages in the process to achieve valued outcomes. Egan lays great emphasis on the needs of the client being the starting point of the helping process. It should also be an active approach in which clients are challenged and encouraged to challenge themselves. This ensures problems and opportunities are explored, goals set and a plan is worked out, as to how these goals will be pursued.

Egan, in emphasising the collaborative nature of the helping process, states that effective counselling depends not only on the competence and motivation of the helper, but also on the competence and motivation of the client in working towards their goals. Helpers-to-be, however, need more than a helping model with which to work. Most importantly, they need a range of skills to make it work. These skills, which Rogers (1951) I am sure would endorse, include basic and advanced communication skills; the ability to establish a good working relationship; the ability to help clients challenge themselves; problem clarification skills; goal setting; skills in developing action plans; implementation skills; and the ability to evaluate both the process of the work and the progress towards the client's stated goals. Many would argue that a lot of these skills come naturally to many workers who are attracted to the field of helping. Whether this is true or not, Egan suggests: "The only way to acquire these skills is by learning them experientially, practising them, and using them until they become second nature" (p. 41).

As a person- (or client-)centred practitioner, Egan argues that because his problem-management and opportunity-development model is embedded in all forms of helping, it can be applied widely across the helping professions. In the chapters dealing with the solution focused approach, it will become clear how the ideas of both Rogers and Egan form a good foundation for the therapeutic work.

COGNITIVE-BEHAVIOURAL THERAPY

Cognitive-behavioural models of suicide are based on the assumption that cognitive processes have a direct impact on the emotions and subsequent behaviour (Beck et al., 1979). It is suggested that there are a range of cognitive processes (assumptions, beliefs, automatic thoughts, expectations, influences, etc.) which influence how an individual responds emotionally and behaviourally to life events. Suicidal thinking and behaviour is caused, the model suggests, by maladaptive cognitive, behavioural and interpersonal processes learned in the course of development (Reinecke, 2000). There are a number of cognitive-behavioural models of suicide: Bonner and Rich (1987); Freeman and Reinecke (1993); and Rudd, Joiner and Rajab (2001).

Cognitive behaviourists and clients work together to examine their thoughts, beliefs and problem-solving approaches. They look, too, at their social behaviour and their skills around regulating their emotions.

Cognitive-behavioural therapy (CBT) is good for treating depression, but there is some controversy around how useful it is in treating severe depression. Therapist experience and competence may be factors in the latter case.

Aaron Beck and colleagues have contributed most to this particular model, when working with depression generally, but with suicide specifically. Their work dates back to the 1960s (Beck, 1963) and various assessment tools have been devised along the way to help practitioners in working with clients on a cognitive level. One of these is the Suicide Intent Scale (SIS) (Beck, Schyler & Herman, 1974), within which there are 15 items. There is also available the Lethality Scale (LS) (Beck et al., 1975); and, the Scale of Suicidal Ideation (SSI). Probably one of the more widely used in depression certainly, is the Beck Hopelessness Scale (BHS). The concept of hopelessness was central to Beck's theory and this assessment tool was developed to measure this construct. The BHS is comprised of 20 true–false statements which are designed to assess the extent of positive and negative beliefs about the future, during the previous week. The BHS score total ranges from 0–20. It is clear to see how this has good applicability to suicidal clients, where hopelessness is invariably a feature. Beck, Brown and Steer (1989) found that mental health inpatients who scored 9 or more were approximately 11 times more likely to commit suicide than those who scored 8 or below. Another researcher, Reich, showed that patients whose hopelessness does not change significantly with mental health inpatient treatment may be more likely to go on to commit suicide (in Dahlsgaard, Beck & Brown, 1998). In an earlier study of suicide attempters, Petrie, Chamberlain and Clarke (1988) found that the BHS provided a unique estimate of subsequent suicide attempts.

From Beck's writings can be found 10 protocol sentences and although space here does not allow these to be outlined in detail, some are as follows:

- Hopelessness (as mentioned above), is a critical factor. The suicidal person views the suicide option as the only possible solution to his/her desperately and hopelessly insoluble problem (or situation).
- The future is viewed negatively.
- The suicidal person's view of self is negative. They tend to see themselves as incompetent, helpless and incurable. It is not uncommon to hear expressions of self-blame, low self-evaluation and self-criticism.
- Feeling hopeless and not wanting to tolerate the pain or suffering, the suicidal person desires to escape. Death is thought of as more desirable than life.

With regard to depression and hopelessness, some research has been undertaken with suicide attempters which showed that most people who attempt suicide or experience suicidal ideation are feeling depressed, hopeless or both (Beck et al., 1979; Brown et al., 2000).

In response to recent research developments, Beck (1996) has refined his original model of cognitive therapy, by the introduction of the concept of 'modes' to account for the diversity of symptoms observed in most mental health states. Within this, he has touched on the 'suicide mode'.

The general cognitive principles used for suicide are: agenda setting, symptom monitoring, reviewing the presenting problem, goal setting, and educating about the cognitive model. Other principles used are: assigning and reviewing homework, obtaining feedback, listing automatic thoughts, labelling emotions, identifying cognitive distortions, completing dysfunctional thought records, activity scheduling and the use of coping cards (Beck et al., 1979; Beck, 1995). The main focus of the therapy is to attempt to help people transform their hopelessness into hope. This is key, as even the most miniscule glimmer of hope can begin to move the person away from the suicide option. In later chapters, it will become clear how this notion of 'hope' is central to the effectiveness of the solution focused approach.

In considering problem solving, one interesting finding was that people who are suicidal often have deficits in this area (Marx, Williams & Claridge, 1992). CBT's problem-solving technique helps people identify clear links between their life problems and their suicidal thoughts and behaviours. Further, it assists identification of strengths, skills and resources, while teaching them a systemic method for overcoming their problems and enhancing their feelings of control and competency. In addition to helping suicidal people discover their internal personal resources, the major goal of CBT is to encourage the development of the person's social resources. This might include weekly scheduling of pleasurable social activities and the broadening of the person's network of social contacts. Identification of strengths, skills and resources is fundamental also to solution focused therapy.

An integral part of CBT is to help people identify and target suicidal cognitions. Part of their learning process — often involving 'cognitive restructuring' — is that they learn to recognise thinking patterns that lead to suicidal ideation and develop strategies that tackle cognitive distortions. One way of doing this might be to encourage the person to address the advantages and disadvantages of taking the suicide option, which would include listing the reasons for living and those for dying.

One of the highly appealing tools of CBT which is a powerful and personal reminder of the person's connection to life is the 'hope kit' (Beck et al., in Jobes, 2006). For use in emergencies, this can be a container that holds various photos, souvenirs, mementoes, letters, symbols and such like, which can serve as helpful reminders of reasons to live.

A client of mine found it helpful to have close by a box which contained photographs of his children, some merit certificates from schooldays, and a shiny piece of coal which was a reminder of his family's connection with mining.

The CBT approach to suicide can be rather long-winded when a 10-or-more session protocol is tailored to individual patients. People in crisis often want things to change quickly. More recently, attention has been given to the development of brief, focused interventions which target suicidal behaviour directly as the primary focus of therapy. Specific cognitive and behavioural strategies have been developed, arising out of cognitive theory, which include a multi-step crisis plan and a detailed cognitive conceptualisation of the suicide attempt. Other aspects of this strategy involve the use of coping cards and the hope kit mentioned above. Also, suicidal people are encouraged to rehearse coping skills at times of crisis, and are assessed regularly as to treatment progress. It is the hope of cognitive-behavioural therapists that there will be a further refinement of these developments, to increase effectiveness of the model in working with suicide. It is interesting to note that there is a growing trend towards incorporating solution focused ideas into this model.

What about some of the other CBT studies which have offered help to suicidal clients? Jansson (1984) found that introducing training in social skills by way of modifying clients' behaviour, can result in both reduced depression and suicidality. Gresham (1998) made similar findings. Other studies (Bostock & Williams, 1974; O'Farrell, Goodenough & Cutter, 1981), in which suicidal clients were treated by reinforcing appropriate behaviours while at the same time not reinforcing suicidal behaviours, were found to be helpful. Therapy contracts were set up as a part of this treatment process. Farrelly and Brandsma (1974) used the simple behavioural technique of paradoxical intention, a technique first described by Frankl in 1946 (Frankl, 1963), who proposed an existential psychotherapy (see below). As mentioned earlier, this technique is now used to good effect within solution focused therapy. Farrelly and Brandsma used it in the following way:

CL: Lately, I feel quite suicidal.
TH: [softening it with humour]: Suicide would be *an* approach to your problem.

Kohlenberg and Tsai (2000), in developing an approach for working with chronically suicidal women, referred to their "functional analytic therapy", which was a mix of behaviour therapy and cognitive therapy. They taught their clients more empowering ways of thinking (cognitive therapy), plus they focused on more activities that brought pleasure (behaviour therapy).

Rosenthal (1986) outlined ways to help suicidal clients within the context of a 'learned helplessness syndrome'. There were five key stages to this approach, the first of which was a written contract for the client to contact the worker if they felt suicidal. Secondly, the therapist intervenes in some way in the client's environment. This might involve talking to the client's parent, spouse, next of kin, or even their boss. This was intended to be a way of the worker showing the client they were on their side. The third stage involves the worker suggesting to the client that they keep a log of self-defeating thoughts and feelings; the idea being this lessens their frequency and impact. (It might, however, be argued nowadays that this is a way of reinforcing these unwanted thoughts and feelings, and could be counter-productive.)

Fourthly, the therapist works on anger, if it is appropriate so to do. Rosenthal believes that there is a close relation between anger and suicide. Many contemporary specialists in the field would, I am sure, agree with this view. (See 'the solution focused feelings tank' in Chapter 8, for ways to dissipate or discharge anger.)

Rosenthal spoke specifically about shy and timid clients and the need to teach them assertiveness skills and how to express anger in ways which were socially acceptable. Aggressive clients could be taught how to be assertive, to replace their aggressive communication style, and were given homework to practise more empathic ways to express their feelings. Last, but not least, of these five stages was for the therapist to hold out hope that solutions are possible to the suicidal person's extreme and/or distressing circumstances. Hope, here again, is seen as an important factor/ingredient. Yufit and Lester (2005): "When individuals can see that an alternative future may exist and that change can be brought about by personal effort, true freedom of action becomes possible. With freedom of action, there is hope" (p. 225).

There have been further offshoots of CBT in the treatment of suicide and one such is detailed below.

DIALECTIC BEHAVIOUR THERAPY

Another form of CBT was developed by Linehan (1993) and is called Dialectical Behaviour Therapy (DBT). It developed out of her theories about suicide. DBT is defined as "A comprehensive, multi-modal approach that balances change strategies with acceptance strategies". Linehan describes how this balance is achieved by integrating CBT strategies with validation and mindfulness approaches, within a dialectical framework. Validation strategies are where the therapist recognises and communicates verbally how the patient's responses make sense. It is interesting to note here that this is a central aspect to Kelly's Personal Construct Approach (Kelly, 1963); and, as will be seen later, this is also a key part of the solution focused approach. In DBT, in addition, validation communicates that the person makes sense. This is referred to as 'implicit validation'. Validation improves collaboration with problem solving and attendance at sessions. Mindfulness (Isebaert, 2005) is a particular way of paying attention, on purpose, in the present moment and doing so in a non-judgmental way. Too often, depressed clients who are prone to suicidal thinking can become overwhelmed with thoughts of past faults and mistakes and also, at the same time, be overwhelmed by frightening thoughts about the future. Mindfulness is a way of calming anxieties and for clients to get to know themselves better. They focus in on listening to what they are actually experiencing and then engage with it. Mindfulness can give a new perspective, from where the individual can judge better what is really meaningful and important to them in the present moment.

In finding that CBT was not enough in her view, Linehan (1993) went on to develop DBT, adding in acceptance strategies (validation and mindfulness) to the treatment, along with dialectical strategies. The dialectical philosophy is the central feature of DBT. What is it? Without wishing to be over-complicated and lost here in the language of philosophy: within the dialectical framework of DBT, the person's reality is seen as continuous, dynamic and holistic. From this perspective, reality is simultaneously both whole and consisting of bi-polar components. Dialectical truth emerges by the process of combining (or synthesising) elements from opposing positions (the thesis + the antithesis). The primary dialectic in DBT is that of acceptance and change. Learning to accept is a change in itself, from a dialectical perspective. These dialectical strategies are woven into all client–worker interactions.

Backtracking briefly, Linehan's earlier bio-social theory (1981, 1986 & 1993) regarded suicidal behaviour as a learned method for coping with acute levels of emotional suffering. Suicidal behaviour was viewed as a skill deficit in that people seek death as their solution to intense pain and/or suffering because they can come up with no other effective options. This makes sense when people who are suicidal go down a path of blinkered thinking as regards possible options. This is a key consideration of the solution focused approach. I call this 'narrowing of the blinkers'. Schneidman (1981) uses the more technical term of 'cognitive constriction'.

Linehan's theory is based on numerous causal pathways to dysfunctional behaviour. She cites environmental causes such as adverse events, lack of social support, and role models for suicidal behaviour (i.e. famous people who have committed suicide). With regard to the feature of emotional suffering, Linehan uses the term 'emotional dysregulation'. Schneidman (2001) used the term 'psychache' to describe this extreme form of emotional suffering.

Hopelessness theory, as described by Abramson, Metalsky and Alloy (1989), features within DBT. It is suggested that depression leads to suicidal thinking and behaviour because of extremes in hopeless thinking. In another study, Brown et al. (2000) found that measures of hopelessness were good predictors of strong suicidal behaviour. Linehan supported the idea that hopelessness and all-or-nothing thinking is likely related to ineffective problem solving.

In considering the 'multi-modal' aspects of DBT, what does this mean in reality, in contemporary approaches to working with suicidal people? Some might describe it more in terms of a 'treatment package', which consists of individual behaviour therapy, skills training, as-needed telephone conversations between face-to-face contacts, and a therapist consultation team, some of whose members could be seeing the suicidal person as well.

DBT is comprised of six broad treatment strategies, some of which have been referred to above. These are the two core strategies of problem solving and validation. A further two are dialectical strategies; and, general change procedures. The last two strategies of the six consist of communication and case management. With regard to problem solving, its goal is to generate effective solutions for crucial dysfunctional thoughts, emotions and behaviours that have been identified during the therapeutic process. Therapists' 'communication strategy' within DBT is somewhat intriguing. Balance is sought between acceptance and change through various communication styles. On the one hand, the therapist can be warm and responsive to the suicidal person, yet on the other may be irreverent by being matter-of-fact or confrontational; or use off-the-wall comments and humour. The aim here is to get the client's attention and to endeavour to get them unstuck in their thinking.

Considering now the 'general change procedures', the purpose within DBT is to modify the suicidal person's dysfunctional thoughts, emotions and behaviours which have been identified by the therapist and/or client as problematic. Cognitive and emotional change is sought. Importantly, during the first session, suicidal and self-injurious behaviours are targeted. Clients are strenuously encouraged to desist from such behaviours. DBT therapists may challenge clients' cognitions directly. For example, they may raise doubts about whether suicide will resolve their problems, anyway. Ellis (2006), in referring to change procedures within DBT, said of the cognitive modification of hopeless thinking, "it involves inspiring hope through verbal cheerleading, generating and highlighting reasons for living, and believing wholeheartedly in patients' ultimate capabilities to succeed" (p. 107). This accords well with the essential beliefs within SFBT of hope and optimism.

In conclusion, DBT was the first therapy, (and is still one of the only therapies), to be shown to have an impact on suicidal behaviour in randomised controlled studies. However, it needs to be stressed that Linehan's work focused a lot on borderline personality disorder, where suicidal ideation and behaviour is often chronic in such individuals. Linehan et al. (1991) showed that there were reductions in depression, hopelessness and suicidal ideation, over time, although the differences between the treatment group and the control group (treatment as usual), were not significant. With their frequently self-injurious behaviours, chronically suicidal individuals are a stressful client group with which to work and are notoriously more challenging to treat.

Linehan offers both clinicians and researchers a model for understanding the onset and maintenance of suicidal behaviours. More data, though, are needed to test the theory. Miller, Rathus and Linehan (2007) used DBT with suicidal adolescents. The techniques of DBT were adapted to treat multi-problem adolescents at highest risks of suicidal behaviour and self-harm.

They looked at who is most at risk and used primary targets and various strategies in the treatment process.

RATIONAL EMOTIVE BEHAVIOUR THERAPY

As a form of CBT, Rational Emotive Behaviour Therapy (REBT) offers a model of working with suicidal individuals. Within the model, there is considerable overlap with other CBTs. In this section, I will look briefly at how suicide and suicidal behaviour is conceptualised; and, how suicidal people can be helped through REBT.

It is accurate to say that there are a limited number of articles examining suicide from an REBT perspective; little research having been carried out to date. One such article was by Ellis and Ratliff (1986). Ellis (1989) described a case of a 27-year-old suicidal woman, and showed how REBT techniques such as unconditional acceptance were helpful. Diekstra, Engels and Methorst (1988) presented a similar theoretical approach, suggesting that REBT could be used as a form of crisis intervention for depressed individuals who are feeling suicidal.

The issue of hopelessness is highlighted in REBT, (Minkoff, Bergman, Beck & Beck, 1973), as it is in CBT outlined earlier. What is acknowledged is that the precise source of this hopelessness is less understood.

Ellis (2006) quoted Ellis and Newman (1996) in highlighting the importance of changing our thinking to produce an effect on our emotions: "The realisation that we can reduce negative emotions and modify dysfunctional behaviours by changing ones' thinking, can have an empowering effect that might be especially beneficial to suicidal individuals" (p. 77). REBT talks of extremes in thinking in suicidal individuals. The terms 'awfulising' and 'catastrophising' are used to describe it. An example of an awfulisation is: 'This situation in which I find myself is so awful that either it will kill me or I will kill myself'. A catastrophising statement might be: 'If I do not get this job, the one I really want, it will be the end of the world for me'.

REBT offers the 'A-B-C model' for working with people who are suicidal, as outlined by Ellis (2006). 'A' stands for an activating event such as some form of loss (a person, health, etc.) or failure (in relationship or job, perhaps). It could equally be some major stressor which has occurred in their life. What then follows is 'B' for beliefs (various cognitive processes). These firmly held beliefs could be the awfulising, catastrophising or hopelessness mentioned earlier, or could simply be some sort of negative self-rating. The third stage in this model is 'C' for the emotional-behavioural consequences.

These consequences can consist of feelings of desperation and despair, with accompanying thoughts of suicide and even suicidal impulses. In extreme cases, self-harming behaviours and completed suicide can result.

From the REBT perspective, some common dysfunctional beliefs in suicidal individuals are:

'If I fail to achieve something worthwhile, I am a worthless person and my life, therefore, is not worth living.'

'I cannot bear to be sad or unhappy.'

'Failure at love is just something too miserable to bear.'

'As far as my family and friends are concerned, I would be better off dead.'

This A-B-C model of REBT is simple and straightforward to understand, both for the practitioner and for the suicidal person. Practitioners can illustrate very easily, how the person's learned thinking processes operate and the dreadful consequences (C) that can result. REBT seeks to help the suicidal person put their beliefs (B) to the test by helping them examine the evidence for and against. Also, the REBT therapist helps individuals to work towards profound philosophical changes in their lives as a whole. An example of one of these philosophical changes is to get some change in the beliefs or thinking around such statements as: 'Life should be fair and it is unbearable when it is not'. As we grow older and wiser, one thing we find out is that life is not fair but unfairness is bearable, depending on the stance we take towards it.

PSYCHODYNAMIC

Freud (1901), in the early twentieth century, was the first to consider a psychoanalytic perspective on suicide. Others have been Karl Meninger, Henry A. Murray and Gregory Zilboorg. Psychoanalysts assert that suicide is motivated by unconscious intentions, the root cause being an experience of loss and rejection of a significant, highly cathected object (i.e. a person). There is some ambivalence in the form of affection and hostility towards the person. As a fulfilment of punishment (i.e. self-punishment) the suicidal person experiences a sense of guilt or self-punishment.

The techniques of psychoanalysis are generally well known as this model has been around for a long time. Probably the best known is that of 'free association', where the client permits his or her mind to wander freely from memory to memory. The psychoanalyst is informed of the chain of associations as the client associates freely.

'Transference' is where the client attributes thoughts and desires to the psychoanalyst that are *not* possessed by the analyst. This phenomenon is worked through over the (often extensive) treatment process. 'Interpretation' is perhaps more straightforward and this is where simply, the psychoanalyst interprets the client's thinking and behaviour to the client.

Psychoanalysis places much of its emphasis and importance on childhood experiences. This is essentially because clients' unconscious desires, say psychoanalysts, are formed from childhood wishes. Additionally, many super ego wishes of the client derive from the commands clients' parents have made upon them; and, in some cases, are still making upon them.

Yufit and Lester (2005) have pointed out that Freud made numerous brief mentions of suicidal behaviour throughout his writings. These have been documented and synthesised by Litman (1967). From a psychoanalytic perspective, Yufit and Lester list the clinical features of suicidal behaviour principally, as follows:

- Guilt over death wishes towards others
- Identification with a suicidal parent
- Refusal to accept loss or gratification
- Suicide as an act of revenge
- Suicide as an escape from humiliation
- Suicide as a communication
- Suicide as a connection between death and sexuality.

There is no doubt that psychoanalysis is helpful in providing a greater understanding of suicidal behaviour: there is a good deal of research which is supportive of theory (Litman, 1967). For example, the experience of loss in suicidal people; and, the relationships between suicide and both anger and depression. It is well known that a healthy expression of anger and the expression of other deeply-held negative emotions can lead to both an alleviation of depression and a reduction in suicidal thinking and behaviour.

It could be suggested that a psychoanalytic perspective is helpful in providing a greater understanding of the reasons behind a suicide (e.g. Sylvia Plath). The precipitating events for strong suicidal thinking and behaviour are obvious: a break-up of a close relationship, financial problems, legal difficulties, etc. *But* the vast majority of people experiencing these life events do not go on to commit suicide. However, as mentioned in Chapter 2, most might think about the suicide option, albeit fleetingly, at some point in their lives. Psychoanalysts are good at probing for possible unconscious motives in cases where serious life events occur. A criticism might be levelled though, that these motives are neither necessary nor sufficient to account for the suicide act.

With regard to psychoanalytic treatment, the goals are many, but one important one is to make conscious to the client what is happening on an unconscious level. If the worker does make these drives conscious, the client will not necessarily want to satisfy them directly. In the future, hopefully, it will enable them to make more appropriate choices.

Psychoanalysis does not attempt to alter the client's choice to suicide, but rather to make it a more informed one. Clients receiving psychoanalysis may become distressed during the process, whereby they are making conscious their various unconscious thought processes, so it is important for the work to proceed slowly and carefully. In many cases, clients are seen for 1–2 sessions a week for a year or more.

The slowness of psychoanalysis makes it unsuitable for crisis intervention work with suicidal clients. It has to be said there are few, if any, cases in which psychoanalytic theory has been described as the preferred method of choice for those clients whose main presenting problem has been a preoccupation with serious suicidal thoughts and ideas.

TRANSACTIONAL ANALYSIS

Within this model the unit of social intercourse is called a 'transaction' (Berne, 1964). Transactional Analysis (TA) can be described as a simplified conception of psychoanalysis. It is a very helpful system for both clinician and patient to understand the dynamics of what has been happening in their relationships, and indeed, what may be happening in the current suicidal state.

Transactional analysts have written frequently about suicide *but* generally have not suggested ways in which TA can be helpful to suicidal clients. Those adopting the TA framework believe beginnings of suicidal behaviour can be found in the client's early years when the injunction 'don't exist' can be picked up from parents or care-givers around at the time. This injunction then becomes incorporated into the growing child's sense of self (Woollams, Brown & Huige, 1977).

TA's three ego states, which are generally known universally, are as follows:

Child (the state of mind the ego had as a child)
Adult (mature, information-processing state of mind)
Parent (based on the person's identification with his or her parent/parent
    substitute).

These three ego states can be helpful in understanding suicidal behaviour. It is the child ego state which feels a sense of hopelessness and despair, crying out to be rescued. As practitioners recognise this, if they can encourage their client's 'adult' to get back in control at times of suicidal crisis, this can prove very helpful (Orton, 1974). This is, of course, a very empowering strategy on the practitioner's part. Nurturing responses from the practitioner's 'parent' ego state are likely not to work because simply, it strengthens the role of the child ego state within the client. Examples of statements from the practitioner's parent ego state might be:

"Promise me you won't take your life"; and, "I will do all I can to stop you killing yourself". Some might wonder if this is a contributory factor to the many suicides amongst patients in inpatient mental health facilities worldwide, because to a lesser or greater extent, they are adopting a nurturing parent role, either implicitly or explicitly. From my length experience of working within such facilities, the patient either accepts or rebels against this.

When practitioners pick up that the child's ego state has strong feelings of despair and hopelessness and is beginning to play with the idea of suicide, simple non-threatening 'adult' questions, which are at first sight unrelated to the problems presented, can enable the client's 'adult' to take control.

Examples of these would be:

"Where exactly do you live; your address?"

"What sorts of responsibilities does your job include?"

"Before things got as they have done, what were your main hobbies and interests?"

Until the child's adult ego state is back in control, it is unhelpful to ask problem/worry/difficulty-probing questions. These would serve simply to strengthen the client's child ego state position, thereby pushing them nearer towards suicidal behaviour.

Once the practitioner sees that their client's adult ego state is firmly established (i.e. 'child' is under control), the client may begin to feel relief as on the one hand, they view their world differently, and on the other, they feel strengthened and more capable of dealing with it. The perceptive practitioner will then gradually move more tentatively towards talk about the problem. If they notice the 'child' reappearing, they can return again to more 'adult' strengthening.

Another way in which TA can be helpful is in the area of communication styles. Many individuals who become suicidal could benefit from information and maybe some training in assertiveness. If they are presenting to the world in 'child', they are more likely to engage the 'parent' of the other person, as illustrated in Figure 5.1 below:

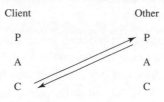

Figure 5.1 'Lose-Win'

What is desirable is that their 'adult' engages assertively, with the 'adult' of the other person (see Figure 5.2). This then becomes a 'win-win' situation, in preference to the earlier 'lose-win' example.

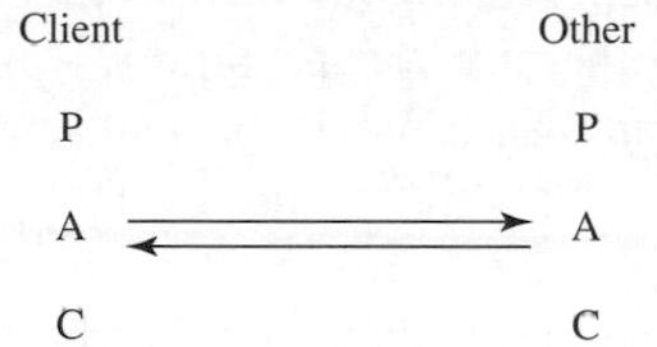

Client   Other

P   P

A ⟷ A

C   C

Figure 5.2 'Win-Win'

From a TA perspective, it is interesting what 'games' people play (Berne, 1964) in their social and family interactions. Some games are passed on down through the generations. Some of these are very maladaptive and can cause unpleasantness to the players on various levels. This historical aspect of games was highlighted by Berne (1964): "Games may be diluted from one generation to another; but there seems to be a strong tendency to inbreed with people who play a game of the same family, if not the same genus" (p. 151). Unless therapists intervene successfully in this process, the game can be passed on to the next generation.

Sometimes with expressions of suicidal intent or risky self-harming behaviour, this too, may have been a 'game' learned from the previous generation. TA can be a helpful way of identifying what is happening on the inter-personal level and maybe to encourage greater client awareness of these dynamics, before moving on to some helpful interventions to achieve permanent change.

A basic awareness and understanding of TA is, I believe, very helpful to all care-givers, whatever their particularly preferred model. It has a certain value, too, for the solution focused approach, especially in cases where self-esteem and self-confidence need strengthening. This can often be so in cases where the context is one of unhealthy interpersonal or intra-familial dynamics.

EXISTENTIAL LOGOTHERAPY

There are various existential approaches to mental health and a few have contributions to make to suicide prevention.

The one which has influenced my thinking and therapeutic practice most over nearly 40 years is 'existential logotherapy'. It was developed by Viktor Frankl: a psychiatrist, a former student of Alfred Adler, and a concentration camp survivor. Many of his writings arose out of his concentration camp experiences, and one of his major discoveries was that the main reason for death amongst inmates was the giving up of hope (Frankl, 1959, p. 81). Frankl was influenced by Nietzche. One of Nietzche's maxims being, "that which does not kill me makes me stronger".

One of the basic concepts of logotherapy is that it focuses on the patient and his/her future. Logotherapy means simply 'meaning-treatment' (from the Greek 'logos' — meaning). Einstein (in Dukas & Hoffman, 1979) spoke about lack of meaning as follows: "The man who regards his life as meaningless, is not merely unhappy, but hardly fit for life". Logotherapy, which has been called the Third Viennese School of Psychotherapy, (Freud and Jung being the First and Second, respectively), focuses on the meaning of human existence, as well as on Man's search for meaning. Frankl asserted that this striving to find a meaning in one's life is the primary motivational force in Man. Throughout his writings, he talks about 'the will to meaning'. When Man experiences difficulties in finding meaning in life, Frankl described this as 'existential frustration'. Existential was used in three ways within his writings. Firstly it could refer to existence itself; and secondly, to the *meaning* of existence. The third was the striving to find a concrete meaning in personal existence (i.e. 'the will to meaning').

Existential frustration can result in noögenic neurosis ('noös' — Greek for mind), which has its origins in the noölogical dimension of human existence. Frankl suggested that noögenic neurosis was behind most mental distress in contemporary society.

How does all this help us with our understanding of suicide?

Frankl (1973) was appalled at the high number of students in American Universities that, despite being surrounded by affluence, decided to take their lives. At one time it was second only to road traffic accidents as the main cause of death in young people. He reported a dean at one such university who, during his counselling work, was ". . . continually being confronted by students who complained about the meaninglessness of life, who were beset by that inner void I call existential 'vacuum'" (p. 28).

With respect to endogenous depression (that which was thought to result from early personality development and intrinsic biological processes), he suggested that patients experience it in a pathologically distorted way, which brings about an abnormal awareness of guilt. Patients who then find themselves confronted with their existential guilt during a depressive state may very well experience intensified tendencies towards self-accusation. This can occur to such an extent that it provokes suicide. Some research in the Czech Republic by Kratochvil and Planova (in Frankl, 1978, p. 31), concerning neurotic patients, found that, in some cases, the frustration of the will to meaning had a relevant role as a factor in the origin of the neurosis or of the suicide attempt.

Within logotherapy, there is much emphasis placed on the role of suffering; and how through it, we can derive meaning. This is the same idea as in some of the main world religions. With the suicidal patient, it is not the suicidal impulses which are important: suicide risk does not depend on the strength of these impulses. Rather, it is the patient's *response* to these impulses which is important. In turn, his reaction, basically, will depend on how meaningful survival will be, however painful it might be (Frankl, 1978, p. 71).

With patients who are experiencing noögenic neurosis, and these were estimated to be a majority of such patients, the logotherapist works on helping the patient rediscover their sense of meaning and purpose in life. It may be that they derive meaning through their pain and suffering, as just referred to. Or, it may be they can be encouraged to strive for higher ideals; goals or pursuits through which they can rediscover a sense of personal meaning to their existence. Logotherapy as a technique discourages people from seeking pleasure directly as a goal in itself, urging patients instead to experience it as a side-effect, as they strive towards their will to meaning. One of the techniques of logotherapy is *paradoxical intention*, which Frankl described first in 1946 and later in a more systematised way in 1960. Solution Focused Brief Therapy has also adopted this technique and it has been used successfully, in recent years, for a variety of difficulties both with individuals and couples.

Logotherapy as a school of existential psychiatry is very effective (Crumbaugh & Maholick, 1963; Crumbaugh, 1968). As an approach to people's problems, like SFBT, it is not afraid to talk about death. It is not pessimistic but realistic in that it faces the tragic triad of human existence: pain-death-guilt. Logotherapy is optimistic because it shows the client how to transform despair into triumph. Rather than existential logotherapy being a psychotherapeutic treatment for suicidal people, it is more of a philosophy of life they can be encouraged to embrace. The result of their acceptance of the basic beliefs and assumptions of the logo-therapeutic viewpoint would be for clients to view their position of pain and suffering caused by the predicament in which they find themselves, in a wholly different way. As they rediscover meaning to their existence, their noögenic neurosis would heal and their existential vacuum be filled.

An instrument called the Purpose-in-Life (P-I-L) test was designed to test Frankl's ideas (Crumbaugh, 1968). Results from 225 subjects demonstrated the predicted differences between clinical and *normal* populations. The data supported the theory that when meaning in life is not found, the result is existential frustration. Within the *normal* range, this shows up as existential vacuum. Among patients in the clinical group, this assumed the proportions of noögenic neurosis.

The purpose of Crumbaugh's study was to gather further quantitative evidence concerning the validity of Frankl's basic thesis. The P-I-L test was a 20-item scale with good reliability. Each item is rated on a 1–7 scale. Some examples of the 20 items include:

'I am usually: completely bored(1)..........................exuberant, enthusiastic(7).'

'If I could choose, I would: prefer never to have been born(1) ....
....like 9 more lives just like this one(7).'

The test was found to discriminate well between 'normal' and 'psychiatric groups', with a high level of significance. The instrument supported, as a reliable and valid measure, Frankl's conception of meaning and purpose in life; and the results favoured the connections of his thoughts and ideas in logotherapy.

CONCLUDING REMARKS

As I have indicated, some aspects of these six models describe, and relate to the underlying assumptions, basic principles and beliefs of SFBT. While putting forward a strong case for the solution focused approach, I am of the view that it is important to highlight some of the similarities to various models, and to acknowledge the root of some of the tools and techniques used. The following chapter will outline SFBT in general terms, as applied to all clients.

6

What is Solution Focused Brief Therapy?

First, you have to walk a path, to generate the path you can walk on.

Steve de Shazer

FOUNDATIONS

Solution Focused Brief Therapy (SFBT) has its origins in the various forms of brief therapy which evolved from the systemic and strategic family therapy traditions in the United States of America. (Watzlawick, Weakland & Fisch, 1974; Watzlawick, 1978). Steve de Shazer, who died in 2005, is regarded as the father of the solution focused approach to people's difficulties which can be described as non-pathological and collaborative (de Shazer, 1985, 1988, 1991; de Shazer & Berg, 1994). He and his colleagues worked at the Brief Family Therapy Centre in Milwaukee, Wisconsin. Prominent amongst his co-workers, who were involved in the shift from problem to solution thinking, were: Insoo Kim Berg, Walter Gingerich, Bill O'Hanlon and Michelle Weiner-Davis.

Brief Therapy of the earlier problem focused variety tended to encourage clients to describe their problems in detail, outline their beliefs on the causation of the problem, and to express a view as to what best may help. However, de Shazer and colleagues (Weiner-Davis, de Shazer & Gingerich, 1987; Berg, 1991; de Shazer, 1988, 1991; de Shazer et al.,1986; O'Hanlon & Weiner-Davis, 1989) discovered that clients achieved their goals quicker by talking more about their hopes for the future and their strengths, rather than describing their problem-peppered past. Furthermore, he discovered that by amplifying the 'solution' behaviour and reinforcing it by giving compliments, the client began to do more of it, thus outweighing the 'problem' patterns. As they began to picture their lives — once the problem had been overcome — and thus experience more of the solution, a return to healthy functioning was hastened. What was noteworthy also was that the problem thoughts and behaviours seemed to have little connection with solution thoughts and behaviours. So from brief therapy origins, de Shazer and colleagues honed their practice and perfected specific interventions by careful choice of language. The name they gave to this specific way of working was Solution Focused Brief Therapy. For over a decade now, it has become a megatrend: being adopted by education, health and probation services, relationship counselling, and more latterly into the business community.

SFBT or SFT (Solution Focused Therapy), as some prefer to call it, is described either in a nutshell or in a comprehensive way in most textbooks on specialist applications of the approach (Dolan, 1991; Jacob, 2001; Burns, 2005).

Some solution focused textbooks are specifically about the approach and contain particular aspects which recommend them. O'Connell (1998) for instance, contains a very comprehensive chapter on the first session interview. Macdonald (2007) emphasises the research and evidence base for solution focused therapy, not only devoting a whole chapter to this subject, but also providing good referencing elsewhere. As with most writers on the subject, both O'Connell (1998) and Macdonald (2007) give good examples of dialogue between worker and client, which is helpful for the newcomer to gain an easy understanding of the language used and how tools and techniques are applied. Macdonald's case study dialogue with a couple in treatment is to be recommended particularly.

THE SOLUTION FOCUSED THEORY OF CHANGE

> Change in therapy is not different in any way from that which occurs in ordinary, everyday life when problems are resolved.
>
> Procter & Walker (1988) p. 133

Newcomers to SFBT are often, at first, disbelieving about the possibility of change occurring after so few sessions, and they remain sceptical for a while until they experience concrete examples of the phenomenon. (See below 'Some Common Myths'.) As a trainer, I am reluctant to announce during an early stage of the training course that actually the solution focused approach lends itself well to one-session therapy. This avoids the obvious uphill struggle that could then ensue . . .

One of the fundamental principles of the solution focused approach is that change is constant: it is happening all the time. By the time I had completed the research for this book, I had changed my views in various ways during the process. You the reader, I suggest, will be changed by the time you have read the last chapter.

If, then, change is occurring constantly, it is important to examine it in order to find clues and keys for solution building. Many workers report that from the point at which a person decides to seek help with a problem, they begin to make small changes. Also, between the time they make their first appointment and their first meeting with the practitioner, further changes are made. Again, more clues and keys are to be discovered within this timescale. This change can be prompted further if the practitioner sets the *formula first session task* prior to their assessment interview: 'What I'd like you to do between now and when we meet, is to notice what is happening in your life that you want to keep happening. Can you do that for me?'

At some point during the first session (usually after the miracle question, fast-forwarding the video or some other goal-finding question has been asked), it is useful to ask, 'What's better between the time you decided to seek help and now?', and 'What's better between the time we spoke on the phone and now?' Asking both these questions maximises the information which may be utilised in later solution building. This is what is often referred to as *pre-session change* (Weiner-Davis, de Shazer & Gingerich, 1987; O'Hanlon & Weiner-Davis, 1989).

Change occurs in a variety of different ways. It is the practitioner's job not to try to persuade or argue with the person to get them to change, but simply to monitor and assist the process of change to the point where the person is satisfied with living the life they want: either without the problem; or, having the problem in check.

Change can occur at any time. It can occur prior to the first session, as mentioned above; it can occur during the first session, either through a realisation or, at the point of the practitioner's intervention. Further changes may be made upon reflection, after the session. There is a gathering body of evidence which suggests that many clients make changes within 24 hours of seeing a practitioner, so it is often worth asking what these were, at the next session. Further changes may occur as a result of a client carrying out a homework task set at the earlier session. Also (rarely), changes may not occur at all if the client is not yet ready or wanting to change.

CHANGING THE DOING OR THE VIEWING OF THE PROBLEM

O'Hanlon (1989) has written extensively on this notion and it is noteworthy to say that one small change in either how the client does the problem, or views the problem, can have a knock-on effect in other areas. An example from my work with trauma survivors experiencing intrusive thoughts about an incident throughout the day, is to request them to use the 'Stop!' technique by pinging a rubber band on their wrist, promising to 'replay the video' in their mind at an appointed time later. An example of changing the viewing of the problem is the case of a son-in-law who found the behaviour of his father-in-law intolerable and the cause of much tension in the extended family. At one session he said, quite unprompted, "That's it! I've decided, as far as Ted (his father-in-law) is concerned: that's the way he is. I'm never going to change him, so I'll just have to find new ways to cope with his behaviour".

ACTIONS, THINKING AND FEELINGS

Extending O'Hanlon's idea of changing the doing or the viewing, and the earlier idea of one small step having a knock-on effect, it is helpful to consider the actions, thoughts and feelings talked about so much within cognitive-behavioural therapy (CBT). It is necessary for the client to make a change in one of these three (see Figure 6.1), for the knock-on effect to occur in the others:

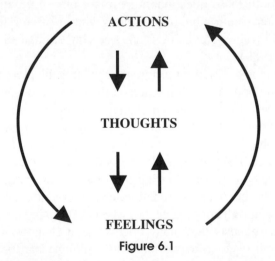

ACTIONS

THOUGHTS

FEELINGS

Figure 6.1

To illustrate this, let us take the earlier example of the trauma survivor experiencing flashbacks (intrusive thoughts). His thoughts about the incident were a severe and disabling problem for him. By taking action with the 'Stop!' technique and following it up later in the day, with 'replaying the video', he managed to reduce the overall number of flashbacks occurring during an average day. As a result, he felt better and more optimistic about the possibility of getting his life back on track. As a result of reduced flashbacks and feeling better, he then felt capable of doing more during the day. As he achieved more tasks he had set himself, he felt better for having done so and began to have even more optimistic thoughts about the future, and so on . . .

Sometimes the practitioner can be instrumental in setting tasks which can encourage this change sequence to get underway; or, can simply note where the change has occurred and amplify it, which, as a process, is reinforcing.

Taking the case of the troubled son-in-law in the above example who simply came out with his decision to view his father-in-law differently, a sequence of questions can follow thus:

- "How did you do that?"
- "How did you know how to do that?"
- "What did you learn by doing that?"
- "What will be the main benefits to you by having made this decision?"
- "What difference will this new decision make to your family?"

These questions are *empowering, pre-suppositional* and *affirming* for the client, with no credit at all being apportioned to the practitioner. Any change reported by the client may be dealt with by some or all of these questions.

This pattern can be repeated from session to session. Lipchik and de Shazer (1986) made the point that, "the purpose of each session is to assess change and to help to maintain it, so that a solution can be achieved". The greater proportion of time spent on solution talk, at the expense of problem talk, will help promote and strengthen this process.

For me, this change business is one of the most fascinating aspects of solution focused working. No matter how complex or long-lasting some problems may be, simply providing for the client a change environment which is respectful, validating and safe, can allow small changes on various levels and in different ways, to occur. Another 'accelerator' to the change process occurs when the practitioner notices or hears about these changes, amplifies and reinforces them, and sees the client go on to achieve more change. This process has a reinforcing effect on the practitioner and has a positive effect on the practitioner's optimism and belief in both the client and the approach. The client picks this up and responds with even more change — and so on . . . (Norman, 2000). The links and crossovers from SFBT to CBT theory and practice are often clear to see.

THE APPROACH

Solution Focused Therapy is described as an approach, rather than a model. This makes sense when it is seen as a set of attitudes; a stance, instead of a model which is applied rigidly to clients.

Being trained in two family therapy clinics by systemic and strategic family therapists, I was impressed by how results were achieved for families, couples and individuals in these two clinics. I began as an observer, moved on to become a co-worker, eventually interviewing clients on my own with up to five others in the back-up team behind the screen. It was in 1993 that I attended a two-day national training workshop in London, facilitated by Steve de Shazer. This was sponsored by Brief Therapy Practice (now known as BRIEF).

SFBT, being a development of earlier brief therapy ideas, utilises much of what the client brings which can be helpful to their building their own solution to current difficulties and concerns. I will describe this in more detail later.

BASIC ASSUMPTIONS, PRINCIPLES AND BELIEFS

Key to the approach are various guiding basic assumptions, principles and beliefs. The first of these is that change is constant: it is happening all the time. As I mentioned earlier, you will be different by the time you have finished this book (*presuppositional language!*) from when you first opened it. I will be different after the final proofreading of the manuscript from how I was at the time of writing this sentence. Each of us, in our separate ways, will have reflected on the material; had various wonderings; made certain connections; and, found that our work and/or thinking have been influenced as a result. So it is, too, with our clients. They will be different from the time they decided to seek help for their difficulties and the time they made contact with the service providing help. And again, they will make further changes from the point of contact with the service to the first assessment appointment with the therapist. It is worth asking, then, *pre-session change* questions such as: "What is different between the time you decided to seek help and now?" and, "Since you made the appointment date and now, what's better?" Research has shown that many clients make useful changes between deciding to seek help and their first appointment (Nunnally, de Shazar, Lipchik & Berg, 1986). Information gleaned can provide useful keys or clues to the client's individual solution building process, and indeed, may form the basis of the homework or task to be set before the second appointment.

A guiding principle of SFBT is, 'If it ain't broke, don't fix it' (de Shazer, 1991). Much of a client's life will be working for them, so it is unhelpful and usually unproductive to meddle in these areas. It may not be quite how we think they should be doing it, but if it is working for them and it is neither injurious nor illegal, it is not for us to say otherwise. A case example might be of a client who works from either a cluttered workbench or office desk. Although we as workers might view that as a problem, if it is not a problem to the client, then it fits into this 'ain't broke' category.

Allied to the principle above is, 'If it's working, do more of it'. The result of asking for *pre-session change* could well be that the client has stumbled on something that is helpful in alleviating the problem or difficulty. As an example, when I was working as a statutory service drugs worker, a heroin addict I was seeing for initial assessment said he had "cut down by a £5 bag a day" in the week before seeing me. Asking him how he had done that, he said he felt he ought to make an effort as he was now seeking help for his addiction. Also, he had made efforts on some days to return home by a different route, to avoid passing a dealer's house. Naturally, as part of the ongoing treatment, I encouraged him to do more of this, as and when he felt it appropriate. He had given me a 'clue' or a 'key' as to what was helpful to him and I was not going to pass it over.

I began by asking him empowering and affirming questions such as: "How did you do that?" and, "How did you know how to do that?" Questions like these invariably get into clients' strengths, qualities and inner resources. Reinforcing their behaviour by following up with, "What did you learn by doing that?" can strengthen clients as they continue moving towards achieving what they want.

Another basic assumption is that when clients get stuck, it is usually because they are doing the same old thing that isn't working.

Case Example 1

Eddie, a young disc jockey, who had been sacked by two pubs in the town in which he worked as a result of a court case for rowdy behaviour, was bound over to keep the peace. His behaviour has been the result of a break-up with his girlfriend and his subsequent shouting up at her flat above a shop in the main shopping street, in the early hours of one Sunday morning. He was feeling suicidal on account of having lost a girlfriend, two evening jobs, and his good reputation in the town, and on account of all the adverse publicity over both his behaviour and the subsequent court case. I saw him in a crisis clinic, following urgent referral by his worried GP. By the third session, he had decided to move out of the area to seek new disc jockeying opportunities in another town. Other changes which followed were to update his hairstyle and seek more demanding day job opportunities which matched his intelligence. Useful questions asked of him were:

- "How did you decide to make these other changes?"
- "What difference did it make?"
- "What will be the benefit to you of a more demanding day job?"
- "Who besides you will be the first to notice these benefits?"
- "What will they notice?"
- "When, in the future, you meet up with people you used to know, what will they notice most that is different about you?"

A key assumption of the solution focused approach is that one small change can have a knock-on effect in other areas of a client's life. Not only can these small changes affect the client's life, but also other parts of their family and/ or social systems. As the therapy moves forward, it is worth asking questions along the lines of, "Who is noticing you are different?"

Case Example 2

Pete had felt for some time that his marriage had become "samey" and was "heading for the rocks". Also, he and his wife increasingly had been living their own lives, becoming more and more independent of each other. Pete came up with the idea that it might make a difference if he surprised her once a week with something she liked: either a present or a theatre show. The knock-on effect of this small change amazed him. She responded by being more chatty and friendly towards him. He then began doing more DIY jobs around the house and suggesting they spend more time out together. Eventually their closeness and intimacy were restored and he felt he no longer needed therapy.

Another key assumption of the solution focused approach is that generally people are competent at finding solutions to most of what life throws at them. This applies to you, the reader, me, and to our clients. Just because the client is having difficulty in one area of their life now, does not mean they are incompetent in other areas of their life. *Problem-free talk*, which I will describe below, demonstrates this point very well. The present difficulty does not necessarily indicate past or future difficulty. In fact, with regard to the latter, what solution focused practitioners find is that clients become equipped with strategies for use with subsequent problems and difficulties. This could be supported by the findings of Macdonald and colleagues in their Carlisle clinic. They were struck by the very low re-referral rate of former patients over a five-year period (Macdonald & Ross, 2003). Following help from an SFBT therapist, there is a reduced likelihood of needing help with future difficulties as experience has shown the approach to have health promotion properties. What seems to happen is that firstly, clients learn or develop particular solution building skills for dealing with the current worry, concern or difficulty that brings them to therapy. Secondly, in a healthy and most constructive sense, they become 'contaminated' (healthily) with the worker's solution focused way of looking at things. This, I believe, occurs at both a conscious and an unconscious level. What happens next is that, in the future, when other problems occur, they use the skills they became contaminated with from the work they did previously. In my experience, generally, clients simply do not return to therapy. Exceptions to this principle are in cases of chronic substance misuse and of severe and enduring childhood abuse and trauma, where a client comes to therapy to make significant progress; and then returns later to move further forward on their recovery journey.

A very important guiding principle is that no problem happens all the time, nor do clients consistently not cope with the problem they may have; whether a client is depressed, drunk, grief-stricken, anxious, having relationship difficulties, or having psychotic experiences, none of these will be happening 100% of the time. There will always be *exceptions* (see below) to the problem. It is of paramount importance, therefore, for the therapist to find these exceptions, as they may prove invaluable clues and keys to the client's solution building.

Another aspect of this guiding principle is in cases where clients have a permanent disability or ongoing, intractable problem. Again, in such cases it will not be true that the client is not coping 100% of the time. There will be times when the client is coping just a little bit better with their disability or ongoing problem; clues and keys can be found for solution building.

TOOLS AND TECHNIQUES

Formula First Session Task

Even before seeing the client, it is helpful to set a task to help clients move mentally from a *problem-orientation* towards a *solution-orientation*. This is achieved by setting the *formula first session task* (FFST) (de Shazer, 1985). Naturally, if we have problems, worries or difficulties for which we wish to have help and we book an appointment to see a professional helper, we will be preparing ourselves by thinking about what aspects of these problems, worries or difficulties we can talk about to the professional. Indeed, generally it is people's expectation that they will be quizzed about these matters, so their thinking goes along the lines that it might be as well to prepare or think about possible answers to such questions. This, though, is the stuff of problem thinking, which could lead to much problem talk. What the skilled solution focused practitioner is wanting their client to do is to re-orientate their thinking towards solutions as far ahead of the appointment as possible. This is achieved by the *formula first session task*, as follows. A typical exchange on the phone, whilst making an appointment for SFT, could be thus:

CL: My name is Freda Hall and I have been recommended to make an appointment to see you. I feel quite stressed at the moment and think I may be heading for a serious depression.

TH: Yes, I am able to see you and can offer you an appointment in about a week's time. Is that OK?

CL: Yes, I can wait, as long as I know I have got a time and date to see someone.

TH: I could see you on either Thursday 15th February at 4.00 p.m. or Friday 16th at 10.00 a.m. Which of these is most convenient to you?

CL: Thursday 15th at 4.00 p.m. would be best.

TH: OK. Do you know how to find me and how will you travel?

CL: By bus and then I'll walk. I'd be grateful if you could give me some directions.

TH: [Gives directions . . .] It would be helpful if you could arrive about 2 minutes before your appointment, to protect the confidentiality of anyone who may be leaving from an earlier appointment. Also, if you could allow about 50–60 minutes for the session, this would be helpful.

CL: OK.

TH: So that's 15th February at 4.00 p.m. And there is one thing I would like you to do between now and when I see you on the 15th [slows down pace of speech and lowers voice tone slightly] and that is [pauses], to notice what's happening in your life that you want to keep happening. Can you do that for me?

CL: Yes, I can do that. There are plenty of things I want to stop happening!

TH: I look forward to meeting you on the 15th [puts phone down].

Some clients forget to do the task, others make a few mental notes and yet others write a three-pager of many and various points they are satisfied with in their life. Either way, the purpose of the FFST has been achieved: to encourage a solution orientation to the thinking prior to the first session.

I saw a middle-aged man who had been diagnosed as having a 'complicated grief reaction' following the loss of his wife to cancer. He had been admitted to an inpatient facility for a month, under a section of the Mental Health Act, but had left as soon as he could, as "the other patients kept talking about their problems; one had committed suicide and another had made a recent attempt". This client brought to the first session a list of some 20 points he wanted to keep happening in his life. Each point was in a bold heading, with various key points clearly entered after each. I saw him for a total of seven sessions over a period of nine months, when he moved from being "a mental and physical wreck . . . and I have just emerged from under the duvet" (his words), to being work-fit again, securing a middle management position in local government. His 20-point list formed the basis of much of our work throughout his 7-session episode of therapy.

Problem-Free Talk

I continue to be fascinated by the changing facial expressions of a new client who is at first apprehensive and slightly nervous about seeing a complete stranger upon whom to unburden themselves; who is then put slightly more at ease by the welcome and explanation of how the service works; and is then all ready to spill out their concerns, only to be asked about something which bears no relation whatsoever to these concerns!

Problem-free talk (PFT) is a great way to tap into the client's strengths, personal skills and resources before even the first detail of the problem is heard. Two questions are most commonly used:

- "What do you do in the day that interests you?" or
- "How do you spend your free time?"

If the client has clearly been in deep distress, severely depressed, or feeling quite moribund perhaps, these two questions may be adapted thus:

- "Up until you got so inactive, what did you do in the day that interested you?" or
- "Before you got yourself this stuck, how did you spend your free time?"

Solution focused drug workers have found the following adaptations useful:

- "Up until you let drugs get out of control, what did . . .?" or
- "Before you got yourself so involved in the drugs scene, how did . . .?"

In a typical first session with a client, the dialogue might go as follows:

CL: [rings bell]
TH: [opens door] You must be Graham? Do come in [welcomes in, shows to seat in therapy room].

[Explains confidentiality, professional body's code of ethics and practice, timings, etc.] Have you any questions about any of that?

CL: No. [Client looks expectant, waiting to be asked about their difficulties.]
TH: Before we start, I'd like to ask you: How do you spend your free time?
CL: Well . . . [gardening, reading, writing poetry, playing with the grandchildren, crossword puzzles, cinema or theatre visits, socialising with friends, walks by the river, etc., to name but a few!]

[After a few minutes, client gives quizzical look to therapist, which seems to say something along the lines of "Have I come here to tell you all about this?"]

TH: ['Quizzical look' cue picked up on] . . . So what brings you here? or, What's uppermost at the moment? or, How can I be helpful to you?

It is interesting to observe how many anxious, depressed or stressed clients particularly, liven up facially, their body posture and their tone of voice improves as they describe what most interests them or how they spend their free time. They can even surprise themselves. I recall a chronically depressed lady in her 60s who described in great detail, in response to the problem-free talk question, how she used to help out at a local playgroup: collecting the money from the parents, taking around squash and biscuits to the toddlers, drawing up rotas for fellow volunteers, and generally ensuring the group ran smoothly from week to week. After a few minutes, she interrupted herself by saying, "Listen to me talking! I sound brighter than I have been for six months!"

Too late. She had said enough for me to learn that she had good interpersonal skills, was good with money, was a good organiser and had general management skills. These attributes were then available for use as the therapy unfolded over the ensuing weeks. Again, as with FFST, the information gleaned can provide clues and keys to later solution building.

Problem-free talk has a four-fold purpose:

• It normalises the interaction between two people (it is an even relationship; not 'one-up');

- It enables the therapist and client together to acknowledge the client's strengths, skills and resources;
- It creates a context of competence (and for the moment, anyway, this over-shadows any incompetence the client may be feeling around their problem, worry or difficulty);
- The worker engages with the *person* of the client, as opposed to the *problem* of the client.

Problem-free talk is not chit-chat or small talk. This is likely to occur as the client is entering the room and may occur around the time they are getting comfortable. Examples are:

"Colder today, isn't it?"
"Did you just miss being caught in that shower?"
"Were my directions clear enough?"
"Did you decide to cycle or come by bus?"

Hearing Out the Problem

Some critics of solution focused ways of working have levelled the criticism that therapists are not interested in hearing about problems. This is not the case, as will become clear below. Clients will always want to describe what is concerning them and if the therapist tries to forestall/shorten them, they will simply come back to it later and will persist until they believe the therapist has heard and/or understood their concerns sufficiently. However, we do not want the client to take up the whole of the first session with problem descriptions. There should be a good proportion of the session comprised of 'solution talk' as opposed to 'problem talk' (de Shazer 1991, 1994). O'Hanlon (1993) went on to develop this idea into clients inhabiting 'solution land' or 'problem land' when they give account of their situation. Symptoms, failures, implications of the problem, failed attempted solutions, etc. are all features of 'problem land'! Our job as workers is to encourage our clients to move to 'solution land' which is comprised of talk about pre-session change, exceptions, the miracle picture, small steps, scaling progress and goals of treatment. To help promote this idea within client sessions, I have devised what I call '*the 5 o'clock rule*' (see Figure 6.2). This rule says that, in the first session at least, if we can encourage the client to describe their problems for approximately 25 minutes of the hour (give or take five minutes), then the majority of the time can be about solutions. Of course, all problem talk will not be at the beginning part only, as *pre-session change* and *exceptions* (both 'solution talk') will arise most likely, early on. *The 5 o'clock rule* simply refers to the overall proportioning of the time available.

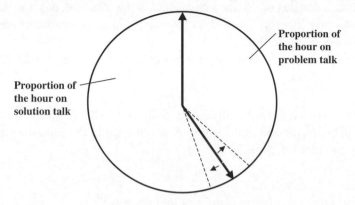

Figure 6.2 The 5 O'clock rule.

What is found to be helpful here is for the therapist to ask clarifying questions and to acknowledge and validate concerns and difficulties as much as possible, as the client is relating their difficulties. This communicates to the client that the therapist is hearing them out and trying their best to gain an understanding. Clients are then far more likely to be open to solution talk.

The Miracle Question

Once the therapist believes they have a sufficient understanding of the problem, they can ask the *miracle question* more confidently. This question, asked for the purpose of producing clear and concise *goals* (see below), is capable of producing some amazing answers from the client. Only realistic and workable answers are useful, so the therapist may have to persist in their questioning to help the client form a useful picture of what they would like to see happen. The therapist may have to discount impossible or unrealistic answers outright, in order to lead the client onto coming up with a helpful answer:

> "Let's suppose that tonight, while you're asleep, a miracle happens, such that all these concerns you have just described have all gone, only you won't know this miracle has happened because you are asleep. What will be the first sign to you, when you wake up tomorrow morning, that this miracle has indeed happened?"

Often, there is a long pause and the client thinks what will be different. In many cases, their first response is "I don't know". Beginner therapists can be thrown by this for a while and be discouraged from asking the miracle question at all. Persistence, however, pays off. Responding to "I don't know" by remaining silent often proves helpful. Other responses such as "Just pretend" (or something similar) can be helpful in encouraging the client to get the hang of what is being asked. The subsidiary questions: "What else?"; "And what else?"; "Who would be the first to notice that this miracle has happened?"; and, "What would they notice?", are all helpful in filling out the detail in *the miracle picture* (the picture of what the client's life will look like after the miracle has happened).

Goals

As the therapist encourages the client to fill out *the miracle picture* even further by skilled questioning, the client will be encouraged to develop *goals* which are what can be called 'SMART+'. This means they are not only small, measurable, achievable, realistic and time limited, they have additional qualities. The first of these is that goals will comprise the presence of some positive behaviour, rather than the absence of negative behaviours (e.g. "When I am not drinking, I will be doing 'X' instead" rather than "My goal is to cut my drinking to 1 pint per day").

Case Example 3

Peter had been referred for therapy because he was "becoming a serious alcoholic". In asking the miracle question, he said after the miracle he would not be drinking any more. The therapist might have been tempted to co-construct goals with the client around 'not drinking'. Instead, to ensure goals included the presence of some positive behaviour, the following questions were asked:

"When you are not drinking so much as you are now, what will you be doing instead?" and,

"What will you want to spend the money on instead?"

Another characteristic which makes the goal 'SMART+' is for it to include some behaviour that is already happening; something the client is already starting to do. This information could have come to light during the client's problem description and may be prompted by the therapist's *pre-session change* questions and *exception finding* questions (see below).

Finally, the sort of *goal/s* that are arising must be something that both therapist and client can agree is worthwhile working towards. So, a suicidal client wanting to establish a *goal* to achieve their own demise within six months' time would be unacceptable to the therapist. A more ethically acceptable goal for such a client might be to help them weigh all possibilities for consideration before having a further life review at an agreed future date. If our work with clients lacks clear *goals*, it is easy for it to become directionless and without focus.

For a variety of reasons, *the miracle question* does not suit everybody. Skilled therapists often get a sense that an alternative may be more appropriate. On other occasions, therapists may change to an alternative in mid-sentence. Some of these alternatives are as follows:

Fast-Forwarding the Video

This is a novel way of achieving the same result as the *miracle question* and sometimes can encourage the client to be more visual. It goes thus:

> "Just imagine we have a TV and video in the corner there [therapist points] and we are playing a video of your life in, say, four months' time when you have sorted all this out [that you have been telling me about here today]. What would we be watching on the video? What would you be doing differently? Who else would be there? What would I/they be noticing that is different about you compared with now? and, what else . . .?, and what else . . .?, etc."

If the therapist's room really has a TV and video in it, the remote control can be used to make it more realistic. If not, a mobile phone can be useful to point at the imaginary TV and video. Again, like *the miracle question*, a good 'video picture' can be constructed of a life without the problem. From this picture, clear goals can be co-constructed by therapist and client.

Magic Wand

This is yet another alternative tool to help the client move from outside the problem to visualising a future where things have been sorted. It goes like this:

- "Just imagine that this pen I am holding is a magic wand [therapist waves pen wand-like in the air]. We are able to wave this wand over your problem, such that it is gone. What would we see that's different?

What would you be doing differently? What else? What would those close to you see that is different about you, compared with now? What else . . .?, etc."

There are other alternatives or variations on the above which can be used. A couple more are:

- "Imagine we have a crystal ball . . ." and,
- "Just visualise we are now sat here (say) six months from now, and your problem is solved . . ."

The purpose served by the *miracle question* or these other tools outlined above, is five-fold:

- To bypass problem thinking
- To create a context for setting goals which are well formed
- To encourage expectations of change within the client
- To get information about how the client can make progress
- To find out about client actions and thinking that will complete therapy.

All these tools can be described as 'non-trance hypnosis', in view of the fact that they are delivered only when the client's attention has been obtained, and they are spoken slowly and in a lowered tone of voice. These points virtually guarantee that the client's attention is maintained throughout.

Key to the success of the miracle question and related tools is for the therapist to be prepared for a change of pace in that part of the session. Also, it is important to be prepared for the client to slow down and be quiet; and, especially for a long silence after asking the question. The client is thinking hard during this silence and so it is vital not to interrupt with any communication, either verbal or otherwise. It is important, too, for the therapist to be prepared to get several answers. Some answers may be totally off beam, unhelpful or unrealistic. For example, asking a depressed and suicidal client the *miracle question*, they might answer, "I'd be dead and gone and all my troubles will be over!" A quick retort would be required in such a case, such as: "Just suppose you are still alive and your problems are sorted . . ."

An example of an unrealistic answer would be for a client who had lost both legs (say) in an accident to answer, "I'd have my legs back". Again, a quick retort of the following may be appropriate: "Well that's not going to happen, so how might you be coping better with your prostheses?" Another commonly given unrealistic answer over recent years is: "I'd have won the lottery"(!)

Exceptions to the Problem

It is always worthwhile asking clients about *exceptions* to the problem. Remembering from the fundamental principles, basic assumptions and beliefs outlined above, no problem happens all the time. A dependent drinker is not a hundred percent drunk a hundred percent of the time; a client who is chronically depressed is not depressed to the same extent every day; and, a suicidal person is not constantly suicidal: there will be times when they are less so, or not at all. It is worth asking, from a range of solution focused questions, to elicit *exceptions* to the problem. Those most commonly asked are as follows:

- "Tell me about a time when you have been less depressed?"
- "When you were just a little less suicidal, what were you thinking differently on that/those occasion/s?"
- "When you felt slightly more optimistic about the future, what was different at that time?"

In cases where the client has an ongoing physical condition which will not improve and may indeed become worse, there is still an opportunity for *exception finding questions*. These are generally around the theme of coping:

- "Tell me about a time/s when you have coped just a little better with this"
- "When you have coped a little better with things, what have you been doing/thinking differently?"
- "What sorts of things do you tell yourself to cope with this situation?"

Often, *exception finding questions* can be asked once the therapist has exhausted the subsidiary questions to the *miracle question*. With the therapist's encouragement, the client will have outlined the *miracle picture* as fully as possible. At this point the therapist may ask:

- "I am wondering whether a little piece of this miracle has happened or is happening already? Tell me what you know about this."

In my experience, in over 95% of cases something useful has happened/ is happening which is an *exception* to the problem . . . and forms a part of the *miracle picture*. It is then over to the therapist to amplify and reinforce this by asking the following questions or similar:

- "How did you get that to happen?"
- "How did you know how to do that?"
- "What did you learn by doing that?"
- "How differently do you feel about yourself and your situation when this happens?"
- etc.

Scaling

One of the most easily adapted tools of SFBT is the 1–10 scaling tool. It is so simple yet so powerful in 1:1 work as both therapist and client together share where the client is and the progress they are making.

Scaling can be used for measuring progress, motivation or confidence. Some colleagues prefer a scale of 0–10, where 0 stands for not having started on the progress scale; no motivation at all; or no confidence at all. My preference is for the 1–10 scale, the main reason being psychological. Even if the client says they have not even started, at least they give themselves a 1. My view is that this is infinitely better than 0. I find this is particularly important when working with suicidal clients as despair, hopelessness and emptiness can pervade their experience and a 1 at least gives them the impression they are at the first point on the scale. Scaling can take many forms. The most common is the linear scale (see Figure 6.3).

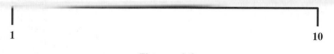

1   10

Figure 6.3

Some therapists prefer 1–10 scale in the form of a ladder, as in Figure 6.4.

Not all clients we see take to numbers very easily. There can be several reasons for this: one being that maybe they did not get on too well with maths at school and so talk of scales and numbers of 1–10 produces unpleasant flashbacks to a particular teacher or schoolroom. Others are simply more artistic and visual and prefer pictorial illustrations instead. I recall vividly a depressed client who when I began asking her to scale where she thought she was now on the 1–10 scale, started to screw up her brow. Picking up quickly on this non-verbal cue, I changed in mid-sentence to 'a hill slope', and she relaxed immediately. From then on, no numbers were mentioned in our sessions. Instead,

Figure 6.4 The 'ladder scale'.

I referred her to the hill slope I had drawn and she pointed to the point in each session where she felt she was at. This novel pictorial representation of scaling is most useful if the slope is made more interesting as in Figure 6.5 below.

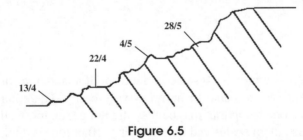

Figure 6.5

Of course, I knew that the bottom and top of the slope represents 1 and 10 respectively. The undulating shape of the slope prompts more creativity in both therapist and client, as there are "steep parts, ledges, rugged bits", etc. This is helpful, especially when it comes to small steps (see below).

Scaling progress is best used first after asking for exceptions ("where a little piece of the miracle is happening already"):

TH: May I ask you another unusual question?
CL: Yes.
TH: On a scale of 1-10, where 1 stands for the miracle not having happened at all and 10 stands for all that you have described happening, where are you now on this 1–10 scale?
CL: About 2–3.
TH: How come you are at 2–3 and not just 2?
CL: [Client gives reasons]
TH: What would you have to do to make that a firm 3 or to go up the scale another half point?
CL: [Client answers]

I have found that a large majority of clients will answer between 2½–4 on the 1–10 progress on the *miracle question* (and they haven't even gone to bed yet!). This seems always to be an encouragement to both therapist and client. It is not difficult to appreciate how important this is for suicidal clients. What suicidal clients need desperately in the first session is some hope to replace their despair; some optimism to replace pessimism; and some sense that the therapist believes that it is possible to go on living. In my experience, the suicidal and depressed tend to give a lower score — maybe 1, 1¼, 2, etc. Sometimes, although rarely, they will give zero or a minus number. The beauty of the *scaling* tool is that any number (up to +10) is OK. Even in extreme cases, no low number is a problem.

Case Example 4

TH: *On a scale of 1–10, where are you right now?*
CL: *–1000 . . .*
TH: *From what you have told me, all these things that have happened, and how you have not been coping too well up to this point, I can appreciate that you would give yourself a very low score. What would you have to do to get to –999?*

[and so on . . .]

Scaling motivation is helpful in cases where the therapist is unsure just how keen the client is about working on their issues. It may be that they are not so much a customer for change. (Rather than talking in terms of motivation — high or low — Fletcher Peacock (2001) in his book *Water the Flowers, not the Weeds* uses a more helpful terminology in the form of 'levels of co-operation'.)

Case Example 5

TH: *On a scale of 1–10, how keen are you to sort out this conflict with your mother-in-law?*

CL: *Oh, about 3½.*

TH: *What would have to happen for you to move up to a 4?*

CL: *Maybe if I could see how getting on better with her would help improve how my wife and I get on.*

Scaling confidence is helpful, especially if clients are feeling de-skilled or unsure about how they can marshall their strengths and resources to make progress. Self-confidence goes hand in hand with self-esteem, so finding ways how a client can increase their confidence by one little bit will lead to a corresponding increase in self-esteem. This then has a further knock-on effect, boosting confidence further.

Case Example 6

TH: *On a scale of 1–10, where 10 stands for completely confident and 1 stands for not being confident at all, how confident are you now in sorting out this problem with your work colleagues?*

CL: *I think, maybe about a 2 only.*

TH: *How come you give it a 2 and not a 1?*

CL: *Well, Jock has a kind streak, deep down.*

TH: *What would you have to do to move up on your 1–10 confidence scale from a 2 to, say, a 2½?*

CL: *Maybe if I could talk to Jock: see if he has any helpful suggestions for moving forward.*

Small Steps

Sometimes our clients want to make huge leaps into a problem-free future, or at other extremes, they feel they cannot make any progress at all due to the perceived enormity of their problem or difficulties. In both cases, the use of *small steps* is helpful. To the client wanting to make huge leaps, it can be explained how important it is to make a *small step* first and then consolidate before moving on to the next one, and so on.

For clients who feel overwhelmed by their situation, suggesting a *small step* they can make can be a helpful way forward. Increased confidence in taking further steps can then follow. When clients suggest *small steps* they can make, it is worthwhile going even smaller, suggesting that this smaller step will be good enough between this and the next session. *Paradox* (see below) plays a part here as invariably clients will do more, the less they feel they are set as a *between session task* (see below) and, conversely, if the step is too large, *paradoxically*, they are more likely to fail at the task altogether.

Small steps (or very small steps indeed!) have proved helpful for suicidal clients, as often they can see no way out of the impasse before coming to the first session. One such a client, who was seen about six years ago, was reminded of the many friends and good acquaintances they used to have before they withdrew from all social contact. In the first session, the client believed it might be worthwhile to reconnect with a number of them, while they were going through this very difficult time, when strong suicidal thoughts seemed to occur at least every three days. The conversation went like this:

TH: Which of your friends would be most helpful to you — as simply a listening ear, maybe — while you are going through this really bad patch?

CL: I used to have some really good friends and lots of other people around. I've lost contact really. I know I could contact them all again, some would help, I know.

TH: That sounds a really big step. I am wondering whether it would be best maybe to contact just one first?

CL: Maybe.

[Session continues until the intervention stage, when the therapist sets a between session task] . . .

TH: Between now and when we next meet, I would like you to do something for me. Because you think it could be helpful to re-contact some of your old friends, what I would like you to do is to write down a list of your 'top six' who you think would be best to contact. Then to put an asterisk against your first choice and tell me who you have chosen and for what reason, when we meet next. Is that OK?

CL: I can do that; no problem.

In this case the therapist went for an even smaller step for the task set. The result was that the client did this and then went on to give them the call to arrange to meet. Also he rang a second friend and had a useful chat over the phone.

Presuppositional Language

The more experienced solution focused practitioners become, the more skilled they become at using presuppositional language. This was one of Milton Erickson's major innovations and his most valuable contribution to the solution focused approach. *Presuppositions* are ways of talking that presume something without stating it directly. They are implicit unconscious suggestions. The therapist can use *presuppositions* to introduce expectations and notions of change during a therapy session. The client buys into the idea without realising it, because it happens mostly at an unconscious level. I have discovered, over the last few years especially, that the more I use *presuppositional language* generally and *presuppositional questions* in particular, the sooner clients begin to use *presuppositional language* back to me. They are then more likely to begin to 'walk their talk'. The more they do this, it seems, the sooner they achieve their goals.

Careful use of *presuppositional language* can be part of the guarantee of the solution focused approach in preventing suicide. The sorts of *presuppositional questions* which are most helpful for the suicidal client are thus:

- "Between now and when we next meet, what would be the most helpful *small step* for you to try?"
- "When you have been up against it before in life, how did you get through it on that/those occasion/s?"
- "When you look back on this really desperately low patch in your life, what do you think you will highlight as being most helpful to you?"
- "What will be different in your life, when you are no longer suicidal?"
- "When you've cracked this really low patch, how will your life be different?"
- "When you are feeling just a little more optimistic, what thoughts about the future might you be having?"
- "When you've got through this difficult time . . .?"
- "When you look back on this testing period in your life . . .?"
- "How have you coped with this situation up to now?"
- "What has stopped you taking your life so far?"
- "Apart from this last resort option, which of the other options do you think are worthy of a try first?"

Complimenting

When clients are lacking self-confidence or have feelings of low self-worth, there is nothing like a well timed *compliment* to lift their spirits a little. *Complimenting* is something Insoo Kim Berg emphasises constantly (Brief Therapy Centre, 1995). We forget, to our detriment, that some clients have had very few compliments from anyone in their lives, to date. I relate the story often at training workshops, about a drug-using client I worked with some years ago. He was 20 minutes late for his first appointment, but arrived for the second session only 10 minutes late. He was quite chaotic in his drug use and I could find little to compliment him on, apart from the fact that he was 10 minutes earlier than last week. His astonishing reply was, "Do you know mate, you're the first person in my life ever to thank me for anything" (. . . and he was still 10 minutes late!).

With suicidal clients, some of the most commonly occurring helpful comments back to the client are:

- "It is good that you've come along here today to give other options a try."
- "Thank you for outlining your current plight for me in such detail."
- "I am impressed by the way you have considered today other options than the suicidal option."

Acknowledgment

Many clients are lost to suicide, in my view, as a result of their pain and difficulty not being acknowledged sufficiently by health professionals. The combination of *acknowledgment, validation* and *normalisation* seems to be a powerful combined tool in the suicide prevention therapist's toolbag (I will explain the latter two below).

Suicidal clients may have closed down much of their lives already in some cases, before seeing a therapist. What is very much sharpened, however, is their 'intuitive radar' which is detecting whether the therapist is sincere and genuine and has some degree of appreciation of their pain and suffering. Suicidal clients might make up their minds one way or the other within the first five minutes. Many health workers in the past, it has to be said, have lacked this ability and clients have been lost to suicide as a result. A typical acknowledgment statement would be thus:

- "From what you have told me about losing your job, your wife leaving you and your home being repossessed, I can get some appreciation of the awful situation you find yourself in right now."

From this statement, the suicidal client will feel that their plight has been *acknowledged* and the therapist is trying to understand what they are going through. Rapport and a working relationship are more likely to be established, as a result.

Validation

The next part, following on from *acknowledgment,* is *validation.* This is where the therapist gives some validity to the feelings and suicidal thinking in the client. This is the opposite approach to the previous traditional containment/risk assessment and management approach prevalent in the mid-20th century where clients might have been told: "You shouldn't think like that"; "It's not good for you to have those sorts of feelings"; "Try and look on the bright side", etc. All these statements are attempts at trying to rob the client of their current suicidal thoughts and feelings. Indeed, there is an attempt at invalidation within this sort of statement. As a result of this style of approach to the problem, paradoxically, the client is more likely to become actively suicidal.

The solution focused therapist is keen to *validate* all thoughts and feelings as far as possible. To illustrate this, a further statement following on from the *acknowledgment* above could be:

> ". . . No wonder you are feeling suicidal and having other thoughts of harming yourself."

Normalisation

The last of this little trio is *normalisation*. Many suicidal clients express the view that, as a result of having suicidal thoughts and ideas, they must be going mad (or similar): a very abnormal experience. *Normalising* feelings can be for any client, a helpful way to reassure them that things are 'not too far gone'. A statement to this effect, following the *validation* above, could be as follows:

> "Most people who are feeling trapped or defeated by a challenging situation in their lives, have suicidal thoughts from time to time. It is a normal response, by normal people, to an abnormal set of circumstances."

So, this combination of *acknowledgment, validation and normalisation* has proved helpful for all clients, but especially for those who are suicidal.

Paradoxical Intention

The use of *paradoxical intention* can be helpful to our clients when used appropriately. It can be defined as: 'Trying to achieve the opposite to that which is stated'. It may be recalled that I referred to *paradox* earlier in the section on *small steps,* and also in Chapter 5.

There are some other novel ways, too, in which *paradox* can be used. One of these is for reluctant clients who seem to be coming along to therapy with either the expectation that the therapist is going to change them, or simply they are not working hard enough on the issues about which they are concerned. A helpful *paradoxical intention* intervention might be:

"I am wondering whether you are ready yet, to work on these issues. Perhaps it may be helpful for you to go away and think about it for a while, then give me a ring when you are ready?"

Case Example 7

This was a couple who had been arguing incessantly, who had separated as a result and were now back living under the same roof. They had been for three sessions and although they were communicating well, they did not feel ready yet to get closer physically. The therapist took the opposite view and so the dialogue went as follows:

WIFE: We are talking again more rationally now. He is showing he cares more, and he is working hard on better listening

HUSB: If I sense things are becoming heated, I will either change the subject or say, "Can we talk about that when we are calmer?"

TH: Sounds like you have both worked hard on rebuilding things between you.

WIFE: Yes, he even held my hand when we were in town the other day. It was nice and I didn't feel I wanted to resist.

TH: I think it's great how you are both working so well, each in your own way. I think it's best we go slowly but surely, so I think, for the time being anyway, we should have a 'no sex' rule. Holding hands and petting is okay, but no further. Is that okay?

WIFE: If you say . . .

HUSB: I suppose so . . .

At the next session, the couple arrived looking very much more a couple; and, looking somewhat sheepishly at the therapist(!)

Stories

The use of stories with clients can be a powerful way of helping them to move forward. Appropriateness of both *story* and the client's current situation is key. Appropriate *stories* can be drawn from well known fairytales, legend and actual clients seen previously. (It is important, however, to change key details to protect confidentiality.) It is always a fascination for me to see clients become 'all eyes and ears' when a *story* is being related as part of the therapy. Other clients' predicaments, which are similar to the client's own and, moreover, how they develop their strategies for dealing with them, are usually the most powerful. A further purpose served is to bring it home to the client that they are not alone in their difficulty: a misperception held by many, whether they are bereaved, depressed or suicidal.

Metaphor

A metaphor can be defined as: 'A figure of speech by which a thing is spoken of as being that which it resembles, not fundamentally, but only in a certain marked characteristic or marked characteristics'.

Case Example 8

A colleague some years ago, was working with a supervisor in an electronic circuitry company. This supervisor was very depressed to the point where he had been so stuck at home that he was unable to go out of doors. By using the language of electronics, not only was the client engaged by the language used, but also was able to see how he could get his life 'back on track'. The dialogue, remembered broadly from a videotape of the session, went something like as follows:

TH: So how long have you been in this state?
CL: About 3–4 months, I suppose.
TH: What would you need to do to make just one small step on the path of recovery?
CL: Maybe, if I could just feel a little more hopeful about the future.
TH: Seems to me that maybe you have let your life be shunted a bit off track?
CL: Yeah. Perhaps I have.
TH: So, to recharge your batteries to get you moving again, what might be most helpful to you?
CL: Maybe, if I force myself to go out for walks, I would feel better for making the effort. It would have to be in the evenings, because I am fearful of meeting other people at the moment.
TH: Sounds a good idea. When would you be up for your first evening walk?
CL: I'll go tonight if it's not raining. If not, tomorrow.
TH: With this and other steps you might take, how will you know when you are ready to throw the switch to make it possible for you to return to your main track in life?

[and so on . . .]

Case Example 9

Another example is the case of a young farmer I saw in a family therapy clinic some years ago. He had inherited the farm from his father, who had retired three years previously. In fact, my client was the fourth generation of the family owning the farm. Due to a variety of factors, my client had become depressed. The main factors were declining farm incomes and his recent wonderings about not really wanting to be in farming anyway. He had agreed to take over the reins from his father, out of duty to him, over and above what career ideas he might have had for himself.

The client was showing all the usual signs and symptoms of clinical depression and it was his wife who urged him to seek help. A section of dialogue was as follows:

TH: So, from what you have said, it seems you are finding it a real effort to take the tractor out into the fields to prepare them for planting?

CL: I'm stuck. I've just got no interest. I wake up early, feel anxious, my heart races and it's all I can do to make a cup of tea and sit by the kitchen stove. I stare into space a lot, too. I feel better towards the end of the day and then don't want to go to bed 'til late. I don't feel like eating anything until the afternoon either.

TH: [taking a chance] I am wondering whether farming is for you?

CL: [sudden head-raising and look at therapist, which communicates: "You've hit the nail on the head"] Well, I've got to do it. My father always intended I take over the business.

TH: Sometimes in life, we find ourselves ploughing the same old furrow, with our head down, concentrating on the earth immediately ahead. We can exclude not only what's over in the next furrow, but also what may lie in other fields? And, also, what may lie further afield.

CL: Yeah.

TH: This may be an appropriate time for you to take a look at those other furrows and also those other fields. You could consider many possibilities for your life. It may be that you will say, "Okay, I've thought about other possibilities long and hard, but no thanks, I'll carry on farming". Would this be helpful to you?

CL: Yes, it could well be.

Generally, I think there is far more scope for use of both *metaphor* and *stories* alike in therapy. When used appropriately, they can be a very powerful tool for helping clients move on.

Client Language

The more a therapist uses the language of his/her client, the more likely rapport will be built; and consequently, the more likely a good working relationship will be established. It is incumbent on the therapist to make a note of particular words used by the client. This applies to idiosyncratic terms of phrase also.

First, I will give some examples of clients' words. A client might describe their response to a disturbing event as being "upset". This is their word and particular meaning or meanings are attached to it. So, if the therapist later refers to them being "unhappy", "cross" or "annoyed" by this disturbing event, what is likely to be conveyed to the client is lack of understanding, or worse: talking at crossed purposes. The therapist would be best advised to use "upset" in subsequent conversations.

Another example might be where a client describes their being "dumped" by a boyfriend. It would be folly, therefore, for the therapist to say they were either "jilted", "passed over", or "ditched" by the boyfriend.

Idiosyncratic turns of phrase can be many and various. Working on the patch of land at the front or rear of one's home can be described in a variety of ways:

- "Gardening"; "clipping and tidying"; and "spuddling in the garden", to name but a few.

Again, it is important to use the client's language when referring later to this activity.

Clues And Keys

I have referred to these earlier. There are numerous keys and clues available to the helper on how helpees can make progress. It is the helper's job to be alert to these at all times during the helping process.

When helpees are describing in minute detail the enormity or severity of the problem, story, clues or keys will be in evidence in the same way that small nuggets of gold might appear in a stream running out of some gold-seam-laden rock mass. They may glint at us momentarily as the water runs on carrying the silt downstream. A good example of this can be seen in the family therapy training video referred to above (Brief Therapy Centre, 1995). In the final part of the first session in this training video entitled, "I'd Hear Laughter", the mother complains at length about how her 15-year-old daughter is refusing to go to school, hanging out with the wrong crowd, is scruffily dressed, and stays out 'til late at night. Inadvertently, as the mother is describing this behaviour in great detail to the worker (Insoo Kim Berg), she slips in the comment that her daughter is intelligent. This is an important clue to be picked up on by the worker for use later in the solution building work.

Information gleaned from the *formula first session task* (see above), if set prior to the first session, can provide many clues and keys to solution building.

Many clients make significant shifts in action, thinking or feeling prior to their first session, prompted or otherwise by the *formula first session task* question. Asking clients directly for information about this at the first session can be helpful. Again there are further clues or keys which may be utilised sooner or later in the work.

Asking clients about their skills, strengths, qualities, personality characteristics or other personal resources can provide useful keys or clues to moving forward. Some of the following questions may be used in this:

- "What particular strengths, skills or personal qualities do you have which could be helpful to you, while working on this issue/problem?"
- "This work that you will be doing with me will be far from easy. What particular personality characteristics or strengths will you be calling on to make sure you are successful?"
- "All of us have a wide range of gifts, aptitudes and personal strengths to use when we are up against it in life. Which will you be calling on here?"

In cases where clients find it hard to name their particular strengths, skills, abilities, etc., questions such as the following can be helpful:

- "What would your spouse/best friend say . . .?"
- "What particular personal qualities, strengths and abilities does your boss appreciate most in you?"
- "On your school reports/individual appraisals, what qualities, strengths, personal values, etc. have been mentioned?"

As the work progresses through the second and third session, clients will begin to make small steps forward, have realisations of what needs to be tried, and start to appreciate some benefits of their progress. These may provide additional clues or keys to further progress.

The empowering, affirming and pre-suppositional questions mentioned earlier are not only ways of flagging up clues or keys, but are a reinforcing process in themselves. This reinforcing and concentration on what is working, what is useful or helpful, has been described as "watering the flowers, not the weeds" (Peacock, 2001). It is more helpful if the worker asks the client about what is working in their lives, rather than what is not working; about their strengths, rather than their weaknesses; and, about what gives them a sense of hope, rather than one of despair. This is desirable 'flower-watering' behaviour on the worker's part.

Generating Possibilities

Bill O'Hanlon, who was greatly inspired by the therapeutic ideas and innovations of Milton Erickson, has variously described Solution Focused Brief Therapy as Solution-Oriented Therapy or Possibility Therapy.

Before encouraging the client to consider other possibilities to their problem situation, it is important to remember the three words 'acceptance and change' (O'Hanlon & Beadle, 1996). Clients must feel that we have acknowledged their worries, concerns or difficulties for what they are. This is to do with the essential solution focused principle of '*going with the client*'. O'Hanlon calls this type of acknowledgment that a solution focused practitioner employs, "possibility-laced acknowledgment" (O'Hanlon & Beadle, 1996, p. 12). This is a form of acknowledgment that lets the client know that the worker has heard and understood their concerns and worries, without closing down the possibility of change. O'Hanlon uses the analogy of curlers on ice. (This has nothing to do with the various techniques employed to unstraighten hair!) It is about the ice sport, curling, where team mates of the one who has thrown the stone across the ice, get busy with brooms frantically sweeping the ice in front of the sliding stone. This helps the stone move forward. As workers, O'Hanlon goes on, we sweep in front of clients we work with, to sweep open possibilities for them. While we are doing this, though, it is important to pay attention to where the client is right now by possibility-laced acknowledgment. Similarly, in the curling analogy above, it is important for the team mates to pay attention where the stone is, as they sweep the ice ahead of it.

An analogy I use often with clients to help with the generation of possibilities is to refer them to a huge junction in Brighton, Sussex, UK: my university town. This junction called Seven Dials is in a suburb called Preston Park. I encourage my clients to imagine they had travelled along one of these roads and they are now at the junction. They have six other possibilities for which way now to travel, in addition to staying put where they are. Further, after choosing one of these possible roads, they may wish to change to another: either by travelling along connecting roads, or by returning to the junction and making a different choice. Additionally, they may choose to travel somewhere along one of the roads from the junction until they reach a further multiple junction. Other possibilities will then exist, from which to choose.

How can we name these possibilities away from Seven Dials? As far as possible, this is client-generated. Some questions for achieving this are as follows:

- "What are these possibilities?"
- "What would your best friend say are the possibilities open to you?"

- "What would your spouse/father/brother/etc. say are the possibilities open to you?"
- "From what you have learned or heard about so far on life's journey, what other possibilities might you add?"

If a sufficiently wide spread of possibilities is not achieved by these questions, other ways of possibility-generation are open to the worker. One of these is to tell the client stories as mentioned earlier of how other clients/people have dealt with similar sets of circumstances. There is a strong permission-giving flavour if the story ends with: ". . . this was helpful to this person and it may or may not be something you might like to consider doing in your situation".

I find it helpful to include in the possibility-generation process, the 'do nothing' option and the 'worst case scenario'. The second of these can take some of the sting out of their worst fears, when it is considered as an equally valid possibility along with the others up for consideration.

Encouraging the client to come up with their preferred future or best hope for the future can be a way of generating most likely possibilities. Sub-possibilities from this could then follow.

The final part of possibility-generation is empowerment. Once all possibilities have been generated, and to some extent considered, it is the worker's job to empower the client to make a choice. It might prove to be simply a first choice or two, or one to experiment with for now. Part of this empowerment process is to communicate to the client that they have full permission to change course at any time, should they choose to do so.

Degrimming

It was Milton Erickson who urged strongly the use of humour in 1:1 work. Humour can ensure there is some balance achieved with all the grief and sorrow that is often brought to the counselling situation. The need to make the work less grim (O'Hanlon & Beadle, 1996), is probably even more important in working with the suicidal. Solution focused practitioners describe this technique as 'degrimming'. Anything which comes within the category of appropriate humour can be used to help the person to see that their situation is not as grim as they think it is. Degrimming is not about laughing at clients, nor is it about being disrespectful in any way. Instead, it is about helping them to see the funny side, and about lightening the session, which might at times be in danger of becoming heavy for both client and worker. Through degrimming, clients are able to leave sessions feeling that counselling or therapy has been both demystified and, at particular moments, fun. Degrimming, which should occur only after the client's situation has been sufficiently acknowledged and validated, can comprise small plays on words, puns, quips or humorous stories which relate to their or the worker's situation.

Degrimming can be a powerful agent of change when working with the suicidal and can make the work more enjoyable — not only for the client — but for the worker, too.

Ending/Intervention

There is always a better way to end a session than: "Well, our time is up for today. I look forward to seeing you next time". Session *endings/interventions* within the solution focused way of working tend to follow a broad general approach, something along the following three steps:

1. Compliments, acknowledgment and validation
2. Bridging statement/rationale for the task
3. Task or homework.

Usually, it is helpful to devote up to about 10 minutes for this part of the session.

Beginning the *intervention* with compliments seems to be helpful, in that the client's attention is held, putting them in a good frame of mind to receive all that is to follow. We all like to hear sincere praise: especially from someone who has been attentive to both our problem situation and to any clues or keys there may have been to making progress.

We can compliment clients in many ways and it is important always to compliment them for something, even if it is only for coming to today's session. An example of a complimentary statement at the end of a session is as follows:

> "It has been helpful to me for you to have explained so clearly what you have been trying to achieve with the situation you are up against. What I am particularly impressed by is your dogged determination to get things back on track."

And another:

> "What I have been struck by from today's session is how well you put into place your new-found strategy for keeping your low moods at bay."

Acknowledgment is the next aspect within this first part of a solution focused session ending. Some examples of these are as follows:

"I'm aware this has been a difficult time for you. In spite of the setbacks you have outlined, you have tried to stick at it, with the result that you have some small steps in the progress direction to be pleased about."

And another:

"With your son being taken so senselessly in that road accident, I can appreciate how terribly sad and upset you are feeling right now, as a result."

The third aspect within the first step of a session ending is *validation*. In addition to helping in the development of good rapport between therapist and client, well timed *validation* of feelings can help the client move on just that little bit quicker in their therapy. Some examples are as follows:

"No wonder you are still in a state of shock. The accident occurred only last Tuesday: it is early days yet."

And another:

"It is not surprising you are feeling a mixture of frustration, sadness and anger: after things seemed to be getting back to normal, your partner simply walked out, without so much as a word of farewell."

The second part of a solution focused ending on intervention comprises the *bridging statement* or rationale for the *task*. Many students of the solution focused approach get confused by this or do not at first understand its purpose. The "bridging" is between what the client has been doing or thinking about in their work towards their goal/s and the actual goal/s as agreed and stated around the time of the first session. The *bridging statement* at the end of a particular session is most likely to refer to something which has arisen during the session that can be used as a small step in their homework before the next session. This is best helped by a few illustrations:

"Because you believe it to be helpful to look up old friends you have let slip out of touch . . ."

And another:

"Given that you have found it useful to take more exercise recently. . ."

And another:

"With your finding it has been so helpful to ask people questions when you are unclear about what they mean . . ."

The third stage in the session ending is the *homework* or *task*. Some therapists, on occasions, may couch it in terms of:

"A little experiment I would like you to try before next time . . ."

For clients who did not get on so well at school, it is generally inadvisable to use the term "homework" for obvious reasons.

Whatever form of word is used, it is important for the *task* to relate to the goal, either directly or indirectly. It may be a *doing task*, a *noticing task* or a *thinking about task*, or with some clients, a combination of two or all three. To illustrate, some examples are as follows:

"I'd like you to go for an energetic walk on at least two days/week between now and when we meet next."

". . . I want you to think about the four options we have discussed today, putting an asterisk against the one you most favour. We can then talk about that one most, next time."

". . . I would like you to notice times when you put your "anti-depression" strategy into practice; and, the benefits to you of doing so at those times."

". . . I want you to think hard about what helpful things you could say to her during this next fortnight. Then, I want you to choose appropriate times for saying something maybe once or twice only. Then, lastly, I want you to notice what difference that makes to your relationship."

SUMMARY

In this chapter I have tried to outline the numerous tools and techniques of the solution focused approach. I began by giving a short history of the approach's origins.

The many tools and techniques are set in the context of the various underlying assumptions, beliefs and basic principles of the approach. Sometimes, newcomers to SFBT find its simplicity and straightforwardness too good to be true. They have yet to experience the power and effectiveness which is available. Others find it totally alien and unfamiliar, compared with many long-established models. From these and other reactions, have grown many misunderstandings. The next section addresses most of these.

SFBT — SOME COMMON MYTHS

Q1 Isn't it really just a 'sticking plaster' approach to peoples' problems?

A. No. What seems to happen is that by concentrating the client's mind on the clues and keys for solution building, they begin to do just that: begin to build a

unique solution to their concerns or difficulties. This can happen in re
sessions. Moreover, what then seems to happen is that the client learns a new ap
proach to dealing with life's difficulties, and then generalises this new learning,
applying the tools and techniques picked up to other situations. It is rare for clients who have been 'worked' using the solution focused approach to return later
with the same problem, 'because the sticking plaster has fallen off'. The underlying 'sore' has in fact healed. Also, as would be expected with this 'new skills
learned' idea, former clients do not usually present with other problems either.

Q2   Surely, unless you get 'to the root of the problem', you can never really help people with SFBT?

A.   This idea has been firmly embedded in the psyche of many cultures for
centuries. The experience of solution focused practitioners, however, is that
the solution rarely has anything to do with the development of the problem.
So, it serves little purpose to go 'digging'. In fact, this activity can actually
be counterproductive as the client can think that by such lines of questioning,
examination of the origins of the problem/s is of great importance. This can
hamper their progress, delay the attainment of their therapeutic goals and
cause them unnecessary expense in terms of both time and money.

Sometimes clients have a real desire to make some connections between
past events and current behaviour, thoughts, feelings. This is all right if that
is what clients want to do. It must, however, be client-led and not therapist-
pushed. Cases in point are those involving adult survivors of childhood abuse,
neglect or trauma. Even in these instances, the way forward with the solution
has little connection with the development of the problem.

Q3   Aren't you really trying to force solutions on people with serious problems?

A.   No, because the SFBT approach is solution focused, not solution forced.
The solution focused practitioner sees their job primarily as one of collaboratively working with the client to help them orientate themselves in a solution building direction. This is achieved by utilising the client's own inner
resources, skills and abilities; and, by considering any changes they may
have made in the right direction prior to their first appointment. Once the
client is headed in the right direction, in terms of their perceived solutions,
this may be sufficient for them while they are working with the therapist; or,
they may want to make much greater progress towards finding a solution to
their difficulties. Either way, solutions are not forced.

Should the therapist attempt to force some sort of solution on the client,
this will not sit comfortably with them. The client may resist such attempts
and may even drop out of therapy.

Q4   Isn't SFBT really just problem solving?

A.   SFBT is solution building, not problem solving.

Solution focused therapy is concerned with the building of solutions. The worker's concern about the nature of the solution, rather than the nature of the problem, helps with the therapeutic task before them: to build solutions. One of the basic assumptions of the solution focused approach is that the client already has the beginnings of the solution as they are sat there before us. This may be discovered by asking about *exceptions* to the problem (see above), which provides us with *keys* or *clues* to how the solution might be constructed. Other clues or keys may be discovered by asking about *pre-session change* (also above).

In addition, the client will have their own unique strengths, skills and personal expertise which will help in the solution building process. These can be utilised, as appropriate, as the work unfolds.

Berg and de Jong (1998) distinguished between problem solving and solution building by explaining it thus:

In problem solving, the practitioner uses their own expertise in trying to resolve the problem for the client. At an appropriate point, they will make an expert intervention to do so. On the other hand, in solution building, the practitioner draws on the client's expertise and then, as the work progresses, the client designs their own solution. In this process, it is the practitioner's job to draw out client expertise and amplify it. Peacock (2001) uses a helpful metaphor: "watering the flowers, not the weeds", to describe this process of concentrating on clues and keys to solution building, highlighting strengths, and amplifying change; thereby paying little or no attention to the problem.

Q5   Is SFBT just for six sessions over as many weeks?

A.   On average, a typical episode of SFBT will be 4–5 sessions over about 8–15 weeks. Some episodes can extend over a year or more, comprising 12 or so sessions. The work is still solution focused and brief ("as few as possible but as many as it takes" — de Shazer, 1985).

Having long gaps between sessions, especially the later ones, allows clients plenty of time to try out their solution building ideas in between times. Also, it reduces the likelihood of dependency and transference, which are important aspects of psychodynamic ways of working, but are not believed to be helpful within the solution focused approach.

With longer gaps between sessions, there are more likely to be further examples of client success to report at subsequent sessions. This provides the therapist with more opportunities to amplify and reinforce any changes reported. Complimenting the client on successes achieved, an important part of the process of change, is more likely to occur, which further reinforces the idea that it is the client and not the therapist who is responsible for the change and therefore deserves the credit.

When sessions occur weekly, there is a reduced likelihood that the client will report significant change, as they have had insufficient time to try out new ways of doing or thinking about things. It is, therefore, more likely that both client and therapist will get into more 'problem talk'.

Q6   Is it true you are only interested in solutions, not problems?

A.   It is true that SF practitioners are more interested in solutions than problems. However, it is important for the worker to gain a sufficient understanding about the nature of the problem: when it began; how it impacts on the client; times when the problem occurs less or is absent; who else it impacts; its severity; how it varies over time; and, what the client has tried to do to improve matters. To this end, practitioners will ask a range of questions in order to gain a sufficient understanding. As the client outlines their problem and answers the practitioner's various questions, the worker will acknowledge, validate and normalise, where appropriate. It is *not* helpful to allow the client to go on excessively with their problem story (see 'the 5 o'clock rule' above). Neither is it helpful to allow the client to continue their problem story without interruption. Helpful interruptions are of the following form:

* To keep the client to the point
* To pick up on any particular strengths, abilities, resources or skills the client has mentioned they have
* To highlight exceptions mentioned to the problem; times when it has been less; or, times when the client has coped better.

Invariably, when a client describes fully their problem situation, there are 'gifts' picked up by the worker in the form of clues and keys which can be used as part of the solution building process.

When clients feel the worker has not heard their problem situation sufficiently (usually because feelings, worries and concerns have not been acknowledged and validated adequately), they will simply return to 'problem talk' again later, even, maybe, repeating it exactly as they did previously.

Q7   Is SFBT simply 'a focus on the positives'?

A.   It is true that the solution focused approach to people's concerns, worries and difficulties adopts a 'half-full' rather than a 'half empty' stance. For instance, when asking clients to answer on a 1–10 scale, "How confident are you in making progress with this particular issue?", the therapist will always respond positively. Below are given the 'half-full' and the 'half-empty' responses.

'Half-full'(solution focused):

TH: On a scale of 1–10, how confident are you that you can make some progress with this?

CL: 5

TH: 5! That's half way. How come you are at 5 and not at 4 or 4 ½?

'Half-empty'(problem focused):

TH: On a scale of 1–10, how confident are you that you can make some progress with this?

CL: 5

TH: Oh. Only 5? Why are you only at a 5 and not 6?

SFT is a focus on solutions rather than a focus on problems, and this may be the reason for the mistaken idea that it is simply a 'focusing on the positives' approach. Also, SFT focuses on 'what works' rather than what is not working. Useful information on what works can give more clues and keys to the solution building process.

Furthermore, SFT focuses on clients' strengths, abilities and resources; and, any other positive attributes they may have, which again, may be utilised in the solution building process.

SFBT is simple, but it is not easy. It is far from being a naïve and simplistic focusing on the positive. Rather, it is a collaborative approach between worker and client in which both are engaged in identifying the resources needed to co-construct solutions which lead away from the problem.

Q8 Wouldn't someone who has been treated by a solution focused therapist, simply come back with the same old problem sometime later?

A. In our experience, largely this does not happen. The 'sticking plaster' myth in Question 1, if true, would suggest that sometime later the client would simply reappear, or seek out another therapist with the same problem.

Developing the metaphor further, what seems to happen is that no sticking plaster is applied in the first place. Instead, both worker and client look at the sore together, deciding which strategy will bring about healing most effectively and in the quickest possible way. From experience, not only does the 'poison' within the sore clear up, the tissue regenerates, as also does the skin covering it. *The client learns much by this process*, such that they are able to avoid similar sores developing in the future, and if they do develop, they are able to apply the same or similar strategy to the one they applied previously. This is an important point and emphasises the health promotion aspect of solution focused working.

Q9   Do the various tools and techniques of SFBT mean that it is a 'techniquey' approach?

A.   Solution focused therapy is equipped with many and various helpful and useful tools and techniques to be used in the work on an as-needed basis. The appropriateness of these techniques may vary from session to session and from client to client. Having many techniques does not make the approach 'techniquey'.

Work with any client should have a sense of 'flow'. Therapeutic conversations flow as subsequent questions are shaped by the answers given to previous ones. So it is with the tools and techniques of solution focused therapy, as most are presented in the form of a question. The reader is advised to study in detail how this is achieved in practice in the chapters on case studies (Chapters 9 and 10).

Q10   Is it true that to use SFBT you need hardly any training and could apply it after reading a book or two?

A.   Some therapeutic models and approaches require several years' training with many hours of supervision. This process has significant financial implications for trainees! In comparison, SFT requires a few day's worth of training only. Kim (2006), in a study examining the effectiveness of SFBT, found that workers were more effective than other models over approximately six sessions of therapy, if they had completed more than 20 hours' training. He showed that if they had undertaken less than 20 hours, they performed worse. As a trainer of novice solution focused practitioners, I have found that those demonstrating the core conditions of effective helping but with negligible past knowledge and experience in matters psychological, often make the most effective practitioners later on.

A three-day basics course, followed up by a one- or two-day refresher/consolidation course six to nine months later, can often get new practitioners well on the way to becoming effective. Good quality supervision by more experienced practitioners is helpful in this process, as is ongoing reading, especially of texts which give plenty of examples of therapist — client dialogue.

Q11   Am I right in saying that you don't go into the person's feelings?

A. SFBT practitioners generally do not go in depth into clients' feelings. There is no evidence that this practice is helpful in the achievement of the client's treatment goals. In fact Bushman, Baumeister and Stack (1999) showed that catharsis can actually make things worse. It is relevant to mention here, that in CBT, from which many SFBT ideas have their roots, workers address behaviour and cognitions, rather than affect directly. de Shazer (1985) suggested that most people experience many emotions fleetingly, every day. Extremes of these feelings could be considered 'high-arousal states' and he found it did not help to lead clients into an examination of them.

What is important for any feelings expressed by clients is for them to be acknowledged adequately. Furthermore, it is helpful if any such feelings expressed are validated and, on occasions, normalised. Some examples are as follows:

- "I can see this is upsetting for you."
- "No wonder you are angry about your being made redundant so suddenly. Your boss reassured you only last month that your position was safe."
- "I am getting just a little more of an understanding about how hurt you are by all this."
- "I can see by your tears that you are still very much in love with him/her."
- "It is understandable you are so cross still, about this whole incident."
- "I am getting a real sense of your grief and loss over all those close to you who died in that incident."

My personal preference, as a practitioner, is to spend a little more time on the acknowledgment, validation and normalisation of feelings. I find this is helpful in letting the client know they have been heard, in building rapport and in the development of trust.

7

Suicide Encounters: The Crucial First Ten Minutes

A strong positive relationship with a suicidal patient is absolutely essential.
Linehan,1993, p. 514

This is probably the most important chapter within this book. It is essentially about building good rapport, trust and a good working relationship. Get it right in this first 10 minutes (or thereabouts) and a life is saved. Get it wrong and the client will begin to close down and withdraw inwardly. Picking up on withdrawal cues, however, practitioners can then claw back the situation during the rest of the session. Failure to, do this could result in yet another statistic.

In preparing my notes for this chapter, I have been wondering: is it best to list the many dozens of factors that can go wrong; or, to list the many factors which ensure the client is heard, understood and helped in these crucial first few minutes of the first assessment interview? On balance, and in keeping with good solution focused practice, I believe it is best to take it from a 'what works' perspective. I hope by the end, you the reader, will have a greater appreciation of the answer to the question: "How come so many hundreds of thousands of people worldwide have taken their lives over the past 30 years or so, *after they sought help and met with a worker*?"

Zunin (1972) in talking about the structure of conversation, suggests that relationships are made up of successive sequences, and that these occur over a 4½–5 minute period. If these periods go well, then the foundations for a good relationship are in place.

THE PRE-SESSION TASK

What is really helpful in getting this first session off to a really good start, is to have had the opportunity to ask the pre-session task — the formula first session task (FFST) question (Adams, Piercy & Jurich, 1991) (outlined in Chapter 6). It runs as follows:

> "What I would like you to do between now and when we meet, is to notice what is happening in your life that you want to continue to have happen. Can you do this for me?"

Ideally, this question can be given over the phone after the appointment has been arranged and agreed. Or, it might occur on a brief 1:1 appointment-making session, the day or so before the first session. Secretaries and receptionists making appointments on behalf of therapists have given potential clients this question prior to their appointment, with useful results. As mentioned elsewhere, this is a powerful way of encouraging a solutions orientation in the client's mind prior to their first meeting. Also, it has a life preserving quality (at least in the short term), as it is a *presuppositional* question: presupposing that the client does have something in their life (amidst all the despair and hopelessness that they may be experiencing currently) that they want to continue to have happen; and, that they will be attending their first appointment. There is a sense, too, with the FFST that the therapist means business with their potential client, rather than simply meeting up with them to see how things might develop.

CLIENT 'RADAR'

In my experience, severely depressed and/or suicidal clients present at their first session with an amazing complexity of emotions, expectations and perceptions. They may be fearful of what the therapist might think of them; they may be embarrassed about having to talk about their suicidal thoughts, ideas and possible concrete plans. They may be feeling sad and/or despairing about the predicament in which they find themselves. They may present as simply 'flat', seemingly devoid of any emotion.

The suicidal person may have few expectations of the therapist as to how helpful they can be, really, given the severity of their circumstances. However, most are open to ideas and are prepared to enter into some sort of dialogue, even though this may be halting and a little incoherent in some instances.

The third aspect of this complexity in the early minutes of the first assessment session, is the person's perceptions. With the various emotions they may be experiencing, their sensitivity to what is happening around them interactionally can be heightened. It seems almost as if invisible antennae are protruding from the person's head, picking up the slightest cues (most often non-verbal) from the therapist. Much has been written about body language and non-verbal behaviour during a first contact (Pease, 1984; Mehrabian, 1981).

The suicidal person, as they meet with the worker, will have questions running back and forth through their mind, such as:

"Might this person be able to help me?"

"Does this person have any idea at all of the depth of pain I am feeling?"

"Is my coming for help going to be a waste of time?"

"If this person has anything to offer me in the way of some help, will I get along with them?"

As their 'radar' is up and working well, they will be looking for the slightest evidence that answers one or several of these questions. I would suggest that the large percentage of people who complete suicide, within a month of seeing a health professional, received some rather unsatisfactory answers to these questions.

NON-VERBAL COMMUNICATION

How we communicate non-verbally is something all need to be aware of. The proportion of verbal (the actual words spoken) surprises many. It has been suggested it is as low as 7%; the remainder of the communication being 38% vocal (voice tone, etc.) and 55% body language, dress, facial expression, eye contact, use of silence, etc. (Mehrabian, 1981).

In addition to what has been said about Zunin's successive sequences in the first 4½–5 minutes, many suggest we come to a view about another person within a few seconds of the first encounter. This is based almost entirely on the non-verbal communication picked up. Again, client radar is up and running at a high level of efficiency, so they will form an opinion quite quickly on whether the worker in front of them feels confident in what they are doing; how hopeful they might be that other options might be worth trying; how warm/cold they are towards the client and/or their difficulties; and, how effective they are in working with clients who are thinking and wanting to talk about ways to end their lives as a solution to problems.

Non-verbal communication will be dealt with again later in Chapter 8. It is sufficient for the purposes of this chapter to say that there are many ways, non-verbally, in which the worker can communicate to the client, within this first 10 minutes to ensure that rapport, trust, a good working relationship and alliance develop.

HOW TO START THE SESSION

It may be of benefit to consider briefly the various models and approaches and how the first session is conducted. If the model requires that a full history be taken before a diagnosis is made and treatment prescribed, valuable time may be lost in these first crucial minutes. If the particular therapy model requires that the first two sessions of treatment are 'getting to know you time', then again, the person may be wondering how helpful this work will be eventually for the current crisis which they feel they are in. If the model requires that the full nature of the problem be outlined, its origins and its effects now on the person's life, with the full impact of signs and symptoms felt; this again may not be helpful for what needs to happen in these first crucial minutes. I could go on, detailing other models and approaches which, I believe, may miss the point of these first vital minutes.

The person's radar picks up signals from the word go, so a friendly, smiling face and a few softly spoken words can go a long way in getting the first session off to a good start. A *brief* introduction to how the service works is all that is needed. Suicidal and/or severely depressed people are neither interested, nor do they hear what they might consider irrelevant or unimportant information.

Also, in my experience, there are few opportunities to use an adapted form of *problem-free talk*. If there is an opportunity, an adapted form of this valuable tool runs as follows:

"Before things got as they have been, in what sorts of ways did you spend your free time?" or,
"Before you got as low as you did, what sorts of things did you do in the day that interested you?"

The client has no time for preliminaries: they want simply to get down to business, if indeed, there is any business to get down to. (NB: The client's four questions at the beginning of this chapter.) Given this, it is best usually for the therapist to get straight to the point, with some useful solution focused questions which are helpful to clients to outline their worries/concerns/difficulties/problems. These are:

"What's uppermost at the moment?" or,

"How can I be helpful to you?" or,

"What brings you here?"

As one of the above is asked, it is important for the worker to be communicating all three core conditions of acceptance, genuineness and empathy (Rogers, 1967). These are communicated almost entirely non-verbally, and unless they are in place, there will be few beginnings of a real working relationship with the client.

I have dealt with Rogers' core conditions in earlier chapters but as they are central to this present chapter, there is merit in re-examining them.

Acceptance is about unconditional positive regard — warts and all — however or in whichever way the client is presenting. He or she may be rather dishevelled; may not have washed much recently; may be perceived as hostile or unfriendly, due to lack of eye contact; or, may be doing their best not to communicate.

Genuineness is about sincerity, i.e. sincerely wanting to try to understand and be helpful to the person. More than this, it is about honesty and congruence. The person must feel, despite any words the therapist may use, that they *really do* want to listen, try to understand, and try to be helpful, even though they may find it hard to. Again, this is almost an entirely non-verbal communication, the client picking up particularly on their radar: tone of voice, quality of eye contact, pace of speech and demeanour. Further questions running through the client's mind may be:

"Does this person *really mean* what they say?" or,

"Does he/she *really care,* or are they merely doing their job?" or,

"Can I *trust* him/her?"

Empathy is about the therapist trying to understand the person's situation, as if they were walking in their shoes, but not losing the 'as if' quality (Rogers, 1967). This is a similar idea to the old native American saying, "You can never understand how it feels to be another person, until you have walked a mile in their moccasins". Empathy, I have found, on its own, is insufficient when working with people who are suicidal. Again, this may be something to do with 'the radar' and the heightened sensitivity. *Deep empathy* is what is required. When the client's radar picks this up, then there are real foundations being laid for a working relationship. Burns and Auerbach (1996) talked about the role of 'therapeutic empathy' and how it can sometimes be missing in psychotherapy. They suggested an 'empathy training programme' be offered to address this problem. This would include listening and self-expression skills (e.g. "I feel . . ." statements). A question might arise here about how far workers can be trained in empathy if they had very little in the first place. Presumably, if there's something there, it can be trained up. I wonder if it is similar to gifted footballers who have their innate ball control skills trained up by professional coaches? Also, it is important to make the point that empathy is not sympathy. It is natural for people to have sympathy for the plight of another human being, e.g. being sympathetic to a person who has lost a limb in a road accident. One can feel sorry for and sympathetic towards an individual or a group of individuals who are suffering misfortune, whether it be financial, economic, physical or mental. I recall an incident whilst travelling on a short train journey a few years ago. The train, a two-car set, on a branch line, with good all round visibility, was approaching a station. Ahead, on the platform edge, was a young man looking disturbed, eyeing the train and its driver as it drew to a halt. There were two elderly ladies ineffectively trying to engage in conversation with the young man. The body language of all three spoke volumes. The ladies, in their way, were trying to be helpful in the words they were using, but they made no impact on the man. Fortunately, both the train conductor and the driver picked up very quickly on what was going on and summoned the emergency services to the young man's aid. As the ladies boarded the train, one turned to the young man with the words, "Don't worry, it'll be all right. Your mother loves you anyway". They were words of sympathy, which sounded insincere and were based on no real evidence in fact. Also, the words totally lacked any empathy.

All that I have written so far about these crucial few minutes of the first session has got us about 2½ minutes into the session!

THE BUILDING OF RAPPORT, TRUST, AND A STRONG THERAPEUTIC RELATIONSHIP AND ALLIANCE

Once clients experience acceptance, genuineness and empathy, there is a basis for the building of rapport and then the early stages of the development of trust. A therapeutic relationship and alliance can then come about (see Figure 7.1 below). 'Alliance' can be defined simply as agreement between client and therapist as to the nature of the problem and what to do about it. In the solution focused approach, the 'what to do about it' is often not made explicit: the client is kept guessing, which is good for client curiosity purposes! There is gathering evidence that the therapeutic relationship and alliance are key variables in predicting successful outcomes across a whole range of different types of treatment. The importance of the therapeutic relationship in psychotherapeutic work generally cannot be overstated. This relationship must be solid, and a cementing of the strong alliance promoted. Simon (1988) and Schneidman (1981, 1984) both emphasised that a strong therapeutic relationship is *essential* to the successful treatment of suicidal thinking and behaviour. They go further by suggesting that without it, it is unlikely that the client will continue. Again, the question can be asked: "Is this what happens in the tens of thousands of lost cases, worldwide, every year?" Was it that the therapeutic relationship did not get established, or was it further back than this (see Figure 7.1), in that there was something lacking in the area of core conditions?

If the worker goes into this first session with the strongly held belief in the importance of establishing an effective relationship and alliance from the outset (Rudd et al., 2001), they increase their chances enormously of making real progress.

Rapport is an interesting phenomenon/quality. I am often struck by the exact point in a first session when rapport seems to be building. Often, there seem to be clear non-verbal signals from the client that this is happening. Usually this occurs in the climate of acceptance, genuineness and empathy, and a general putting at ease by the worker.

Sometimes it can be a quick smile from the client; at others it can be an opportunity taken for the use of 'black humour' (*degrimming* — see Chapter 6). In other cases, the client may be showing some slight relief from their pain, having outlined a small part of their story. The 'problem shared is a problem halved' principle may have started to apply. They may appear just a little less tense or they may have become slightly warmer towards the therapist: these can all be signs that rapport is building.

TRUST

The next stage in the process is *trust*. I find it difficult to describe exactly how and when trust grows between client and worker. Again, like rapport, it just seems to come about as the earlier foundations have become more firmly laid. These earlier foundations include the core conditions of effective communication mentioned above. It is my firmly held view that there is a process at work here; and, at various key points, clients will be asking themselves additional questions about trust along the following lines:

"Can I trust this person with my worst thoughts and fears"

"Can I trust this person to take me seriously"

"If I put my trust in this person to help me, are they both able and willing to get me through this?"

For exactly how I believe the development of trust fits into this process during the first 10 minutes, please see Figure 7.1 below and refer to the flow diagram in Appendix 1.

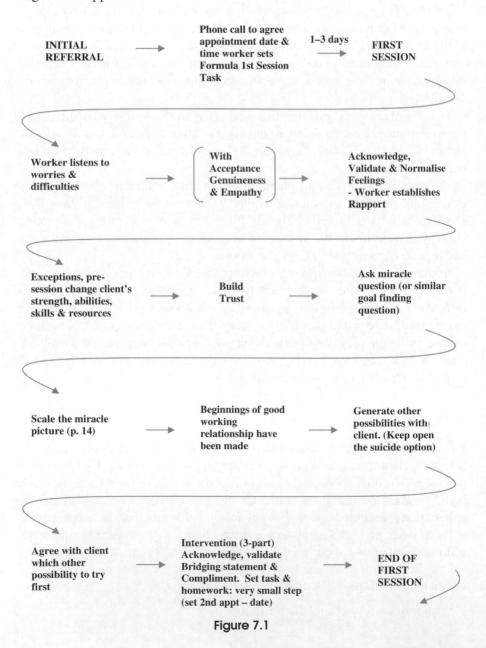

Figure 7.1

ACKNOWLEDGEMENT, VALIDATION AND NORMALISATION

During these first 10 minutes, opportunities should be taken to acknowledge, validate and normalise the client's experiences described and feelings expressed. This is good, basic solution focused work in any context. By acknowledging that we have heard what someone has told us, it lets them know that not only have we been listening, but also that we are trying to understand. It is important, especially, to acknowledge any feelings expressed: e.g. "Seems like you feel really upset by this". We can never know exactly how another person feels, but we can try, based on our own experience and knowledge, to get some understanding. One of the most common communication spoilers is for one person to say to another: "I know exactly how you feel!" It is far better to be more tentative by saying something instead like: "I am beginning to get an understanding of how painful this is for you".

Validating suicidal experiences and feelings in these first few minutes is very important, too. This is a similar idea to 'reflecting meanings' within various person-centred models. So what we endeavour to do, is to link the feeling to the fact: e.g. "No wonder you have felt so devastated by your boyfriend's departure: he just texted you that it's over, and disappeared".

Normalising feelings and any other experiences expressed is also a great way of reassuring the suicidal person that they are not alone: that their feelings and reactions are quite normal for normal people in everyday life. It is good for them to know that they have not developed some unique mental illness or have crossed the line into 'madness'. A good reassuring statement which aids normalisation of feelings and thoughts is:

> "What we find in this work is that the thoughts and feelings you are having are normal; and are experienced by normal people within an abnormal set of circumstances."

HOPE, OPTIMISM AND CONFIDENCE

Hope

Another quality which is essential to communicate within the first 10 minutes is *hope*. Hopelessness is a key factor in people who successfully suicide (Rudd et al., 2001). This important factor is dealt with more fully in Chapter 8, but suffice it to say here that within the first 10 minutes, some sort of grounds for hope must be evident in the suicidal person's mind for them to want to continue. This may not yet be hope that they can climb out of their morass of difficulty. However, they need to feel hopeful that the therapist may have some thoughts, ideas, clues — anything that can give them a reason to continue with the process.

Optimism

People who are feeling suicidal may have had thoughts dominated by pessimism for some time. Negative thinking may abound also and this in itself can lead to further pessimism in the suicidal person. Pessimism and negative thinking are closely related to hopelessness and can lead to a further closing down of possibilities in the mind of the client as to what the best solution to their difficulties might be. I have often likened this 'closing down of possibilities', which eventually leads to suicide being chosen as the preferred option, to a racehorse with its blinkers firmly in place during a race. In the horse's case, the blinkers enable the horse to keep its focus on the track ahead, regardless of distractions along the route (e.g. fences), until it reaches eventually the finishing line. It is the worker's job with the client (not the horse!) during the course of the work to 'widen the blinkers' in the client, to allow more possibilities in the form of other options than suicide, which may be their correct focus.

Both pessimism and optimism are contagious. When therapists are optimistic about their clients transcending current difficulties and having a future where they not only survive but live a better quality of life, then clients become 'infected' by this in some way. Ideally this process should show the beginnings of happening within the first 10 minutes. The result of clients being infected with optimism is that they become curious as to what it might be that the therapist can possibly feel optimistic about. They are then open to other possibilities for moving forward. With my many years of experience in both working with suicidal people and training other health and welfare professionals to work similarly, I have on the one hand experienced countless successful outcomes of severe suicidality; and on the other, heard numerous accounts of services in which the suicide rate has been reduced significantly. This factor alone can give workers grounds for optimism when working with this challenging client group.

Confidence

The above points on optimism related to successful outcomes can apply equally to grounds for feeling confident.

In my experience, being both confident in one's approach to suicidal clients and confident in their inner strengths and resources, (which may be somewhat hidden during a first session), to enable them to deal with the causal factors can again have an infectious quality and raise client curiosity.

The challenges of working with suicidal people may result in a lack of confidence on the worker's part. Non-therapeutic reactions in a worker may occur (Rudd et al., 2001). Examples of these reactions are fear, dread, malice, aversion, empathic dread, hate, anxiety and worry. Rudd et al. (page 13) suggest that this may lead to an avoidance or fear-based treatment, which is against the client's best interests. There is no doubt that in my mind, given the above discussion about clients' radar, heightened sensitivity and contagion, that these will be picked up by clients very easily.

Confidence, then, is a very important quality to communicate to our clients: confidence in communicating the core conditions; confidence in building rapport and a therapeutic relationship; and, confidence in the client's abilities to experiment with/choose other options other than that of the last resort (suicide).

CONCLUSION

My hypothesis is that the many thousands of people who take their lives each year, within a month or so of having consulted with a practitioner, did not have a satisfactory experience within the first 10 minutes of their first meeting. (In most cases their only meeting.)

This hypothesis, as mentioned in an earlier chapter, could be tested by interviewing survivors of serious attempts, based on the key factors mentioned above. Also, there may be sufficient data from suicide notes, clients' diaries, personal logs, etc. of those who completed suicide to gain more information on what their experiences were when they sought help. Such a retrospective study could prove both interesting and useful in future prevention planning.

There is much that can go wrong during these early minutes of a first encounter with a practitioner and yet, there is much to get right. Setting a formula first session task firmly and professionally, prior to the appointment; smiling in a friendly and sincere manner on first meeting; ensuring the core conditions are in place; building good rapport and trust; communicating hope; establishing a good therapeutic relationship and alliance with the client; *and*, communicating all of these non-verbally, is a very good start.

There is much scope for training here. Not all practitioners in the field of mental healthcare are recruited because they display all or most of the above. Many apply to work in health, social care and welfare as a career choice and are selected using other criteria (e.g. exam qualifications). Some in this group come into the work with some basic skills and the best motives to be helpful to their clients. Part of a social contract could be to reward these attributes by providing the highest quality of ongoing development training.

My firmly held belief is that if, worldwide, it is suicidologists' aim to make further significant reductions in the suicide rate, then attention needs to be paid to further fine-tuning by way of good training for this crucial first 10 minutes.

8

The Solution Focused Approach in Working with the Suicidal

The problem now is to identify what works, i.e. what is cost-effective.

Jenkins et al., 1994, p. 186

INTRODUCTION

The basic tools and techniques of the solution focused approach have been outlined in detail in Chapter 6. There has been some outlining too, of the basic assumptions, beliefs and fundamental principles of the approach. All of these can be applied when working with suicidal service users.

Alongside the basic solution focused tools and techniques, a range of specialised solution focused tools and techniques have been developed and field tested over the past 10 years or so. Some of the more basic tools have been adapted in specific ways. Both these specialised tools and techniques and the various adaptations will be outlined below.

Additionally, at the end of this chapter is a section entitled 'Key Points to Cover'. On many occasions over the past few years, I have reflected on the solution focused approach to suicide prevention, paying particular attention to the successful outcomes aspect of the work. In addressing the question 'What works?', there arose nine key points which hearteningly, in various combinations (or maybe all nine together?), seem to be responsible for these highly significant successful outcomes. I spend some time examining and discussing these, for you the reader, in an attempt to shed further light on 'what works'.

THE SPECIALISED AND ADAPTED SOLUTION FOCUSED TOOLS AND TECHNIQUES

Before examining various tools and techniques specifically, I will begin by out-lining basic counselling skills used, and their part in determining suicidal think-ing and behaviour. These are all applied from a solution focused perspective.

DEEP EMPATHY AND QUICK RAPPORT

It is incumbent on any health professional, welfare or social care worker, to develop a good degree of rapport with their clients. As mentioned in earlier chapters, rapport develops as a result of the three core conditions for effective relationships being in place (Rogers, 1951). Once rapport has been estab-lished, trust can follow and the basic foundations for a working relationship are then laid.

The importance of the first 10 minutes is dealt with at length in the previ-ous chapter, but suffice it to say here that a lack of felt empathy is one thing that can occur during the first few minutes of contact.

The solution focused approach with its emphasis on 'brief' lends itself well to working with suicidal clients. (Some solution focused practitioners work on a basis of a one-session episode of therapy.) This first session, then, must count, and start to count quickly.

How is this achieved? Through the establishment of *quick rapport* devel-opment and *deep empathy*. I have been amazed in many instances, when severely suicidal clients have been referred, at how this can be achieved so quickly. This is crisis intervention work at its most fluid and fast moving. By using the following case example, I will endeavour to illustrate how this can be achieved:

[Ring on bell]

TH: Hello. Graham Fuller?

[Client nods]

TH: Do come in. We are in the first room on the right. Do take a seat.

[Client looks fidgety, eyes darting left and right and lowered, slightly un-kempt and has a slumped posture.]

TH: [Therapist decides not to give formal welcome and introduction, out-lining how the service works, as the client looks not the slightest bit interested. Also therapist decides it would be inappropriate to ask problem-free talk.]

TH: [Experiencing fully the core conditions of acceptance, genuineness and empathy; lowers and slows voice.] What brings you here?

CL: My life's just hit the buffers! [in a lowered voice] I'm all washed up.

TH: [Endeavouring to communicate deeper empathy] I'm really sorry to hear that right now [presuppositional flavour], this is how things are for you. Tell me a little more about how things have developed to this current state.

CL: Well, it all started when . . . [Client outlines the problem in some detail. During this time, therapist uses various 'minimal encouragers' such as, 'Aha', 'I see', 'Mmm', head-nods, etc. Therapist communicates more of a sense of deep empathy as he/she tries to get a fuller understanding of the client's desperate situation. Throughout the problem outlining, the therapist interrupts with coping questions, clarification questions, and statements of acknowledgment and validation. Therapist soon senses that rapport is building well.]

—5 minute mark—

In this case, it was clear from the outset by the client's body language that he felt suicidal. Also, I had had some scant information from the referrer that this might indeed have been the case. What of 'run-of-the-mill' depressed clients who may not at first sight appear to be suicidal? How does the principle of establishing deep empathy and quick rapport operate in these cases? Should not all workers endeavour to establish deep empathy and quick rapport with all clients, regardless of presenting concerns, issues or worries? In considering these questions, of course we need to feel empathy towards the client from the outset and endeavour to develop good rapport as early as possible, but what is very important is that when suicidal thinking or plans are spoken about, we need to move up a gear into the area of deep empathy and quick rapport. This session may be our one and only chance to connect with the person and their pain. The second session will then not only be looked forward to, but will actually happen.

ASSESSING FOR INCONGRUENCE

In the example of Graham above, it was clear from both his non-verbal behaviour and his spoken words, that he was suicidal. There was a match between these two communication types, so he came across as congruent. However, it is often not that easy. Some people who are very depressed can exhibit a whole range of signs and symptoms which indicate 'depression'. They may or may not feel suicidal as a result. They may say they are not suicidal, in response to a direct or indirect question about intent, and yet they are within a few hours of completing the suicide act. This business of verbal and non-verbal communication about suicidal intent has baffled many a health professional and others alike. Some, who have been less well trained, have been shocked on being informed about the suicide of a service user they saw only a few days before.

How can we tell? We tell, by looking for discrepancies (incongruence) between the spoken word and all the other (non-verbal) communications. Within ASIST (Applied Suicide Intervention Skills Training), which is a form of suicide first aid training, these are referred to as 'invitations' (ASIST, 2005). In some cases, clients will come straight out with it, being totally congruent as they do so:

> "I've failed miserably to get her to come back. Death is the only way out. I've already planned the when, where and how."

In other cases, there can be just some fleeting sign or throw-away remark which gives us the clue we need.

Firstly, let me consider the verbal part of communication in more detail than appeared in an earlier work (Henden, 2005).

Verbal Communication

These include the following:

(i) **An overt statement of intent,** e.g. "I am going to kill myself". This statement, like the last one given above, is fairly clear as to what the person intends for themselves. Unfortunately for the worker, few fall into this straightforward category.

(ii) **Talking in the past tense.** This verbal communication gives the worker a sense that the client is not or will not consider a future. They are here now before us, in the present, but something about the dialogue indicates they are referring to a past only. Some examples of this are:

> "I used to think things would get better."

> "I had some very good friends, one time."

> "I have had some happy times, it's true."

> "Back along, life used to be fun. We would do all sorts of things together. Things were different then: they were good."

Often, accompanying these statements, clients seem distant, lost in thought or musing over happy memories. There is often a sense they are detached from the present, and certainly, the future.

(iii) **Obscure references to, or an inability to envisage a future.** This sort of statement can be quite subtly dropped into clients' conversations and workers need to be able to tune in quickly. Some examples might be:

"Sometime in the future, these difficulties might work out, I suppose."

"One can, I suppose, find a way forward, if one really wants to."

"I can't really see how this problem can be sorted out."

"Answers to this situation will be hard to come by."

Often, it is the somewhat resigned way that these statements are made which gives a clue or key as to suicidal intent.

(iv) **Statements that indicate that affairs have been/or are being put in order.** This is part of the preparation process for the aftermath of the suicide act, in the mind of the client. Not all clients make such preparations, but many do and evidence can emerge as to what actions have been taken to date, or at least, thought about. 'Affairs in order' statements could include the following:

"I always wanted my granddaughter to have my jewellery."

"I don't want all the fuss any more with the car. I think I'll give it to my brother."

"I've been finding I've sorted quite a few things out recently. All my financial documents are now in a marked box."

(v) **Almost inaudible throw away remarks.** It is incumbent upon workers who come across people who are suicidal, to be attuned to this sort of verbal communication. The most commonly occurring are as follows:

"Sometime in the future . . ." [mutters quietly under breath] "if I'm still here — I'll get around to sorting that out."

"One day," [more quietly] "pigs might fly — I'll have got through all this and be living a full and happy life again."

"One's just got to survive" [muttering] "some hope! — this sort of tragedy."

"I know there are more constructive ways . . ." [sarcastically and muttering] "blah, blah — of finding a way out of this exit-less maze and my job is just to find it."

Non-Verbal Communication

As discussed in an earlier chapter, it has been suggested (Mehrabian, 1981) that the verbal percentage of any 1:1 communication is as small as 7%, and that everything else — the 93% — falls into the category of non-verbal communication. This comprises facial expression, body posture, tone of voice, pace of speech, dress, eye movement and so on. I will consider the most important of these first.

(i) **Eye contact.** Clues or keys to suicidal intent, with eye contact can take three main forms. The first of these is where the client fixes a stare to a spot on the floor, during the bulk of the interview. This performs the role of 'non-communication' or 'non-connectedness' with the therapist. The second eye contact, or more accurately, lack of it, is where the client focuses steadily onto a point either beyond and behind the worker, or on a part of the worker's face, other than the eyes. This is another form of non-communication or non-connectedness and is more subtle and therefore not so easy to pick up.

The third form of 'faulty' eye contact is where reasonable eye contact is being maintained for much of the session, but on a crucial word, the eyes flick momentarily away to the left. This is most commonly noticeable in certain politicians who, when being asked a direct question on a key policy issue by a skilled interviewer, feel a need to avoid the truth!

With suicidal clients, some examples are as follows:

"Of *course* [eyes flick to the left] I wouldn't do such a dreadful thing."

"Me, suicidal? Far from [eyes flick to left] it."

"Some people have asked me if I have considered ending it all, but I would never [eyes flick . . .] do that."

All these three instances are good examples of incongruent communication.

(ii) **Slumped posture.** On its own, this form of non-verbal behaviour does not necessarily indicate suicidal intent. It may be simply that a person is depressed, feeling hopeless and despairing in some way or of low self-esteem, without any strong thoughts of suicide. Alongside other cases, though, such as one or two of the verbal cues described above, they could present a completely different picture.

(iii) **Appearing superficially joyful, when all factors indicate that the opposite should be the case.** Many practitioners, across all disciplines, both professional and otherwise, have been caught out by this one.

Practitioner comments such as, "Well, she was referred to me as highly suicidal, but I found her just now to be quite upbeat"; "He appeared very low and despairing last time I saw him, but today he seems full of the joys of spring"; and, "At last, he appears to be getting better". In all three cases, the service user took their life within the following week. What was happening in the service user's mind when they were seen by their practitioner was they were now feeling a sense of peace. No longer was the internal struggle or conflict raging about whether to live or die: the decision had been made and the action plan set.

In recent years, on occasions when I have experienced this form of communication, I have been struck by its unreality in some curious way or other. There is a side of me that shares in the relief the service user is experiencing. Suicidal feelings and intent in the person potentially can be upsetting and distressing for workers, so reported improvement is always welcome. However, it is the unreality which is the alarm bell, indicating that closer questioning is needed with a concentration on any incongruence which may then appear.

It is helpful to mention here about 'the trough of depression' into which some people descend over a period of time. This has been well documented in the literature on depression. As they are sliding down the side of the trough, they may have suicidal ideas, but choose not to implement them. Then, whilst at the bottom of the trough, the ideas may become stronger, but they feel incapable or unable to action them. However, just as they begin to climb up the other side, usually with the help of medication in these cases, this is the point of highest risk. At these times, patients can exhibit this superficial joyfulness, which then catches out their clinician.

(iv) **Recent lack of attention to personal hygiene, personal care and appearance.** Again, taken alone, these cues could simply be some among a host of depressive features. However, alongside other cues such as putting personal affairs in order, throwaway comments and insincere eye contact can indicate suicidal intent.

Every client is different and cues presented by one may differ completely from those of another. This lack of attention may include unwashed or unbrushed hair, lengthening fingernails, wearing the same clothes as the day before, unpolished shoes, and some buttons on clothing left undone. The point to be clear about here is that this behaviour is out of character and not something the client would be satisfied with, under normal circumstances. The point to stress here is to be alert and watchful for these out-of-character lack-of-attention signs. It is the close questioning (see below) which will then provide a clearer impression, as the client's incongruence begins to show.

(v) **An anxious or frightened facial expression.** In some cases, this form of non-verbal communication is evident. There is something about the client's whole face, including the eyes, which communicates fear. The muscles of the face may be taut; the expression is held in an unnatural position; and there may be an absence of expression of any other feelings. This can be as a result of strong suicidal thoughts over a long period; a feeling of being out of control; or, a feeling that they are moving closer to putting the thoughts into practice. A simple question about thoughts or intent often provides immediately a clear picture of the extent of the suicidal intent.

Both with the verbal and the non-verbal cues, neither should be taken in isolation. They are simply cues which could provide keys and clues as to how the person is feeling and whether they are thinking about putting into action the last resort option to problems, worries or concerns. It is *incongruence* we as practitioners should be on the lookout for as we question the person sensitively on issues, their thoughts about their situation, feelings about the future and their individual coping threshold.

QUESTIONS TO ELICIT SUICIDAL IDEATION

When a practitioner's 'alarm bell' begins to ring, as a result of a selection of either the verbal or non-verbal cues, or a combination of both, outlined in the previous section, a question or two should be asked to confirm or deny any hunch they may be having.

Over a number of years, various questions of this nature have been field-tested. A question one might ask one service user may not feel appropriate for another, so a different question may be the one of choice. The table below is a battery of 10 questions:

1. "Seems like you are having quite a time of it at the moment?"
2. "When everything comes at once, sometimes it can seem to get on top of one?"
3. "At this point, how much more do you feel you can cope with?"
4. "How far is all this getting you down right now?"
5. "How often, recently, have you felt you are getting to the end of your tether?"
6. "I expect sometimes you feel you have had your lot?"
7. "At the moment, how far do you feel able to go on?"
8. "How close do you feel, right now, to ending your own life?"
9. "On a scale of 1–10 (where 1 is 'not at all well' and 10 is 'very well'), how well do you feel you are doing at the moment?"

10. "If you decided to go ahead with the last resort option:
    (a) What method would you use? (i.e. pills, rope, razor blades, vacuum cleaner tube, firearms, etc.)
    (b) How prepared are you should you decide?"

Experiences show that asking one of the list of 1–9, followed by 10, is a foolproof way of assessing suicidal intent.

Questions 1–9 are all about how the client is finding their situation, currently. It is important to point out that although some clients can feel close to breaking point and may have thought about the suicide option, something or other would stop them even making a plan, let alone carrying it out. A dialogue of this sort might be as follows:

TH: [Asks Q3] At this point, how much more do you feel you can cope with?
CL: Things have been awful for so long. It started when Barry was made redundant last May. Then mortgage payments were stopped a couple of months later, so we are now in this dump [client points to dilapidated surroundings]. In August our Peter was hit by that car as he played in the road; and I've this health scare over this lump in my neck [points to undulation in neck]. Sometimes I feel at breaking point and wonder how much longer I can keep going. But, I think of what my Gran had to put up with during the war: she did it, so I think I should be able to do it, too. We'll get there in the end.

Alternatively, in response to any one of the 1–9 list, the answer might not be as clear and the client not so congruent in their overall communication. This would indicate the timely asking of Question 10, from the list. The dialogue in this case might run as follows:

TH: [Asks Q7] At the moment, how far do you feel able to go on?
CL: On some days, I feel I can keep going as there is a very small light at the end of the tunnel, but on others, which seem to be happening more and more, I don't know [client averts eyes] if I can get through this.
TH: [Asks Q10] If you decided to go ahead with the last resort option, what method would you use: pills, rope, razor blades, vacuum cleaner tube and tape, firearms, something else?

A client who is actively suicidal might answer as follows:

CL: [Becomes very still and maintains a scared, but fixed stare at the therapist. Great congruence is communicated.] I have been saving up loads of different tablets for the last few months now. I have been looking at Internet sites to try and find out what the right quantity would be to take. I have been up on to the Moor and have found a very lonely, but comfortable looking place. I would slip away quietly up to the spot late one evening.

A client who is not actively suicidal, tends to back-pedal at great speed when asked this question. The following reply is typical:

CL: [Looking at the therapist surprised and amazed; and again, with great congruence.] Oh! No, I wouldn't do anything stupid. I would upset too many people. I couldn't lay such a heavy load on my kids — and for the rest of their lives.

While both of the above replies are communicated congruently, the therapist should be aware that in very rare cases, deeper suicidal intent may be present.

With the latter reply, the therapist can usually take comfort and continue with both the session and the work as if they were working with a normal client with the normal difficulties of life, which are causing extreme distress, but not to the extent that the person is actively suicidal. However, quite normally, as outlined in Chapter 3, they are having suicidal thoughts from time to time.

Alternatively, with the former reply, a second battery of questions can be selected. These questions appear in the next section.

QUESTIONS TO ASK, ONCE SUICIDAL IDEATION HAS BEEN ESTABLISHED

As with the battery of questions to elicit suicidal ideation, this one has been field-tested over many years. The questions, all of which are solution focused, are all to a greater or lesser extent presuppositional in construction. Most are empowering in some way or other and others are very affirming of the client. It has been found that these attributes all contribute to the 'guaranteeing-against-suicide principle'.

1. "Tell me about a time in the last week when you felt least suicidal?"
2. "Before you were feeling as you do at the moment, what did you do in the day that interested you?"
3. "What has stopped you taking your life up to this point?"
4a. "On a scale of 1–10 (where 1 stands for very suicidal and 10 stands for not at all), how suicidal do you feel right now?"
4b. "On a scale of 1–10 (where 1 stands for very suicidal and 10 stands for not at all), how suicidal were you before you decided to seek help?"

4c. "What would you be doing/thinking about/feeling to be another half-point higher?"
5. "What have you done in the last week/couple of weeks that has made a difference to this terrible situation you are in?"
6. "On a scale of 1–10, how determined are you to give other options (other than suicide) a try first?"
7. "What would have to happen here today (i.e. in this counselling session), for you to think it was worthwhile coming?"
8. "Let us suppose you went for the last resort option and actually died. You are at your own funeral as a spirit looking down from about 10ft at the mourners below:

   a. What might you be thinking about another option you could have tried first?
   b. At this funeral, who would be most upset amongst the mourners? What advice would they have wanted to give you regarding other options?"

9. Miracle question . . .
10. "When was the last time (before this current time in your life) that you thought of ending it all?"
11. "What did you do then that made a difference and enabled you to pull yourself back?"
12. "Suicide is the last resort as we know: what other ways have you tried so far to crack this problem?"

The purpose of this selection of questions is to find clues and keys of any sort, in order to help with the solution building, no matter how desperate and sad the client might be at this point.

In order to unlock the power of the basic solution focused questions in this list, which have been specifically adapted to suicidal clients, I would examine each individually. Others in the list are of the specialised or adapted solution focused question type I referred to at the beginning of this chapter. These will be dealt with separately towards the end of the present chapter.

THE QUESTIONS

Q1   Tell me about a time in the last week when you felt least suicidal?

A.   This question is presuppostional and a direct request to come up with an exception to severe suicidal feelings. We know from our experience of clinical work, there are always exceptions, so the sensible thing to do is ask about them. Within the answer, there may well be some helpful clues as to how the client can make progress. A typical dialogue might be as follows:

TH: [Asks *Q1* (above)]

CL: Well, last Thursday evening for about 5 minutes I felt just a little less suicidal.

TH: Great to hear. How did you get that to happen?

CL: I was talking on the phone to an old school friend who said she had been severely depressed a few years ago and was quite suicidal. I never knew. She told me how she got through it. After I put the phone down, I felt slightly less suicidal for a few minutes. *Then all my problems flooded back into my mind.*

TH: What was it particularly that your old school friend said which gave you maybe, just the slightest morsel of hope?

CL: She said she was up by the bridge looking around and then decided to write down as many possible alternatives to killing herself as she could — including back-packing on her own around Australia!

TH: In what ways was it helpful to hear about this list?

CL: I thought I could do one of my own.

TH: And . . .?

CL: Well, I haven't done it yet.

TH: How helpful might it be to make a start on such a list?

And so on . . .

Q2   Before you were feeling as you do at the moment, what did you do in the day that interested you?

A.   The aim of this question is two-fold. Firstly, it reconnects the client with happier or more normal times and with all the associated thoughts and feelings around at that time; and, secondly, it is a way of discovering inner strengths, abilities and personal resources, which have become dormant. With the first, what is implicit is that such times are possible again in the future, albeit of a different form. With the second, further clues and keys can be elicited by the therapist, for use in the work, either in the present session or in later sessions. Again, the client leaves the session having been reminded of their capabilities, even though they may not have seen much of them lately. This particular question is a small part of 'widening the client's blinkers', referred to in Chapter 6.

Q3   What has stopped you taking your life up to this point?

A.   Another presuppositional question, this question encourages the client to search for reasons how come they are still alive up to this point. It is also a way of the therapist showing the client that they are not afraid of them talking about killing themselves. Talking sincerely and genuinely about living and dying is an essential part and a particular strength of the solution focused approach to suicide prevention.

Q4a   On a scale of 1–10 (where 1 stands for very suicidal and 10 stands for not at all), how suicidal do you feel right now?

Q4b   On a scale of 1–10 (where 1 stands for very suicidal and 10 stands for not at all), how suicidal were you before you decided to seek help?

Q4c   What would you be doing/thinking about/feeling to be another half-point higher?

A.   These three scaling questions are used to gain an accurate understanding of how suicidal the person is right now. If you like, it is one of the solution focused therapist's assessment instruments. Scaling, generally, has proved to be a highly accurate way of gauging progress, confidence or motivation. These three questions are about scaling progress in reducing suicidal intent, specifically. The very fact that the client has made the effort to be in front of the worker indicates that, more than likely, they are further up the scale than a 1. For those wondering how 'very suicidal' scores low as a 1; and, 'not at all suicidal' scores high as a 10, the reason for this is that the 1–10 scale is a progress scale upwards in all cases, whether it be a measure for client progress, confidence or motivation. These questions are merely being consistent with this rule. The answers to questions *4a* and *4b* can be very encouraging to both worker and client and can be a part of the process of the promotion and growth of hope. A typical dialogue might run as follows:

TH: [Asks *Q4a*] On a scale of 1–10 (where 1 stands for very suicidal and 10 stands for not at all), how suicidal do you feel right now?

CL.   About 2.

TH: 2! How come you're at 2 and not 1?

CL: Well, I've made the effort to come here to give this a try.

TH: That's good to hear. And [asks a variation of *Q4c*], what would have to happen here today to move you along this scale maybe just a little bit further, say to 2¼ ?

CL: Maybe to have you shed some different light on my predicament. Look, right now I can't see any way out of this. I've pretty much decided I am going to do it. I've got a plan. And, I've been thinking a lot recently that everyone would be better off if I was out of the way.

TH: I can see you are very close to the edge at the moment and have been a lot recently [*acknowledging*]. In what small way might I be able to shed some different light on your current predicament? [using the *client's language* and being *presuppositional*]

CL: Not sure. People say hearing an independent view can be helpful. You've seen similar cases to me, right?

TH: I certainly have.

CL: And they've lived?

TH: Yes, indeed, they have.

CL: Well, you may have some ideas from those people.

TH: How helpful to you would it be to hear about these ideas and have this different light shed?

CL: It would give me something to think about.

And so on . . .

Pre-session change with highly suicidal individuals is a very common occurrence. It is a gift the therapist should not ignore. Something will have happened in the person's thinking and feeling, and maybe, in some small actions they have taken, prior to being sat in front of the worker. As pre-session change occurs in the majority of cases, it is well worth asking about it, in order to discover some useful keys or clues which may prove invaluable in the solution building process. Question *4b* achieved this purpose. A typical Question *4b* dialogue would be as follows:

TH: On a scale of 1–10, (where 1 stands for very suicidal and 10 stands for not at all), how suicidal were you before you decided to seek help?

CL: 1 or even minus 1.

TH: And where are you right now at 9.20 a.m. on 2nd November?

CL: Well, surprisingly, I am at about 2½.

TH: 2½! How have you done that?

CL: Well, dunno really. It just feels like I'm at 2½.

TH: [Remains respectfully and expectantly silent]

CL: I've heard about Samaritans and people like that. My doctor said it might be helpful to talk to someone. He wanted me to go into hospital, but I wasn't having any of that.

Since I have booked this with you, I've been thinking. Maybe people like you know what you're doing and can help. I've also written to the credit card company about this £13½ K debt that's hanging over me.

TH: [In a slightly upbeat tone] You've written to the credit card company? How was that helpful to you?

CL: Well, at least I felt I was doing something at last. For months, whenever one of their white envelopes with their grey logo arrived, I stuffed it unopened in a drawer with all the others.

TH: What else might have got you to 2½, so far?

CL: Well, I was thinking a couple of nights ago, when I woke early in a sweat: at the end of the day, it's only money.

TH: [Asks a variation on *Q4c*] What else would you have to do, or think about, over the next few days, to move another half-point up the scale?

And so on . . .

Q5   What have you done in the last week/couple of weeks that has made a difference to this terrible situation you are in?

A.   This is another direct question into pre-session change which is available for the counsellor to ask, as and when appropriate.

Q6   On a scale of 1–10, how determined are you to give other options (other than suicide) a try?

A.   Often, it is helpful for the worker to get some measure of the client's willingness or motivation to work on other options, rather than suicide: the last resort option. As with the scaling questions in *Q4*, the worker finds out where they are now; how come they have this score; and, what they need to do/what has to happen/etc., for them to be half a point higher. From my own clinical practice over many years, approximately 95% of clients presenting with suicidal intent, score between 2½–9 on determination to give other options a try.

Q7   What would have to happen here today (i.e. in this counselling session), for you to think it was worthwhile coming?

A.   This is a good question to address directly the person's hopes and expectations of either the worker, the service or the appointment. It is important to be aware of these because if the client's hopes and expectations are 'wildly unrealistic' and we don't know about them, they may well go away disappointed and therefore will continue to be 'high-risk'. Some of these more wildly unrealistic expectations have been: a magic pill; a direct piece of advice or suggestion; some miracle cure occurring within the session; or, the worker taking over the client's problem from them. It is important, on discovering any of these or other unrealistic expectations, to disabuse the client of them immediately in a direct, respectful, caring and honest way, explaining that the session will comprise what is realistic, achievable, measurable and something that the client wishes to do.

The majority of clients are realistic in the answers they give to this question and an exchange such as the following might be common:

TH: What would have to happen here today (i.e. in this counselling session), for you to think it was worthwhile coming?

CL: Dunno really. Maybe to have talked through my frightening worries with someone neutral.

TH: How might that be helpful?

CL: My old man used to say "A problem shared is a problem halved". I know that used to work for him.

TH: What else?

CL: I might find that my situation is not as diabolical as I think it is.

TH: How might that help?

CL: Well, perhaps I would feel less overwhelmed by all that's been happening and so struck down by all these illness feelings I've been having.

TH: And when you're feeling less overwhelmed, what difference will that make?

CL: Well, I might sleep a bit better, perhaps! I keep waking up about 1.30 a.m. and then again at 4.

TH: And when you're sleeping a bit better, what might be the first benefit you'd notice?

CL: I'd have more energy and might be able to tackle the smallest of my worries first.

TH: Mmm, more energy. And what would be the smallest or easiest of your worries to tackle first?

CL: The car. It's been lying outside the house, covered in road dust, with the clutch seized.

TH: What would be the first baby step towards getting the car sorted out?

And so on . . .

Q8 **(This question will be dealt with later in the chapter.)**

Q9 **(This question will also be dealt with later in the chapter.)**

Qs 10 & 11 **When was the last time (before this current time in your life) that you thought of ending it all?**
What did you do then that made a difference and enabled you to pull yourself back?

A. These questions are part of the process of normalising suicidal thinking. Once the message has been communicated to the client that most people, when they find themselves in severe circumstances, consider the suicide option, this can be very reassuring. ("Suicidal thinking is a *normal* response by *normal* people to an *abnormal* set of circumstances?" See Henden (2005) and Chapter 3.) The other message this question communicates is that they have been here before. They survived it then, so what needs to happen to survive it this time? Past resources and strengths can be tapped into, which may wholly, or in part, be used as a part of the current solution building process. So, in short, this question is both feelings-normalising and resource-seeking.

Q12 Suicide is the last resort option as we know; what other ways have you tried so far to crack this problem?

A. This powerful question serves to show 'no fear' on the part of the practitioner and also has strong presuppositional and empowering qualities. It provides also, good opportunities to affirm the person. I will illustrate these features with a likely dialogue:

TH: [In a matter-of-fact way, which shows no fear of the suicide option; also it presupposes other ways have been tried already.] Suicide is the last resort option as we know; what other ways have you tried so far to crack this problem?

CL: Not sure that I have.

TH: Maybe something you have thought of doing, ideas that have come to mind, or even something else you've heard about . . .?

CL: I tried ringing the bank about my escalating overdraft.

TH: How did that go?

CL: I got through to one of those annoying automated phone conversation things . . . [sarcastically] "Select from the following options — 1, 2, 3, 4 or 106. Now select 1, 2 or 3. Now go back to the start, but do not pass go!"

TH: What else have you tried?

CL: I've tried phoning my son. We haven't spoken for three years since a big row about some nasty family business with my sister.

TH: How helpful was that?

CL: Not very. It felt good to have made the effort, but I think he saw on his mobile that it was me and ignored the call.

TH: [Affirmingly] It's good that you made the effort and felt good about doing so. How else might you contact him, letting him know how you feel towards him nowadays?

CL: I could write, I suppose.

TH: What might be the benefits of that approach?

CL: I could draft out what I want to say and then edit it afterwards before posting.

TH: Sounds a good idea to try.

CL: Yes, I might think more about that.

TH: [Presupposing again] What else have you thought about or tried?

CL: I wondered about just selling up everything here in town, cutting all ties with lots of so-called friends and moving up country to live near my sister. Make a new start, you know?

TH: Sounds like you are prepared to consider some quite radical alternatives . . .

And so on . . .

NORMALISATION

This is an important part of working with suicidal service users. Many feel that what they are experiencing (suicidal feelings and ideas) are very abnormal and that they are in danger of losing control. Some suicidal people have even gone as far as to question whether they are losing their sanity. Certainly, feelings of loss of control — losing one's mind; losing control of actions; or needing to be controlled by others — occur not infrequently. So to hear the solution focused 'normalising' statement outlined above can be very reassuring.

In many cases, the worker actually notices that the client's shoulders drop a little and their feelings become slightly calmer, on hearing this normalising statement.

HOPE

Much has been written about hope over many centuries. For its importance in bringing about therapeutic movement — especially with the suicidal — I will refer to some of the ideas which have been put forward since the 1980s. Wikepedia (2008) defines hope as, "a belief in a positive outcome related to events and circumstances in one's life"; and, "[it] implies a certain amount of *perseverance* (i.e. believing that a positive outcome is possible — even when there is some evidence to the contrary)."

Hope, hopefulness and optimism are of vital importance when working with the suicidal; and crucially, both should be communicated to and engendered in the client within the first ten minutes of the first session (see Chapter 7). Hopefulness is somewhat different from optimism. Hope, which is commonly contrasted to despair, is an emotional state, whereas optimism is a conclusion made by the person as a result of deliberate thought processes, which leads to a positive mental attitude.

Hope theory in 1:1 working as described by Snyder and colleagues (Snyder, Michael & Cheavens, 1999; Snyder, 2000) talk about goals, pathways to goals and the resources involved in embarking on those goal pathways.

How does the solution focused worker apply various theoretical considerations about hope and hopefulness to the desperate situation in which the suicidal client finds themselves? Fiske & Taylor (2005) see hope as the one, if not the *central* guiding light, to the successful outcome of therapeutic conversations. So, both applying our own hopefulness and tapping into the client's hope is key to the process.

In my own clinical practice over the past 15–20 years especially, I have been struck by the ways in which clients begin their goal-ward journeys. This applies to both the suicidal and non-suicidal. Such observations give workers grounds for optimism; and, knowing both the incredible natural resourcefulness of most people when confronted with extreme difficulty, and the effects of certain lines of questioning, workers can remain hopeful that they will make progress. This hope is communicated by the worker/sensed by the client at a non-verbal level. The communication occurs via tone of voice, eye contact, facial expression, demeanour, etc., and it would be difficult to say which is *the* most important of these. In fact, it is likely that a combination of several is most effective. This hope communication, in turn, initiates client hope. Whether it be worker hope which is sensed or a spark of hope within the client which is kindled, either way, a triggering of the client's curiosity is unavoidable.

Presuppositional questions in the first interview may be: "How are you going to sort this mess out?"; and, "What will be the first small step away from all this hopelessness and despair?" Both these communicate worker-hope and give grounds for client-hope. I have outlined elsewhere the power of the opening question: "What's better?" at second and subsequent sessions. Fiske and Taylor (2005) suggest that when this question is asked confidently and with ease, the small spark of hope can be nurtured. Again, practice based evidence shows that eventually this and similar presuppositional questions fan the flames of hope.

With the "What's better?" question, in my experience it is important to ask it with hope and to maintain the sense of hope, despite initially in a few cases, the answer being negative. With some clients, seeing their expression and demeanour to be dampened or worsened on entering the room, I might amend the question thus: "What's just a little bit better since we last met?" The reply: "Nothing's better!" or "Worse!" *is not a problem*. It is vital to maintain hope and to persevere, *in the expectation* that eventually you will find something for them to be hopeful about. It may be simply that on one brief occasion, the client copes a little better with things being worse. Subsequent questions can then follow, of the nature of: "How did you cope with things being worse?"; "How did you do that?"; "How did you know how to do that?"; "What difference did that make to you?" etc. This line of questioning then gives grounds for hope within the client and can displace any despair which may have crept back in. It is almost as if the client, on seeing the therapist's hopefulness, begins to feel more hopeful themselves; and when eventually the evidence gathers (even the tiniest morsel), this then gives some grounds to justify it. However, even in the absence of evidence initially, hope can remain alive. In working with clients (who are customers for change) over many years, I have yet to be disappointed with this hope communication and hope engendering process. Fiske, in Fiske and Taylor (2005) suggests that the process whereby solution focused practices convey the therapist's hope and elicit the client's hope, are one and the same.

Returning to the power of presuppositional questions, both to communicate and engender hope, it is easy to see their function in the process. They are never "If . . .?" but "When . . .?"; they are never "Maybe someone . . .?" but "Who . . .?"; and, they are never "Might it or not . . .?", but "How . . .?"

Another key part of the hope communication and engendering process is the highlighting of client's resources, strengths, abilities and skills. These can be those which they have applied to their lives generally and/or which they can apply now and in the future to the current difficulty. Questions abound to acknowledge these qualities which Snyder et al. (1999) would include within 'perceived capacity' to follow routes to desired goals.

Hope then, is of vital importance when working with suicidal people. If therapist despair or hopelessness creeps into the relationship — this is bad news for the client. There is more risk of this happening if the client is encouraged to labour each point or problem which is contributing to their profound negative stance. Unfortunately, some approaches to 1:1 work encourage this process. Suicidal clients who pick up feelings or thoughts of despair and hopelessness within the worker might simply have their fears confirmed: that their situation *is* hopeless and the only way out is suicide. One might wonder what proportion of the high rate of those who go on to take their lives within a month of seeing a practitioner, have picked up some degree of worker-hopelessness.

Fiske (2006) has produced a sizeable list of practice principles of suicidal interventions. Some of these are: utilise what the client brings; make every encounter therapeutic; collaborate with clients; and, what I believe to be the most important of all: tap into *hope*.

EMPOWERMENT

Many newcomers say of the solution focused approach, "It seems very empowering". Indeed it is so. To students of the solution focused approach, I often liken empowerment to the way a builder deals with a weak brick arch within a walled garden. Rather than removing some of the loose bricks from above the arch, after a little tidying up, he will actually add weight to it. The result: the brick arch tightens and therefore functions better as a result. The same is true for our clients. If we add some weight (in the form of a task such as thinking about, noticing or doing something), this has the result of strengthening them in readiness to take on more. This is somewhat paradoxical as common sense might suggest we 'take off some of the load'; 'reduce their level of responsibility'; 'take them away for some respite'; etc. However, all these actions could be regarded as 'disempowering' in some way. Other forms of disempowerment would include removal of pyjama cords, disposable razors, knives and tablets. While it has to be acknowledged that a few lives are saved in the short term by such strategies, many more are lost in the longer term on account of the disempowering and devaluing effect produced by such actions. These strategies are central to the risk assessment and management approach described in Chapter 4. This can have a knock-on effect on self-esteem and self-confidence which is more likely to push service users further towards suicide and away from constructive solution building activities. The more we empower helpees to take responsibility, the quicker they will recover their normal level of functioning. It is interesting to make the point here that the ASIST (2005) training encourages care-givers to ask clients to surrender any equipment they have which might be used in their suicide. This is part of the 'safe plan' stage in the ASIST model. One of the most empowering statements a solution focused practitioner can deliver to a client is as appears below. These are especially appropriate when practitioners sense that a client might be relying on the practitioner to 'come up with the answers' or 'do something for them'. The solution focused empowering statement and follow-on question:

> "Although these sessions are very important, what is even more important is what you think about, notice or put into practice between sessions. It involves hard work on your part. How willing are you to do this?"

THE MIRACLE QUESTION (ADAPTED)

There are various solution focused tools and techniques which help clients envisage a future where the problem or difficult situation is resolved and life is being lived again. One of these is the *miracle question* (MQ). For the purposes of working with suicidal people, this has been adapted in such a way that the exclusion of suicidal thoughts and feelings is the miracle. It reads thus:

> "Let's suppose tonight when you go to bed [pause] . . . you go to sleep [pause] . . . and a miracle happens such that all these suicidal thoughts and feelings are

gone [pause] . . . Only you won't know this miracle has happened because you are asleep at the time [pause] . . . What would be the first sign to you, when you wake up in the morning, that this miracle has happened?"

This powerful solution focused question addresses suicidal thoughts and feelings directly. It would be unhelpful to ask about a future, once the problem is solved, because currently, the client sees no future. Indeed, an end is being thought about or planned in the present.

The adapted MQ is a neat way about finding out about some future behaviours in the instance of an ending of suicidal thoughts and feelings. This might best be demonstrated by an illustration:

TH: Could I ask you a rather strange question?

CL: Yes, go ahead.

TH: [Slows down pace of speech and lowers tone slightly.] Just suppose that after we have finished our session here for today, you go home and do whatever you have got to do for the rest of the day. Then this evening, you go to bed. Let's suppose tonight when you go to bed . . . [pause] you go to sleep . . . [pause] and a miracle happens such that all these suicidal thoughts and feelings are gone [pause]. Only you won't know this miracle has happened because you are asleep at the time [pause]. What would be the first sign to you, when you wake up in the morning, that this miracle has happened?

CL: [Thoughtful silence] I'm not sure [pause]. Well, I wouldn't wake up with my heart racing and those scary palpitations. I wouldn't have the sweats and churning stomach. The dread would be gone.

TH: [Because the client is saying what would no longer be happening, a prompt is given.] What would you be noticing instead?

CL: I would feel calmer; more at ease. I would have more energy because it wouldn't be being wasted on my negative thoughts.

TH: What else?

CL: I might be feeling a few glimpses of hope about sorting things out, just a little. I might actually *do* something about my predicament.

TH: Who would be the first to notice that this miracle has in fact happened?

CL: I live on my own now, so it would be my dog, Jimmy.

TH: What would he notice?

CL: He would just sense I was different; slightly better.

TH: How would you tell he is noticing you are better?

CL: His eyes would be brighter, his ears would be arched higher, and he would have a slight smile. Dogs are very expressive, you know!

TH: With Jimmy being different in this way: eyes bright, ears arched, and him smiling at you, what difference would that make to how you are towards him?

CL: I'd probably give the old boy a hug and pat him more. And . . . I'd probably give him his breakfast on time, for once!

TH: You mentioned you would be feeling the [therapist presupposes a continuous process by adding in 'first'] first glimmers of hope about sorting things out and actually doing something. What might that be?

CL: Over the last five or six months I've withdrawn from most of my family and all my old mates. It's just me and Jimmy. I might give Alex a ring. We used to go for a drink together and go for trips out and things.

TH: How might that be helpful – to give Alex a ring?

And so on . . .

From this dialogue, the therapist is provided with information, clues and keys as to how to move the work forward. Also, the client is visualising the situation without suicidal thoughts and feelings. By taking some form of action, this in itself has been found to reduce the severity of the suicidal ideas and feelings. Hope begins to seep into the picture.

WISE OLD YOU

When helpees are stuck and find difficulty in answering questions, a helpful 'getting unstuck' question is *wise old you* (WOY). Dolan (1991) first described this as the 'older, wiser self' (p. 36) and WOY is an adaptation of this. It has the effect of transporting the helpee years hence to a point where they are older and wiser, such that they can offer some good advice about how to deal with the current impasse. It reads as follows:

Just imagine you are much older and wiser than you are now, say 70 or 80 (or if a teenager, 25 or 26!). What advice would you give to you now about how best to get through this difficult time/sort things out for yourself/get more control over the situation?

(With full acknowledgement to Yvonne Dolan, for the original version.)

The presuppositional quality of this question is evident and hooks well into long held cultural beliefs that the older we get, the *wiser* we get. Somewhat amusingly, we say 25 or 26 for teenagers because often in their minds, 25 or 26 is very old indeed! In many instances, clients will answer a future oriented question as "I don't know", but when asked the WOY question to shed some light on the same question, they will come out with a full and vivid description. Of course, the helpee has not reached 70 or 80 years of age: in fact, they have barely lived another two or three minutes!

Rather subtly, in addition, the WOY question has a 'living guarantee' quality in that it presupposes that not only is the client going to grow older and wiser, but also that they are going to live beyond their current period of difficulty. Like much of what is presuppositional within the solution focused approach, this works at an unconscious level within each individual.

WORST CASE (GRAVESIDE OR CREMATORIUM) SCENARIO

This question has saved many lives, as has been testified by many former suicidal patients who have been asked it. It cuts across any form of pretence or other false realities:

"Just suppose you decided to take this last resort option before considering all the other possibilities. You are in the grave but your spirit is hovering 3 metres above looking down on the assembled crowd below."

a) Who is there?
b) Who is most upset?
c) What advice would they have liked to have given you before you took the 'last resort' option?
d) What would you be thinking of in terms of other options you could have tried?
e) Who would throw some soil in first? What might they be thinking as the soil hits the lid?
f) As the guests walk away from the graveside/crematorium, who might say what to whom about how you might have sorted things differently?"

Some of the following statements have been collected from colleagues, former course students and personal clients:

"It was that scary question you asked me that really made me think."

"You certainly knew how to ask some hard-hitting questions. That one about me being in my grave was a real turning point."

"Do you know why I am here today talking to you now? It was that question you asked me about hovering above the guests at my own funeral!"

Some trainees on first hearing the *worst case scenario* question say they find it disturbing and upsetting and that they would not be able to ask it of clients. I would suggest though from my observations, that says something about them, rather than the value of the question.

Some earlier treatments for suicidal thinking and behaviour have disempowered patients in some way by instituting personal restrictions on freedom, or by putting other controls in place. What was often absent with this approach, was a direct conversation about the implications of taking the last resort option — completed suicide. 'Cat and mouse' games often resulted with staff having covert conversations amongst themselves without anyone actually speaking directly to the patient. Staff would 'sense' how suicidal the patient was and then tighten or ease the controls accordingly. Patients were quick to pick up on this way of operating and would either co-operate with it, play their own games, or pretend to be 'the model patient' in order to be released or observed less. Some would then go on to take their lives later when a good opportunity arose.

DEATHBED SCENARIO

Another adapted solution focused tool used particularly for abuse and trauma survivors (Dolan, 1991); drug and alcohol abusers; and others with long-standing difficulties is the 'deathbed scenario' (DBS). There are a variety of useful versions and my current, preferred one is:

"Imagine a date some 30, 40, 50, 60 years from now and you had decided not to take this last resort option, choosing other options instead to sort things out in the best way possible and you went on to live a full and rewarding life. You are on your deathbed, looking back. What would your life have been like?"

Some subsidiary, trigger questions:

"What sort of things would you have done?"

"What people would you have known and met?"

"What new places might you have visited?"

"What sorts of holidays would you have had?"

"What other challenges in life might you have had to resolve?"

"How would you have allocated your time in retirement?"

"Where might you have seen the best sunrises and sunsets?"

At no point throughout this elongated question, does the worker disempower the person in any way. The suicide option is kept 'on the table' alongside other options which might be available to sort things out.

It is a helpful question because like the generation of other possibilities, it helps 'widen the blinkers' with regard to other possible/achievable futures. The question serves as a form of *visualisation*, and it is well established that the more a person is able to visualise the future, the more likely they are to move towards it.

Another aspect of this question is that, while the practitioner is enquiring about aspects of life in the future, he/she is also talking about the client's eventual death, and what they would be thinking about, presumably in some way which expresses satisfaction of things in life achieved ("… a full and rewarding life").

This question, like the *miracle question*, the *worst case scenario* and *wise old you*, is best introduced as follows:

TH: [With a slight air of mystery] Can I ask you a rather unusual question?

CL: Yes, do.

TH: [Slowing down pace of speech, lowering tone of voice and fixing eyes on the client] Imagine a date . . .

. . . your life had been like?

CL: [Thinks hard, then gives a considered answer.]

This is indeed a very powerful question. It is clear to see the potential from what could be a very full answer, and that there is great scope for some long-term goals to be agreed on; and, for the purpose of the work, some short-term ones which could become small steps towards achieving them.

THE SOLUTION FOCUSED FEELINGS TANK

As referred to in Chapter 5, this tool (see Fig 8.1), has proved to be very useful in helping service users to discharge or dissipate strong negative feelings.

This tool was constructed on the hoof by me in 2006, when a client displayed such a high level of anger in a session, while expressing ideas about "putting the frighteners on" a couple of colleagues who had betrayed him. He threatened to do this by using a sawn-off shotgun. By the end of the session, the new tool had proved so successful, that my thoughts about breaking confidentiality to protect others, had evaporated completely.

Since this occasion, I have used the idea with a large number of clients and for a whole range of negative feelings expressed: shame, disappointment, grief, despair, hopelessness, frustration, and sadness — to name but a few.

With clients who are suicidal, it seems the most commonly experienced negative feelings expressed are anger, hopelessness and frustration

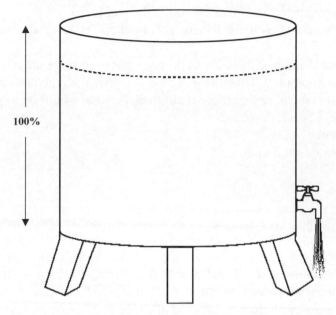

Figure 8.1 The Solution focused feelings tank

I will demonstrate the solution focused feelings tank by the following case example in which a male client was feeling angry about being made redundant under suspicious circumstances:

T: Just suppose all this anger you have been sitting on/pushing down for this past week or so could be represented by this tank (therapist sketches quickly an outline of a garden water butt, on a stout plinth. The water butt has a tap but, deliberately, no inlet pipe. Therapist writes in capital letters above the sketch: 'The Anger Tank').

When your anger was at its maximum (100%) the tank was full to the brim. Probably, you will have run some off already, via the tap here (points to tap), so at what level is your anger right now? (Therapist points to area on tank, between halfway mark and the top).

C: About 8%, I suppose

T: How have you done that?!

C: Well, I have spoken to a supervisor friend of mine in another department.

T: How was that helpful?

C: He sympathised and said he would try and find out stuff.

T: What would you need to do to run off, say, another 1% (to get down to 92%), over the next couple of weeks or so?

C: Maybe try and speak to my boss to get the *real* reasons.

T: What else could you do to run off another 1% over the next few weeks?

C: Talk more to my best mate about it: he might have some ideas.

T: Sounds a good idea. Given that the tap is higher than the bottom of the tank, and you can never empty it completely, what would be a manageable level to get it down to?

C: Oh, I dunno — say 30%?

T: OK. Sounds good to me…

…and so on.

The solution focused feelings tank, whether it be named 'The Anger Tank'; 'The Sadness Tank'; 'The Hopelessness Tank'; etc., has proved to be a very visual representation of strong negative feelings, with which the client feels more in control. Of course, with suicidal people, these strong feelings — if not dealt with — can lead to a serious suicide attempt or at worst, completed suicide.

The tank is a way of empowering and affirming service users, giving them back control for reducing the high level of any negative feelings expressed. It has proved helpful when used from session to session, or at every other session; and, in most cases, the level drops over time. As with scaling, if the level in the tank rises temporarily, this is not a problem, as the following solution focused questions may be asked.

"What do you need to do to run off this recent 'build-up'?"
"How will you get back on track?"
etc.

THE VERY, VERY SMALL STEP

Small steps or 'baby steps' as they are sometimes described, referred to earlier in Chapter 6, are an important tool in the solution focused practitioner's toolkit. Often, small steps towards the goal are discussed within a session and then the small step, or maybe an even smaller one is suggested as the between-session task or homework.

The adaptation of this tool for working with suicidal service users is the *very, very small step*. People who are deeply depressed and suicidal regard anything as involving a huge effort. In setting very, very small steps, service users can feel that it is more achievable, as they have been asked to do very little. Between-session tasking can involve either 'thinking about', 'noticing' or 'doing something'. Experience of working with suicidal people, shows that a noticing task is generally the best type to set. An illustration appears below of a severely suicidal person of a few months' duration who has come for help:

TH: [Towards the end of the session] You mentioned earlier there was one occasion only over this past week, that you have felt slightly less suicidal. What I would like you to do between now and when we next meet is to be on the lookout for just a brief time — it may be a fleeting moment only — when you feel just very slightly less suicidal. I want you to notice this time and notice what is different about it compared to the rest of the week. Can you do this for me?

CL: Yes, I'll try.

TH: Good. I look forward to your telling me about it at our next session.

KEY POINTS TO COVER

As a result of reflecting on 'what works' with the solution focused approach to suicide prevention, nine key points arose. Questions asked in relation to these key points might be: "Which is the most important one?"; "Is it really a combination of a few only which is key?"; and, "Do all nine points need to be in place?"

It is not necessary to go through each in turn within this section as they have been discussed adequately in other parts of the book.

WHEN SOMEONE EXPRESSES SUICIDAL IDEAS: KEY POINTS TO COVER

- Always Take Them Seriously
- Be Sincere And Genuine As They Are Relating Their Pain
- Show Deep Empathy
- Don't Show Fear Of The Worst Scenario
- Acknowledge And Validate Feelings And Thinking
- Together, Generate Other Possibilities
- Ensure They Understand <u>They</u> Are Responsible Ultimately, For Any Decisions They Make
- Compliment For Being Here Now And For Talking It Through (And Anything Else Worth Complimenting)
- Set Either A 'Noticing', 'Thinking About' Or 'Doing' Task, Prior To Your Next Appointment Or Session

Considering these questions in more depth recently, my view is that by far and away the most important to have in place are the first three in the above list; and the last. These, I am sure, are some of the points which have been little in evidence or less clear in cases where patients have gone on to take their lives following a first consultation session. If a tenth could be added to the above list, it might be as follows:

Be presuppositional in your language generally, and in your questions, specifically.

There is potential here for some future research, in that two groups of service users could be assigned randomly to two treatment groups. The first would be where practitioners ensured they scored well on all nine of these key points; and the second, 'treatment as usual'.

One empirical finding so far has been that, in cases where all these points have been in place, the suicide rate amongst service users worked with, has been reduced significantly.

SUMMARY

Within this chapter, I began by describing how basic counselling skills are applied to the suicidal. Then I endeavoured to outline the specialised solution focused tools and techniques which have proved to be helpful to people contemplating suicide. Also, I have described some of the basic tools and techniques which have been adapted specifically for use to good effect with this challenging client group. For a fuller outline of the basic assumptions and fundamental principles of the solution focused approach and a description of the many basic tools and techniques, please refer to Chapter 6.

9

Case Study: Reg and 'The Demons Calling from the Deep'

This case study is of 'Reg' aged 55, who is married with three grown-up children. I am deeply indebted to him for giving me permission to use 'his story' for the purposes of this case study. I have changed many details to protect his confidentiality, but he told me he would not mind if someone worked out, by chance, his true identity.

He was referred to me by his organisation's employee assistance programme after he had phoned them for help for his "feelings of anxiety and depression".

Reg was removed to an orphanage when he was seven years old, after his single parent mother became ill and was eventually incarcerated in a mental hospital's long stay ward. He never knew his father and has felt desperately sad on occasions since. He was close to his wife, to whom he would tell everything, including the vivid nature of his nightmares — most of which were about death or suicide. He was director of a local voluntary service; and, whilst feeling supported by his deputy, felt criticised by many of the staff.

PRESENTING ISSUE

Frequently occurring were feelings of despair, despondency; wondering who he really was; of being unappreciated; and having extreme anxiety when thinking about work. When these were at their worst, he imagined demons' hands reaching from the bottom of the sea (one mile away from their bungalow) and beckoning him to wade in towards them. His crisis was precipitated by seeing a small boy run to hug a work colleague of his, someone for whom he felt brotherly concern. (Comment: This man was the most actively suicidal client I have worked with in recent years. On two occasions — once before seeing me and once during — he had walked into the sea during the night, up to his waist, before returning in tears to the cliffs.)

SESSION ONE

About 10 minutes in . . .

  R: I have got an obsession with a close colleague. I see him every day. He is a lovely person called Dennis and is good with computers. At times, he is quite a brother to me. I've got a wonderful marriage and have told my wife about it. She is very understanding and is helping me deal with it. She trusts me to keep the boundaries in place. I am better about it lately though.

TH: How have you done that?

  R: I was quite distracted and quite suicidal. I went into my room when the house was quiet. I felt on the brink and had written a note.

TH: How did you manage to get yourself back from the brink?

  R: I realised, it's all to do with my childhood: my origins; who I am, etc. I said to myself, "You don't have to do this, you can get help".

TH: Besides coming to therapy, what else have you found helpful?

  R: I've spoken to a close friend over in the Home Counties who is a social worker. He has been suicidal himself in the past. He thought I was dealing with it very well. He said I should "Hang on in there". He realised how desperate I was, when I said I was going to scramble down the cliffs and walk into the sea.

TH: In what ways particularly was this close friend helpful to you?

  R: He suggested I write all my thoughts and feelings down on paper. This really helped get things in perspective. I wrote three sides of A4.

TH: And what else?

  R: He seemed to understand what depths I had plummeted down to. I suppose you could say I felt his empathy.

Later on, in the first session . . .

R: You see . . . my early life, just before the Second World War had many hurtful aspects. I was taken into the mental hospital to see my mother on a couple of occasions. That was very distressing for me, seeing her like that. I found it hard to make friends because I felt I was different from other children. I've lived and wrestled with horrible thoughts and dreams over years and years. They are demons which can't be killed or destroyed. They are locked away in a chest which sits on the seabed. While they are there, they can't do me any harm: they are under control. Every now and then, something or someone unlocks the chest and they get out. Dennis has done that.

TH: It sounds like you had a really hard time in your early years. There was a lot of hurt around and I am thinking that you were unloved for much of that time. No wonder you have had those thoughts and dreams you have just described. I am struck by how effective you are at keeping that chest locked away at the bottom of the sea for much of the time. What might be the smallest step to get those demons swimming back to the chest, before you relock it?

R: I've got to make more sense of my early years first. You know, talk about it, write things down; that sort of thing.

TH: How will you know when you've done enough talking and writing about your early years?

R: I'll just know.

[Therapist 'goes with the client' on his wish to delve for a while into his 'psychological archaeology']

TH: Which aspects do you consider most important to talk about first?

R: I need to understand this emotional trigger thing. There are many strands in my past. I've worked hard to rise above them. My early memories were of extreme poverty and deprivation in South London. I didn't have a clue about who my father was. I always wondered whether my mother was a prostitute. I know her three sisters were. My grandmother (my mother's mother), didn't know of my existence for a few years. I was told later that my mother had schizophrenia. She was terrifying at times. In those days, there was no help like today and I think she just did not know what to do. She was institutionalised and died before I was thirty. I was never hugged or kissed during my early years except once when I was twelve: my mother kissed me when I visited her in hospital. I'll never forget it.

TH: How did you survive all this?

 R: Sheer guts and determination not to go under!

About half way through the first session . . .

TH: Can I ask you a rather unusual question?

 R: Sure. Go ahead. [Client looks most mystified and expectant.]

TH: [An adapted miracle question.] Just suppose that after we've finished here today, you go home and do whatever you do this evening . . . Then you go to bed . . . And go to sleep . . . And while you're asleep . . . a miracle happens such that all these suicidal thoughts and feelings you've been having over these past few months are gone . . . Only, you won't know this miracle has happened because you have been asleep at the time . . . What will be the first sign to you in the morning that this miracle has happened and all these suicidal thoughts and feelings are gone?

 R: [Long thoughtful silence]

Well, my first thoughts would not be about Dennis or about the demons. I would be thinking more about the day ahead; what I needed to do in my role as Director. I would be knowing and feeling normality again. I would be feeling a sense of my own place in the world and not having these suicidal thoughts. Also, I'd feel more strongly about the more important things in life. I would be thinking more in the future and less 'in the past'. I have a great love for people. My pain and suffering helps me empathise.

TH: What else?

 R: I would be feeling my life's come right at last.

TH: And what else?

 R: I would be feeling more contented with what and who I've got in my life now. I am not a great seeker of material things. I'd be appreciating the benefits more to me now of my early experiences, rather than concentrating on the hurts that I am left with.

TH: Who'd be the first to notice the miracle has happened?

 R: My wife, Sylvia.

TH: What particularly would she notice?

 R: She'd see that I was more level; more normal; and less worried.

TH: What else?

 R: I'd have more life about me. I'd be looking forward to the day.

TH: I'd like to ask you another strange question, because I'm wondering whether a little piece of this miracle has happened already. Just suppose this long edge here . . .

[shows client edge of clipboard]

> . . . is a scale of 1–10. The left hand end stands for 1 where the miracle hasn't happened at all; and the right hand end stands for 10 where the miracle has happened in all regards.
>
> Where are you now on this 1–10 scale?

R: About 3½.

TH: 3½! That's over a third of the way along. How come you're at 3½ and not 3?

R: Well, having talked to my social worker friend helped. Also writing things down has been useful. Talking to you like this has helped get things straighter in my mind, too.

TH: What would you have to do to get to 3¾ or 4 over the next three to four weeks?

[. . . and so on]

SESSION TWO

This second session was eight days after the first.

TH: What's better?

R: It's been terribly erratic. I've written loads down. Here.

[Gives pages to therapist . . .]

> Sometimes I've felt more positive, hopeful and confident; then at others, I've felt I am not going to get out of this.

TH: When you're more hopeful and positive, what's happening at those times?

R: I've been enjoying things. Instead of focusing on the problem, I've been focusing on constructive things. I've taken a rational perspective on it.

[Client goes back into problem . . .]

> I went to my GP initially to get some tablets. Not had any good night's sleep lately. Sometimes it is like living with a cancer that's not terminal. When I'm at my worst, usually in the middle of the night, I go downstairs and batter myself again with all the things that have been in my life.

TH: This sounds very upsetting for you. How have you coped with these occasions during the night?

  R: I've put pen to paper, to try and make sense. It has helped, there's no doubt.

TH: What else has helped?

  R: I get up and make myself a weak cup of tea and have a bowl of cereal. Also, I make sure I get cold just sitting there. This makes it easier to go back to sleep when I get back into the warm bed. The contrast, I suppose.

   I've got to tell you about a trigger I had the other day! Dennis's nephew came in to see him at work with his Mum. He ran over to Dennis and hugged him. I felt a whole range of emotions well up and had a burning desire to go over and hug Dennis too! It was all I could do to restrain myself. The thoughts around this incident have festered and grown. The 'little boy' within me seemed to be crying out to be loved and hugged: something I never had when I was young. The words 'desolation', 'wasteland', 'arid desert', 'greyness' and 'coldness' seemed to reverberate in my mind. You see, not only did I never know my father; it was as if I didn't have my mother's love either. She couldn't show me any because of the circumstances.

TH: This incident which acted like a trigger into your past experiences seems to have been very powerful. Sounds like it was very upsetting for a while after. Given what you've said about your mother and father, no wonder you have been vulnerable to this type of event. If you could learn a technique to have available for similar triggers in the future, might that be helpful to you? Would you like to try it out?

  R: Yes, I would. I'm prepared to try anything!

[Therapist outlines the technique and gives second copy of handout to client.]

DUAL AWARENESS EXERCISE FOR DEALING WITH FLASHBACKS

(Adapted from a protocol drawn up by Babette Rothschild)

It seems we have got two things going on here.

Right now I am feeling . . . (isolated/lonely/etc.).

And I am sensing in my body . . . (3 things: i.e. heart racing, perspiring, etc. . . .).

They are real sensations; that's what I am experiencing, because I am remembering 'childhood scariness' (or another similar name that you would give to your memory).

However, <u>at the same time</u>, I am looking around where I am now here (the place/room where I am now) and:

I can see 5 things . . .

I can hear 5 things . . .

I can sense the following 5 things . . .

<u>And so I know,</u> 'childhood scariness' (or similar name), is not happening now or any more.

I went through this with him, explaining its purpose. I encouraged him to practice it at least three times, if possible, prior to our next meeting. By the end of this second session, the client was beginning to look less haunted. He seemed to be making sense of things and felt more optimistic about getting more control over his future thoughts and actions. He seemed particularly keen on the trigger-tackling technique (above).

Part of the intervention was for the client to keep making more use of his writing. He continued to keep a diary and, in addition, wrote letters on his computer which were then not saved. As the therapy unfolded, he would send me these letters between sessions. One such arrived about 10 days after the second session.

Some selected extracts follow:

Wednesday 16th April

Lighter of spirit, following our time together. Sunshine and music on car radio evidence of goodness of life — I intend to enjoy more of same and WILL beat this cruel thing. At home Sylvia is putting together a collage of family photos of the five of us to hang on a wall. In several of them I am with the children when very young and appear as a protective figure. Reminds me of how much I value our family life and, considering I was never fathered (in the wider sense!), I haven't made a bad job of it where Sally, Jamie and Fraser are concerned. I enjoy a very good relationship with them all — a fact which was pointed out to me recently.

Monday 22nd January

Awoke before 4 a.m. and feeling the onset of 'wobbles'. Am so annoyed with myself . . . battles . . . I haven't the total confidence that it can be done again . . . suicidal thoughts looming again.

Tuesday a.m.

. . . [A]m startled out of sleep at 3 a.m. by a very bad dream in which my mother is tying me down in bed (the 'me' being adult, not child). I awake feeling that my demons are on the rampage again and lie awake going over some of the old, familiar ground and end up feeling desolate and sobbing. Amazingly, Sylvia doesn't awaken (she always has been a very sound sleeper) and I resisted temptation to wake her and share my thoughts. Drift off eventually, having decided to consider asking for sleeping pills . . .

I've achieved something worthwhile and have worked so hard to make something of myself and overcome my handicaps, when in fact I amount to nothing and never will. This is a totally new and frightening thought and, at bottom, I cannot believe it — but in the small hours it was very real. Weighed up the pros and cons of ending my life, again, and found in favour of staying alive — but what a struggle it's going to be. Sylvia and I agree, for all my dark times in the past, this one is decidedly different — and I cannot account for it. Have an 11.15 a.m. appointment with GP re sleeping pills. My willingness to accept this kind of help is a further sign that I really am up against it and cannot possibly come through all this without maximum help.

A week after this letter, another arrived with a covering note, saying:

John — my instinct is to apologise for all this (enclosed) and to shred it — but it was you who suggested I wrote down something . . .

The letter was comprised of three sides of dense text and reading through, it seemed this was becoming a therapeutic activity all of its own. In addition to recording unpleasant events by day (the recurring disturbing thoughts); and, the events by night in the form of nightmares and dreams, he described better times too. Amongst the many setbacks, he was beginning to show evidence of progress in both his thinking and actions. Some examples of progress from this letter are:

. . . [T]here are many men and women who grow up without feeling they matter. They do not feel acknowledged. Instead they have grown up with a feeling of insignificance. They do not feel wanted, indeed they feel unwanted or rejected and far from feeling appreciated, they feel worthless . . . [W]hat a long way I've come, but how difficult the remaining road appears to be — but I WILL get there . . .

And:

. . . [F]eel really good — my true, old self. No sleeping pill and I didn't wake until well after 6 a.m. Sylvia and I exceptionally close and I feel considerable enthusiasm for work and life in general. Have just read an article by a prominent business leader in which he refers to his own childhood: this brings home to me the undeniable fact that most certainly I am not the only person alive who didn't have the best start.

And some of the not so good:

Awake at 4.30 a.m. feeling terrible — very alone despite all I have. Wonder, again, if I've got a completely wrong angle on my problem and if there's something I have not even considered — but if so, what can it be? Terribly withdrawn and consider that putting an end to it all might possibly be the solution — but . . .

. . . [E]ven Sylvia admits that she cannot give me the comfort I so desperately need. In some strange way this crisis is the worst of the many in my life, but more so because there is no obvious cause. The feeling began to overwhelm me. My mind was filled with the horrible demons beckoning me from out to sea. I found myself getting out of bed quietly, so as not to wake Sylvia. I went out to the landing, got dressed, put on my coat and went down to the cliffs. I was frightened and trembling as I scrambled down to the beach. In seconds, I found myself wading out to the demons. Once up to my waist in the cold water, I got a grip. I said: "This is ridiculous! There is another way! I'm doing well with the therapy. I'm not going . . ." I returned home, bagged up my wet clothes, had a shower and got quietly back into bed.

And:

. . . [A]wake after 4 a.m. and my mind filled with memories of when I was very young and my yearning for my father to find me. I ended up feeling very sorry for myself and crying.

SESSION THREE

My next appointment with Reg was two weeks later. In this session, he was more upbeat and there was evidence of a real shift in his thinking. He had found it helpful to boundary the thinking time about his early childhood desolation, neglect and lack of parental love. He had tried to restrict this to 30 minutes each evening, but admitted he had allowed it to spill over into other times too. He said he had identified two extreme positions in his thinking. One of these was when he was feeling "positive, hopeful and confident", and the opposite was, "feeling down; not going to get out of it".

Evidence that he was making small steps forward was in the following statements occurring in this third session:

"I've decided to broaden my life into other areas";
"I think I'm the sort of person that needs my own personal space a lot, but also need to spend time in the company of others";

"I need a best friend in addition to my wife";
"I have a sense it will come right in the end"; and
"This diary work and letter writing is really helpful".

The therapist's intervention at the end of this third session went thus:

TH: You have certainly had some more struggles over these past few weeks
and at times this has been upsetting for you. However, I must say how impressed I am with some key shifts in your thinking. You are recognising
that you are the sort of person that needs a lot of your own space, *and* you
do need friends, too. You are keen also, to broaden your own horizons by
developing other interests. Because the writing has been helpful to you,
I'd like you to continue to do this. Also, I'd like you to notice occasions
when you are withdrawing temporarily into your own space, which is a
healthy thing for you to do. You might think, too, about possibilities for
your suggestion of identifying a best friend from either within or outside
your existing circle of friends and acquaintances. These three small tasks
I am setting you may be helpful to you between now and when we next
meet. You might, of course, think of something to notice or think about
that is different from these, and is of even more help to you.

SESSION FOUR

Approximately two weeks later.
   Prior to this session, I noted down a reminder of Reg's strengths and resources, thus:

   Has a strong inner dialogue which tells him he is going to get through this; is
   able to cry in private, when necessary; is able to recognise he needs to take
   time off/give self breaks; has decided it is beneficial to broaden his life interests; is wanting to counter loneliness and self-sufficiency; and, has a very
   loving and supportive wife.

Also I felt it was important to remind myself of his stated goals from our
first session. With clients who need to talk things through in great detail, as
part of their therapeutic process, it is easy for both client and therapist to lose
sight of the goal. I penned his stated goals thus:

   Goals:
   I will be better focused on the moment (>70% of the time);
   I will be more confident (>60% of the time);

I will have the demons under control;

I will feel secure within my friendship with Dennis;

I will have someone who I could describe as 'a best friend' by 1st June next year; and

I will have broadened my life interests in at least two ways.

The fourth session began thus:

TH: What's better?

 R: *Much!* Although, I'm not there yet.

TH: How come?

 R: Sylvia. I can tell her anything. She's one of my great resources. She's much more of help now. The act of sharing with her helps.

TH: I'm wondering how far along you are towards achieving your goal . . .

[Therapist reiterates goals above]

On a 1–10 scale, where are you right now?

 R: About 5.

TH: 5! That's half way! What would you have to do to move along another point — to 6?

 R: To feel more secure about not regressing.

TH: How will you do that?

 R: To hold on more to positive things . . . to what I've got. And, to know I can and will beat it.

TH: What else?

 R: To have the 'wobbles' under control more. Also, to be less obsessive in my thinking about Dennis.

TH: How have you done this, to some extent, already?

 R: Well, the other day at work: he came into the office with this quiz he had put together for a staff social. I complimented him for doing it so thoughtfully and I found I was acting and feeling quite normally in doing so.

Later on in the session . . .

TH: Tell me about some better nights' sleep you've had recently.

 R: I have had two good ones since I saw you last.

TH: How did you get that to happen?

 R: Well, I told myself: "It's not helpful to dredge up the past too often"; "There are plenty of people worse off than me"; and, "I can deal with this".

TH: This sounds really helpful to you. I am very impressed by your strong, positive internal dialogue that you use at appropriate times. How did you learn how to do this?

  R: Dunno. I've just found it helpful, I suppose.

Later on . . .

TH: How are you doing with the chest of demons?

[Client's expression was a mixture of seriousness, anxiety and triumph]

  R: They're mostly back in the chest. The lid is still open slightly and the seaweed has yet to grow back around it, to hide it from view. The thing I am dealing with at the moment is not one of the demons — it's to do with friendship. Can I be a friend to Dennis; and he to me? I am working well on not being obsessed about him. I do have a yearning for another friend to talk to — someone companionable; someone male.

Later . . .

Intervention:

TH: Our time today is nearly over . . . What I'd like to say to you is how impressed I am by what you have now got under control. It's good to hear how hard you have worked on getting the demons back in the chest. Also, again, I am struck by how powerful and useful your positive internal dialogue is. You are keen to work on establishing close, companionable friendships — sharing helps, and you are determined to establish a close male friendship at some point.

   I have to say that, because you are making such good progress in many areas, I want to express a note of caution. Rather than make any more progress at the moment, I would like you to 'go slow' for a while, to consolidate what you have already achieved. Can you do that for me?

  R: Yes, I'll try.

[Therapist and client make fifth appointment for two weeks hence]

SESSION FIVE

Two weeks later.

TH: What's better?

R: Yes, I am! Much! I've had a real downer though. I nearly fell apart. It was an intense emotional thing. I felt my skull might crack or my head explode. It happened in the night. In the morning, I booked an urgent appointment with my doctor for some antidepressants.

TH: How did you cope with it at the time?

R: I awoke Sylvia and she cuddled me; reassured me. I was completely obsessed again with Dennis. He was invading my thoughts very strongly. I forced myself to think of other things and that helped. I do need to find other interests — part of the broadening-my-life strategy. I have seen 'Chess for Beginners' advertised at the village hall. I think I might go along. Also, there's this Ramblers' Group which meets every other Sunday afternoon. Sylvia and I might go along together.

Later in the session . . .

TH: With your goals in this work we are doing together, where are you now on that 1–10 scale?

R: 7.

TH: 7! Nearly three-quarters of the way along! How come you're at 7, not at 6 ½, say?

R: Well, I seem to be getting more satisfaction and fulfilment now. I feel I am heading in the right direction, in spite of some real low spots and times of despair. I can see no reason why I shouldn't get through all this.

TH: I agree with you. You have worked really hard at conquering your fears and worries. I am particularly impressed at how helpful you find writing a diary and the letters you send me between sessions. It seems to me it enables you to make sense of things — both past and present.

As you find this approach so helpful, there is an exercise I would like you to try between now and when we next meet. It is called the 'Healing Letters Exercise' and was developed by a colleague called Yvonne Dolan. You may find it slightly helpful or very helpful indeed, for the sense you are trying to make of your father. Many other clients have found it really useful in their healing. There are four stages to the exercise and it is important to read all the instructions fully before beginning it. From what you have told me so far, it seems as though it might be helpful to use this healing letters exercise with your father. Do you think it might be something you would like to try?

R: Yes, I'm prepared to try almost anything.

TH: Okay, here are the instructions.

[Therapist hands over a copy to the client] — see Appendix X.

> You will see from this, it is important to be as frank and detailed as possible in your first letter to your father. Express your emotions as fully as you want. After you have written the second letter, it is very important not to dwell on it, but to write the third letter *immediately* afterwards. Is that clear to you?

R: Yes.

TH: Once you get back home today, you might decide to delay doing this exercise for some weeks or months, or you might decide to complete it within a few days. Either way is okay.

After this fifth appointment, I received two more very long letters (four and three typed pages respectively). The contents of each indicated further improvements being made, whilst at the same time flagging up low spots.

The first letter:

Reg sent a covering letter with this one, which I discovered was, in fact, letters numbers 1 and 3 of the Healing Letters Exercise. The following are extracts from his covering letter:

> Thank you for giving me the Healing Letters material. I know I am not supposed to be sending the attached to you, but I am doing so firstly to show you what I have written; and, secondly it might prove of some use to another client who can benefit from this course of action. Do feel free to use me, by way of an example.
>
> . . . [Y]ou will notice that, in effect, I have amalgamated letters 2 and 3 — all this came very quickly, unlike letter number 1 which I laboured over for some considerable time.
>
> . . . [T]he fourth letter isn't 'around' at present — I shall wait until it comes. I'll tell you about that when I see you.

Extracts from his letters nos. 1 and 3 of the Healing Letters Exercise:

> Dear Dad — I never thought I would be able to write those two words in conjunction, but as I say so often, life is full of surprises. You don't know me, or know even of my existence I suppose, and I can never know you which I happen to believe is a personal tragedy for both of us. For me this fact of

my life has brought me a measure of unhappiness I'd never really measured until recently, despite its overshadowing every part of my life to date. Until last summer I knew absolutely nothing about you, but on the basis of things I had heard, believe that I was conceived as a result of you having sex with a prostitute — not exactly the ideal circumstances in which to begin life, I think. I grew up believing I was just about the most unwanted person alive and, to make matters worse, other adults around me effectively reinforced my sense of worthlessness. In my teens I believed myself to be totally unloved and unlovable . . . for years I found it virtually impossible to say or write three words: Love, Father and Dad.

. . . [T]he one thing that the Children's Home was totally incapable of giving me was affection. As a child I longed for the day when my daddy would come and find me and take me away to begin what I thought must be my proper life, as a member of an 'ordinary' family . . . [M]y mother's story proved to be genuinely tragic: soon after I was born (and remember she was only 18 at the time), she developed rheumatoid arthritis, which quickly crippled her; but much worse, she became 'paranoid-schizophrenic' and ended up confined in an asylum . . . [B]ecause I have so little to go on (a great void, in fact) at some time in my life I reached a point where I forgave my mother for all the hurt. I never loved her and believe that she never loved me.

. . . [M]any times in my life I have wished genuinely that I had never been born.

. . . [T]hose first 30 years of my life were very difficult in all sorts of ways and many times I reached breaking point and always I had a deep longing for you. I wanted to know that you cared about me; I wanted your encouragement and guidance; I wanted you to help me feel that there was a place for me in the world (to say nothing of in your own life)   [I] wanted you to show that you loved me and that I was lovable and that you could accept my love; and, I wanted our love for each other to be expressed in such simple (yet so important ways).

. . . Sylvia is a wonderful person and gives me so much, but neither she nor anyone else can ever be what I needed you to be. I have no idea, of course, and never can know what life gave you after my mother and you went your separate ways. Did you ever give ME a thought?

. . . [I]'ve worked hard at trying to make something of my life and overcome what I regard as quite a few disadvantages and sometimes I feel I have done quite well and that, were you to know me, you wouldn't be ashamed of me.

Ironically you have been responsible for a huge volume of pain and suffering: which has clouded my whole life. The past five months have been the most testing time of my life, and that's saying something . . . [H]owever, since my little discovery about you, my whole world seems to have come tumbling down.

. . . [I] wanted you and, ideally and very selfishly, a brother too. I know many people, like me, have neither, but that's no comfort to me — many do have both. In August a surprising and cruel thing happened: someone came into my life who in some strange and mysterious way fascinated me from the moment we met. Then, totally innocently, he touched my most raw nerve: he was hugged by a little boy — the very thing that I have craved all my life — and still do. That tiny incident triggered off a whole chain of emotions and memories which came to a climax, I believe, on the first day of this new century. On the night of January 1st, I was overwhelmed by a sense of isolation, desolation and despair, such as I have never known before, and that, believe me, is saying something. I sat by the sea and sobbed as I have never cried before (and I've done an awful lot of that in the past weeks). I cried out for you . . . I longed for the sea to swallow me up . . . in fact I began to walk towards it — but would you believe it was low tide and before I could reach the water, something told me that that was not the answer.

. . . [W]ithout ever having known you I have to let you go. To me that is so terribly cruel and I curse you for bringing all this about and for bringing me into the world.

. . . [T]here can be no appropriate final greeting to a letter of this kind . . .

As I mentioned above, he omitted letter no. 2, but then went on to write letter no. 3:

My dear son, I don't know where to begin, nor end; like you, all I can do is try to put the record straight. Yes, I did love your mother and we both wanted you, but, for my own selfish reasons, I realise, I felt I couldn't accept the responsibility which clearly I ought to have done. To say that I am sorry goes no way towards telling you what I know you want to hear and what I genuinely want to say to you. I can only ask your forgiveness and repeat, so very, very humbly that I am genuinely sorry for all the pain, hurt and suffering that I have caused you. From what you say, you are a son to be proud of and, yes, it is my great loss that I don't know you, and as you point out, never will.

. . . [Y]ou are so fortunate and blessed to have such a delightful family. And your work, too, is so worthwhile . . .

Know that you are loved and maybe more than I could ever have loved you, much as I would like to have had the opportunity of being a Dad to you. I am sure you are a great dad . . . [F]or my sake and that of your mother, to say nothing of your real family's, be as strong and brave as ever and carry on living for other people. Thank you for overcoming your hatred of me and forgiving me; it takes a rare kind of strength to do those things. You must be quite a boy — a boy I would have been proud of. Yes, you do have to let me go, even though you have never found me. I know how hard that can be, but I know also that somewhere within you, you have what it takes . . . [E]ven though I have no way of showing my love for you, I believe that there is a tie of love between you and me and that you can pass it on to others.

The second letter, of some three typed pages, came about a week after the first one. I have highlighted some pertinent parts thus:

Friday evening: Have recorded nothing for a whole week; I must be getting better! Yes, I am. Since our meeting on Monday have felt decidedly improved — while recognising that I still have some way to go; and I still fear that at any time I could regress. However, am much more positive and, as Jim said last night on the phone, vibrant.

. . . [W]ith friends and I felt very 'normal', although my thoughts kept going to Dennis, but not as overwhelmingly as until now. Monday night before leaving, I spent nearly two hours at Dennis's home . . . we had some business to discuss . . . at the personal level I continue to feel that we are establishing a good rapport.

Today have enjoyed tidying up the garden and other odd jobs . . .

Sylvia and I continue to be amazingly close while Jim and Pete, both of whom I phoned last night, are closer friends than I had appreciated. Maybe good has already come from this terrible business — and who knows? Maybe the best is yet to be ... [S]on's going to the toilet awoke me early and my mind turned to 'me'. Felt somewhat weepy, but not depressed.

Strangely, had worst night's sleep for weeks — awake at 3.45 a.m. — and great difficulty getting back again — but no unpleasant thoughts.

Tuesday a.m.: Full of enthusiasm for work and appreciating my many blessings. Thoughts of Dennis less frequent, but he continues to monopolise and fill many empty thought-spaces . . .

Much better night's sleep. Am definitely 'getting there': if only I had the security of a close friendship with Dennis and the conviction that I won't plunge into my black pit again, I'd be so happy . . .

For all kinds of reasons, I am unable to begin to look for someone else with whom, ideally, to establish some friendship.

. . . [F]eeling of rejection (my biggest bogey, perhaps) coupled with self-disgust that I am so dependent upon other people. Talked things through with Sylvia (as ever totally understanding) and wrestled with familiar problems of making new friendships. Awake far too early feeling decidedly lower in spirit than for some time. Having felt well on the way to recovery, I know that I have a long distance to travel.

Early this a.m. hit rock bottom!!! Awake around 5 a.m. and lay feeling very sorry for myself. Sylvia reminds me how strong I am and, if only for her sake, I mustn't give up hope — so I must soldier on.

. . . [W]hy can't I be thankful for all I have and rejoice in that? At present, all I can say is that if I am not to progress beyond where I am, I cannot see how I can go on living. What's the point? Yes, I am that bad and, no, the demons aren't loose again; I assume it's the damage they have done which is the problem.

Saturday a.m: Yesterday proved to be (I sincerely hope), the *turning point*. Too much happened and my mood was all over the place, to record in detail. Essentially, when I felt I was at the bottom of the deepest and darkest pit imaginable and that there could be no way out and God seemed to have abandoned me entirely, Dennis phoned. I seized the opportunity to talk with him very frankly; in reply to my question about what he values in life (shades of your approach, I realised on reflection later!), he listed health and possessions, but his first, immediate thing was . . . friendship! . . .

[I]n summary, I would say I am almost back to where I was this time last week which is really a rather good feeling . . .

Sunday p.m: . . . [I] suppose it *is* good for me to have to pass through all this, but I don't relish the prospect of much more!!!

Monday a.m: Remainder of yesterday in top form. Much recovered and wondered how on earth (or in hell) I find myself in that other condition . . .

As usual, I awoke too early, but then slept again and currently am fine … Sylvia and I are so happy with each other that it's strange, to say the least, that I retained this very real need for 'friendship with a man'.

Tuesday: 10.30 p.m.!: Such a 'normal' day that I have omitted to think of recording anything — must be getting better! Feel really good — best since all this began . . . [I] was sharing thoughts with Sylvia about my current 'reasoning' re Dennis. Having resolved my 'father complex', in the sense that I know as much as can be known, I suspect I have directed my emotional needs in the direction of 'the brother I never had and longed for, in addition to my father'; and, for some reason(s), Dennis fits the bill …

Thursday a.m.: . . . [H]e still continues to flood my thoughts far too much and I remain fearful that I might relapse . . .

Ultimately (whenever that is!), I'm certain something good will come from all this . . .

SESSION SIX

Five weeks later.

TH: What have been the highlights of the last five weeks?
 R: I am gradually getting a grip on things — on the normality of life. Work, at times, is my salvation: I get a lot out of it.
TH: That sounds good, what else?
 R: I'm working things through more. Also, I've been broadening my interests. I've booked a couple of tickets for a play put on by our local amateur dramatic group.
TH: That's what you wanted to do — broaden your interests?
 R: Yes, I know. It's taken me a while.

I realised the other day, I am bringing too much work home with me. I need a healthier separation between work and home.

TH: How will you do that?
 R: I'll just have to be firmer with myself and say 'No' to it.

> Sylvia and I decided last week, we need to get away for a bit. I need and deserve a holiday. All this stuff I have had to work through has left me exhausted. I picked up some brochures from the travel agent yesterday, to give me some ideas.

Later in the session . . .

TH: Where are you now on your 1–10 progress scale?
 R: I'm now at 7½, most of the time.
TH: That's higher than you were five weeks ago. How have you done *that*?
 R: Just keeping going; riding out the bleak patches; the diary -- that sort of thing. That Letters exercise was so helpful to me. As I said in my last letter to you, you are welcome to use it for other clients!

Later . . .

TH: When do you think you will be ready to have a conversation with your doctor, about cutting down the anti-depressants?
 R: Maybe in another couple or three weeks.

Later still …

Intervention:

TH: Our time is gone today, but what I would like to say to you is well done for maintaining progress overall, this past five weeks, despite the bleak patches you have had. It is normal for these patches to continue for a while yet, although predictably they will become less frequent as you continue to make more sense of things and move further towards achieving your goals.

What I would like you to do between now and when we meet next time, is to continue working on the things that have been helpful to you. Also, I would like you to notice times when you nip the bleak patches 'in the bud', such that they are shorter and/or less severe.

To give you another good length interval for you to continue working on these things, when would be a useful number of weeks before we meet next?

R: Six?

TH: Okay. I was thinking along the same lines.

I received a further letter indicating more consolidation of progress and, of course, further detailed descriptions of the predicted bleak patches, although they had been occurring less frequently. In one entry, he says, "You did warn me!"

I had emphasised in the first session that although our sessions together were important; what is even more important was what he put into practice between sessions. Throughout the work, he has shown good evidence of this. Also, it is important to make the point that throughout, Reg has felt empowered to consider choices and make decisions. At no time have I attempted, either overtly or covertly, to take away his suicide option. It has been, and always will be there. Simply, I have been encouraging him to consider other options to his pain which involve living as opposed to taking his life or simply existing.

Here are some extracts of both 'highs' and 'lows' from the letter:

Friday 10th: In part out of consideration for your reading time and also because I haven't felt the need, I've recorded nothing for the past week. I have been feeling really good and getting on with things, including having to deal with some particularly difficult situations at work. I appreciate the importance of doing something positive towards making other friendships . . .

Sunday a.m.: You did warn me! Awoke early this morning, feeling very sorry for myself and had a cry and a talk with Sylvia. I came over weepy . . . contained it until I was driving home when I was wracked with crying and a feeling of utter despair. Could barely see my way home, literally . . .

I feel terribly drained and look bad, but that awful blackness has lifted.

Monday a.m.: Got back on track yesterday amazingly quickly. Several good things happened which brought home to me the truth that life is good and that I can cope! I suppose Saturday's episode was one of those blips you warned me about — must say, I don't look forward to more — but then if, ultimately, 'I get there' it's a price worth paying . . .

Tuesday a.m.: Very happy, relaxed two hours talking with Dennis . . . and I walked home with him, feeling very brotherly and walking back along the beach very content and optimistic about my future. Shared with Sylvia and went to sleep very much at peace.

Tuesday 21st: What does this say: not occurred to me to write down anything since the above?! . . .

Really lovely little gesture from Jim which affirms a deepening of our friend-ship — which is a bonus from 'all this'. Would give myself an 8 on your score-sheet, at present — but ask me when we meet!!

Wednesday 29th a.m.: Coped remarkably well on Sunday a.m. and since then have been okay. What is very noticeable now, in contrast to some weeks ago, is that my 'lows' are of shorter duration. Even though at the time it seems as if I'm overwhelmed and will never resurface, I find that within a few hours, not days, I am back up again.

Tuesday a.m.: Hit another very bad low after lunch yesterday, but after telling Sylvia how I felt, got over it surprisingly quickly.

Saturday afternoon: Since above, have had an excellent run – would award myself an 8 again! Can't explain. No obvious reasons for my feeling generally healthier. If I were to continue like this, life would be okay, although I haven't the conviction that this will be the case. Standby for the next dip . . .

Prior to my next session with Reg, I had a group supervision session, where I brought up the case. The main suggestions from the group were thus:

- With his night-time waking, ask him to notice the frequency and the tim-ing; looking for particular patterns or changes in pattern.
- Also, with his waking in the night, ask him to consider things to *do* or *say* at those times.
- Encourage him to take on Ben Furman's idea as expressed in the title of his book: 'It's Never Too Late to Have a Happy Childhood' (Furman, 1997). This could go some way, maybe, towards compensating him for the loss he feels about his childhood years.

SESSION 7

Six weeks after the sixth.

TH: What's better?

R: Have had highs and lows again, as you saw in my last letter.

> I have now completed letter 4 of the Healing Letters! I had to wait for the right moment. I know it has been weeks since I did the others, but I just found myself alone in the home one evening and was in the mood. I found it well worth doing and now can say, it's the end of the matter. I know I've still got some unpleasant things, but with respect to my childhood, I don't dwell on it now — I can't forget it, though.

TH: I'm impressed by how you have tailored the letters exercise to your own particular needs. That's absolutely fine. With all these things, it is most useful when clients do things that work best for them. No two people are alike.

> How did you know that particular evening was the right time for you to do this?

R: I dunno. I just felt a zest for doing it. The circumstances were right at home at the time, so I went for it!

Later . . .

TH: How much nearer are you now towards your goals in the work we have been doing together?

R: I have good days and not-so-good. I can say the latter are now less frequent. I think I told you that in the letter.

> Things are okay with Dennis. We get on pretty well now. I told him the essence of the Letters exercise. He's a superb listener. I gave the third letter to him to read as long as he destroyed it afterwards. Was that okay to do that, do you think?

TH: It sounds to have been very helpful to you in various ways.

[Session continued for approximately another 35 minutes, talking about more achievements, but also some misgivings he was having about his current job. He was thinking maybe it was time to consider other job possibilities . . .]

SESSION 8

This was the final session and was held three weeks after the seventh, as he was going away for a long break "to reflect and meditate on life". He came to the session looking a little despondent, so I shifted away from my customary "what's better?"

TH: What's different?

  R: I feel trapped by my job. I am questioning both my role there and the values of the organisation as a whole. It's this counselling that's doing it. It's made me question lots of other areas of my life.

TH: That can be a good thing?

    Later in the session . . .

TH: I am both encouraged and impressed by all the work you have put in over the months since we first met. Have you heard the expression: 'that we get out of something, in direct proportion to the effort we put in?'

  R: Yes.

TH: Well, you are a good example of that. Where are you now on the 1–10 progress scale?

  R: 7½ to 8.

    I've decided, I've had enough of my life being 'on hold'. This all stems from that early encounter I had with Dennis and all the feelings it brought up.

TH: What would you say you are most proud of in terms of your achievements with Dennis?

  R: The fact that we have a genuine two-way friendship now. I feel brotherly towards him, too, which is good. I have met his girlfriend: she is very nice. The three of us met for a coffee in town recently.

TH: It seems as though you have worked hard to develop the friendship.

  R: I've got to do something about this work thing. I have been having outlandish ideas that I would like to buy a sports car and drive around wearing a stetson and playing loud music! What can that mean? I am nearly 55 after all!

TH: Maybe it's a symptom of your needing to make further changes, in addition to those you've achieved already.

  R: Yes, perhaps.

TH: I am wondering whether you are ready now to continue consolidating your improvements some more; and, making other changes without my help. You will continue, of course, with Sylvia's support and that of your friends — both near and far. They seem to be great resources for you. What do you think?

R: Funny you should say that. I was thinking yesterday, shall I cancel my appointment tomorrow: because I am doing so well on my own now.

[Being ready for this eventuality, I had a long intervention prepared, which was a brief outline of his original concerns and a summary of all his achievements to date.]

I acknowledged and validated all the 'lows' and 'bleak patches' he had experienced. I normalised again his strong suicidal thoughts when they had occurred.

During this final intervention, I emphasised the 'hard work' nature of things; and, that there was more yet to do, as he was not yet fully 'out of the woods'. He accepted this.

My final task was to invite him to notice what he was doing to stay on track; and also, to practice his 'nipping-in-the-bud' strategy for the low patches, which latterly, had been occurring much less frequently.

At the end of this last session, I calculated the eight occasions had spanned a period of just over five months. In my experience, this is unusual for the solution focused approach to suicidal clients. A typical episode would be about four sessions over some two months. He was an exceptional case, though, on account of the severity and persistence of his symptoms.

About nine months later, I had a surprise letter from Reg, quite out of the blue. Extracts from this letter follow:

Dear John,

A 'voice' from the past! You may recall our sessions last winter/spring, after which I enjoyed a period of 'normality', although without any deep satisfaction from my work.

Cutting a long story short, as they say, in early August I suddenly found that I had nothing to give to the organisation and could no longer cope with its demands upon me . . .

. . . [W]hat may interest you, I think, is that in essence I feel that I can no longer function in my job, because the pain which was the driving force of my creativity and motivation is no longer there. I am like an engine deprived of its fuel (pain). An interesting paradox: in consequence of that Healing Letters exercise you made possible, I was able finally to lay to rest some terrible demons, for which I will ever be so grateful; but in being healed I have lost 'that thing' which enabled me to reach out to others.

With hindsight, I look back upon my crisis of the past 12 months as a period of grief following the 'death' of my father. Now that I have put that behind me and accept my own personal history in a somewhat different light, I feel as if, in some respects, I am a new person -- or at least ready to begin a new phase of life.

May I re-iterate how much I valued and appreciated the help you gave me during that very difficult time. The eventual outcome might not be what either of us anticipated; nevertheless, I believe it is to be a healthy one — and, after all, life is full of surprises, isn't it?

I trust all is well with you. Kindest regards, Reg

To conclude this case study on Reg, what was particularly of note was that, although he wanted to delve back into his past, to make sense of his present, this did not result in protracted psychoanalysis or depth psychology of another sort. It is possible for therapists to persevere with the tools and techniques (miracle question, scaling, goal setting, small steps, possibility generation, presuppositional language, etc.) of the solution focused approach, whilst 'going with the client' and adapting it in such a way as is most helpful to the client.

In retrospect, what seemed to have been helpful to Reg, was for me to acknowledge and validate fully his pain; to acknowledge, validate and normalise his suicidal ideation; to encourage him in his diary keeping and letter writing between sessions; and, to coax him gently in the direction of his stated goals whilst, at the same time, supporting him in his quest to unravel his tragic past. What seemed helpful too, was his feeling empowered to act in ways he felt constructive; and, to be affirmed in the progress he had made and 'the new person' he was becoming.

What was interesting also about Reg's case is that it is possible to work in a psycho-social way with someone, whilst they are at the same time 'under the doctor' and receiving medication (in Reg's case this was sleeping tablets and at one time an antidepressant). It is in keeping with the brief therapy tradition to work with other approaches, models, rather than in opposition to them.

From a financial resources point of view, this is a very economical way to work with suicidal clients. Generally, they are able to stay at work (for most of the time); continue living at home; and, maintain family and social contacts. By contrast with other ways of working, the cost of a few hours of counselling/therapy is minimal.

Another reason for bringing Reg's case is to show that, even in 'extreme' or 'serious' cases of suicidal thinking and behaviour, it is possible to work with them towards a successful, hopeful and constructive conclusion. Whilst not wishing to suggest that more-junior practitioners take foolhardy risks with people they are seeing, what is important for the practitioner is for them to remain hopeful and optimistic, knowing and believing in what works with such clients. The greater experience and confidence that results, enables them to take on even greater seriousness or severity presented. As with other types of crisis intervention, it is rewarding and fulfilling work.

10

Some More Case Vignettes

In over 30 years, working in mental health services, I have come into contact with a few hundred clients who have expressed either suicidal ideas and/or shown suicidal behaviour. They have taught me a lot about how best to work with them in order to preserve life and encourage them away from taking the last resort option (completed suicide).

Initially, in the 1970s, whilst working in mental health inpatient units, being bound by policies, procedures and structures, I found myself being an accessory to the fact of patient suicides. The explicit policy was to adopt a risk assessment and management approach; and this, combined with drug treatments often meant that we/the organisation were out-smarted by patients who found themselves in a 'cat and mouse' game with the multi-professional team.

With many of these patients, rarely did anyone sit down and have an honest conversation about how the severity or complexity of their difficulties was contributing to their consideration of the last resort option. Invariably, a problem focused approach was adopted towards them and there was a general identification with their hopelessness and despair. Staff were ill-equipped and ill-trained to deal with the existential questions that were being asked either explicitly or implicitly by patients in their charge.

In the case studies below, drawn from my solution focused work over the past 10 years or so, as with earlier examples, I have disguised personal details to avoid risk of identification, without losing the poignancy of each case. I have chosen these particular cases to illustrate the effectiveness of the solution focused approach in steering clients away from suicide as an option, and to show how powerful some of the fundamental principles, basic and specialised tools and techniques are when applied appropriately.

Case Study 1 – 'Determined To Do It'

Barry (28)

Referral: via GP

Setting: Community Mental Health Centre

Family/Social situation: This man was divorced and had three children who were living with his ex-wife. He had had a serious machinery accident at work which had left him with a limp. He was estranged from his extended family and had recently lost his job and lost touch with friends.

Presenting issue: A break-up with his girlfriend was the last straw.

(Formula first session task)

Phone call from client to book appointment:

B: I am not sure you can be of any help to me. I have been in mental health units in the past and have been given diagnoses such as 'manic-depressive' and 'schizo-affective disorder'.

TH: I don't find labels particularly helpful but there is one thing I would like you to do between now and when we meet: I would like you to notice what is happening in your life that you want to keep happening. Can you do that for me?

B: There's plenty of things I want to stop happening!

At the beginning of the first session . . .

TH: [Usual welcome, introduction and explanation of service . . .]

B: I thought I'd give this a try, but just to let you know, if it doesn't work, I've got in the boot of my car a vacuum cleaner tube, a roll of tape and a 4-pack of extra strong lager. I've already picked a quiet spot on the heath, so if this doesn't work, I'll be driving up there.

(Going with the Client and Worker not showing fear of the worst case scenario)

TH: That's your choice, as it would be mine, if I found myself up against things in life.

B: [Lost for words at the response] Well, we'll see what you can come up with.

TH: ...

Case Study 2 – 'Punchy And Desperate'

Peter (30)

Referral: via GP

Setting: Community Mental Health Centre

Family/Social situation: Estranged from family who lived in another part of the UK. Only friends and associates connected to football club (youth team), which was his life. He was the team coach and also treasurer.

Presenting issue: Got drunk on a Saturday evening and went round to the Chairman's home to continue an argument. Police called and by 11 a.m. on Sunday, club had sacked him.

(Outlining the problem)

P: That's it. My life's finished. I lived for youth football. That club was my life.

(Acknowledgment, validation and normalisation)

TH: I can see it is very upsetting for you. No wonder you are feeling as you do. Others in similar circumstances might have the same reaction.

P: I don't know what to do. I know I shouldn't have gone round to Bill's house after drinking in the pub for a couple of hours. He was totally out of order in getting me sacked. I feel like jumping in the lock basin. There are no steps down there, so I would be sure to drown.

(Generating possibilities)

TH: That is an option open to you. How keen would you be to look at other options too?

 P: I could try.
TH: What comes to mind first?
 P: Dunno.
TH: [Silence] What would your best mate suggest?
 P: He'd say 'Find another club' but, feeling as I do right now, I don't want
        anything to do with football ever again.

(Acknowledging)

TH: I can see things are still raw for you. It is only Tuesday today . . .
 P: I feel like going round to the Chairman's house and giving him 'what
        for'!

(Generating other possibilities)

TH: What other options come to mind?
 P: I could go back to my cycling. I used to compete in area rallies.
TH: What else?
 P: Just get all the overtime at work I can and forget about it.
TH: And what else?
 P: Dunno. Maybe go back to the club and apologise.
TH: Worth a try?
 P: No, that Pauline, Bill's wife: she never liked me from the start. I know
        she's got some part in this.
TH: How keen are you to look at possibilities of finding another club you
        could approach; or, maybe look at something completely different?
 P: . . .

Case Study 3 – 'Despairing Over Lost Love'

Alex (20)

Referral: via GP

Setting: Community Mental Health Centre

Family/Social situation: His parents separated when he was very young. He lives
with his father and a younger brother. Alex always had difficulties in relating to
the opposite sex.

Presenting issue: Was besotted with a girl he had been going out with for seven
months. Worshipped the ground she walked on. They had been making plans for

their joint futures together. She announced, without warning, she didn't love him anymore and wanted their relationship to end.

For the first 20 minutes of the session, Alex was expressing suicidal ideas, describing his plan to take tablets which he had bought earlier that day. He had described a mate's house where he would take his life, knowing that his mate would not be returning for a couple of days.

Later on in the session . . .

(Worst Case Graveside (or Crematorium) Scenario)

TH: Can I ask you a rather unusual question?
 A: Go on then.
TH: Just suppose you went for the last resort option and actually died. You are at your own funeral as a spirit looking down from about 10 feet at the mourners below. What might you be thinking about another option you could have tried first?
 A: Could have gone right away from here, I suppose. Maybe a course of training to John O' Groats to think.
TH: At the funeral, who would be most upset amongst the mourners and what advice would they have wanted to give you regarding other options?
 A: There wouldn't be anyone else at the crematorium.
TH: What about the minister and the crematorium staff?
 A: I suppose they would have to be there.
TH: How many?
 A: Maybe three in total.
TH: What about just one member of your family?

(Reconnecting client with family)

 A: I suppose my Dad would be there . . . and he'd bring Jamie, my kid brother.
TH: Maybe one or two mates? How about your friend with the house you mentioned?
 A: Crispin? – yeah, he'd probably want to make it there.
TH: What might Crispin be thinking as he watched your coffin moving towards the purple curtains?
 A: Silly b—! There are many more fish in the sea. Why couldn't he have talked to me about it?
TH: What else would he be thinking?
 A: If only he wasn't so stupid!

TH: What might your Dad be thinking?
 A: He'd be really upset. He would be bawling . . . and that would set Jamie
        off too.
TH: What might Dad be thinking?
 A: That I shouldn't have done it. He would have lectured me about Lisa
        being only my first serious girlfriend.
TH: What might the minister be thinking?
 A: That it was a waste of a life.

(*Generating other possibilities*)

TH: What might he be thinking in terms of what you could have done in-
        stead of taking this last resort option?
 A: Maybe that I could have written a pleading letter to Lisa.
TH: What else?
 A: That I could have chatted things through with a mate or gone and seen
        someone like you.
TH: . . .

Case Study 4 – 'Tired, Hard-working Carer'

Josephine (49)

Referral: via Employee Assistance Programme

Setting: My home office

Family/Social situation: Hard-working professional carer. Married 24 years. Husband has permanent disabilities due to a boating accident at sea. Has a 22-year-old
son with learning disabilities who has been in trouble with the police; and, a married
daughter with emotional problems. She has three children. Client tries to help her
daughter whenever she can, by way of keeping her family together.

Presenting issue: Feels she has been caring for everyone for years now and can
no longer cope. Her full-time job has become more demanding recently and the
last straw was when two friends, each independently, asked her if they could come
and talk to her about their particular problems.

At about one-third into the session . . .

(*Questions to elicit suicidal ideation*)

TH: Sometimes in life, we can feel that everything is just too much?
 J: Yes, you can say that again! I don't think I can do this anymore . . .

TH: Just suppose you considered the last resort option, how would you go about it?

  J: You mean kill myself?

TH: Yes.

  J: I've been thinking about it a lot recently. I would either use pills (and I've saved up a good lot over the last few months), or I would drive my car at full speed into the docks.

(*Acknowledgment and validation*)

TH: I can see things are really tough for you at the moment. What's stopped you doing either of these things?

  J: I've been that near [uses gesture of small gap between forefinger and thumb of right hand] on about half a dozen occasions recently. Last time I went to suss out the dockside. I worked out how to remove the chain between the bollards. Then I noticed there were dog walkers randomly crossing to and fro. I wouldn't want to take anyone else with me — and I'm rather fond of dogs!

(*Degrimming the session*)

  TH/J: [Laughter]

(*Scaling*)

TH: Just suppose, on a 1–10 scale, where 1 stands for you feeling totally suicidal, and 10 stands for you not being at all suicidal, where are you now on this 1–10 scale?

  J: I was almost a 1 or a 2 the other week, but making this decision to come and see you, I think I'm about a 3 now.

TH: A 3! That's almost a third of the way along! What would you need to do to get to 3½?

  J: Dunno. I love my husband dearly, but I know he's never going to get any better. My son and my daughter are a constant worry . . . [thoughtful]. Maybe if I could learn to look at it all differently. I was talking to my friend Susan last week and that was something she said.

(*Looking for clues and keys for solution building*)

TH: Tell me a bit more about that?

  J: She said, "You can't take on all the responsibility for your daughter's family. Step back a bit. She and her husband are both adults".

(*Coping question for inner and external resources*)

TH: How have you coped with all that you've had to deal with up to now?

J: I've got a few really good friends. We phone each other a lot and meet up. I think I'm a strong person.

(*Amplification*)

TH: How do you know you are a strong person?
J: I try and take care of myself. I go cycling; I read poetry; I treat myself to reflexology occasionally; and, I go to the local folk club. I have kept going up to now with all of it, so I must be doing something right.
TH: Can I ask you a rather unusual question?
J: Yes, go ahead, ask me anything you like!

(*Miracle question – qualified version*)

TH: Just suppose, after you've finished here today . . . you go home . . . do whatever you do this evening and tonight you go to bed and go to sleep . . . While you are asleep, a miracle happens, such that all these strong suicidal thoughts and feelings are gone, just like that [clicks fingers]. Only, you won't know that the miracle has happened because you were asleep at the time . . . When you wake up in the morning . . . what will tell you that this miracle has happened . . . and all these suicidal thoughts and feelings are gone?
J: [Very thoughtful. Silent for about six seconds.] I'd wake up feeling happier. I would have slept for at least five hours at a stretch with-out waking. I would not be afraid of my son's law-breaking. I would tell myself more that he is responsible for his actions because I have taught him right from wrong. I would no longer be worried about my daughter's marriage and I would be looking forward to 'me' things that day. I would be able to love and support my family and friends, without going under myself.

(*Third-party noticing questions . . .*)

TH: Who would be the first to notice that this miracle has happened?
J: My husband.
TH: What would he notice?
J: That I'm less tired, got more energy. I'd be laughing more. I've got a good sense of humour when I'm on an even keel. I like a good laugh.
TH: What would work colleagues notice?
J: I'm popular at work. I work across three health centres and have a really good secretary at one of them. I always chat to the clerical and support staff. They would notice I'm different.

TH: What would they notice specifically?

J: That I show more interest in what they say to me; that I have more of a spring in my step.

(*Questions for post-miracle information*)

TH: How else would you be different?

J: Having more energy, I would be thinking about something I could do for myself – a treat or something.

TH: How would this be helpful to you?

J: I might feel a little better in myself; less put on by others.

(*Going for a piece of the miracle picture that may be happening already*)

TH: From all that you have told me I am wondering whether a little piece of this miracle is happening already?

J: Well, since booking this appointment today, I have decided to ask Olivia – one of my friends who has problems – to go and see a counsellor herself, rather than for me to try and help her. She just seems so hopeless and stuck right now.

(*Affirming client*)

TH: That sounds a good decision to have made. Can I ask you another unusual question?

J: Yes, sure.

(*Scaling the miracle*)

TH: [Shows client edge of clip-board] Just imagine along this line here is a 1–10 scale. This left end stands for 1 – where nothing of the miracle has happened at all; and at the far right end is 10 – where everything you described to me is happening in total Where are you right now on this 1–10 scale?

J: . . . About 2¼.

TH: 2¼! How have you managed to do that?

J: . . .

Case Study 5 – 'Everything's Busted'

Simon (20)

Referral: via Employee Assistance Programme

Setting: My northern office

Family/Social situation: He left his parents to go away to a northern university to read biological sciences. He has three older sisters, all married and living away. Simon's mother and father are enjoying life and looking forward to their daughters' and grandchildren's visits.

Presenting issue: He was on a secondment to a laboratory and hating it. He was wondering whether he had made the right degree choice. Simon's car was at home on his parents' drive with an oil-leak, which was annoying his father. His motorcycle was in the back garden of his digs at university. Currently it was not working, due to an electrical fault. He and his girlfriend had decided on a mutual separation, but he was now missing her greatly. Recently, he had been feeling more homesick. As a result of "everything busted" in his life, he has been contemplating suicide as an escape.

[I was informed by the EAP that he had expressed a strong wish to die.]

(*Introductions and welcome*)

I explained how the employee assistance programme works; the nature of confidentiality; and that I would be taking notes. There were two reasons for the note-taking, I told him: firstly, to make sure I recorded important details; and secondly, so that I can go through the notes between sessions to ensure I steer the work in a direction which is most helpful and useful to him.

TH: Have you any questions about that?
  S: No.

(*Problem-free talk*)

TH: Before we start, when things were more normal for you, what did you
        most enjoy doing in your free time?
  S: Spending time with friends: socialising, having a few beers, that sort
        of thing. Also, I play basketball for the university second team. [Gives
        me a wondering, quizzical look, which is my cue to ask him about the
        problem.]

(*Finding out the nature of the problem*)

TH   So what brings you here?
  S: Everything's busted. My car, my motorbike, and I'm on the wrong de-
        gree course, I miss my girlfriend terribly – although we agreed to split.
        Recently I had an argument with two of my best mates over some petty
        thing. Now they're cool towards me. I don't know what to do.

(*Questions to elicit suicidal ideation*)

TH: Seems like you are having quite a time of it at the moment?

   S: You can say that again!

TH: At this point, how much more do you feel you can cope with?

   S: I can't take any more. All I need now is to break my leg or something – that would be the last straw. I'd think about ending it all.

(Pressing further to determine level of suicidal intent)

TH: If you decided to go ahead with this last resort option – ending it all, how prepared are you, should you decide?

   S: [Back pedals rapidly] Oh no! Don't get me wrong. Although I might be thinking about it, I wouldn't do anything stupid.

TH: What's stopping you?

   S: My mum would be devastated. Also, two of my nephews, Jack and Sam, would cry non-stop. They really look forward to my visiting them. I could always drop out of uni and do something different.

(Goal-finding question)

TH: [Now satisfied, client not actively suicidal.] What would have to happen here today to let you know it was worthwhile doing this (therapy)?

SUMMARY

From these case vignettes, I hope you can see more clearly how the basic tools and techniques of the solution focused approach are applied. Additionally, I hope you have gained a better appreciation of how the specialised solution focused tools are used as and when appropriate.

These cases have been well chosen, in order to provide you with a maximum understanding of both basic and specialised applications.

Although there are many solution focused tools and techniques available for use with clients, 1:1 work is a skill. For any 1:1 work to 'flow', it is important to be natural; and, for it to be a genuine conversational interchange between two people. As I mentioned in an earlier chapter, our approach to clients should in no way be 'techniquey'. Such practice will stick out like a sore thumb and be felt by the client as insincere and less-than-genuine.

Helper–helpee dialogue of the above form is a good way to learn how to improve interpersonal communication when working in helping contexts. There is a growing range of solution focused texts from which to examine more of this type of dialogue. Some of these include: George, Iveson and Ratner (1990); O'Hanlon and Beadle (1996); Jacob (2001);

Sharry, Madden and Darmody (2001); Burns (2005); O'Connell (2005); and Macdonald (2007).

In addition to reading about this effective approach, participating in training workshops, casework practice and high quality supervision, all help to improve both competence and confidence. For information about courses and training workshops worldwide, please see back pages.

11

Where Do We Go From Here?

There is now a burgeoning literature on treatment of suicide individuals — but we still lack a comprehensive treatment strategy and set of alternative approaches to the treatment of self-destructive behaviours.

Silverman & Maris, 1995, p. 10

Over the past 20–30 years especially, much has been written on preventing suicide. This literature has addressed various points along the prevention continuum. It has addressed the primary prevention level in the form of greater public awareness and the targeting of high-risk groups. It has also addressed the treatment aspect of suicide prevention: the subject of this book.

The literature grows, but suicide rates overall do not fall. In fact, for some groups, the rates continue to rise at an alarming rate. Something is going wrong here. I suggest a different approach is now essential if further significant improvements, worldwide, are to be made in reducing suicide rates.

Within existing helping models applied to the suicidal, a greater training emphasis on connecting well within the first 10 minutes, as outlined in Chapter 7, could I believe, improve outcome rates significantly. Also, within these models, a move away from problem-focused questions, and more of an emphasis on those which are solution-focused, would capture the imagination and curiosity of service users currently in despair.

ACCESS POINTS FOR THE SUICIDAL

Various access points have been looked at within the suicide prevention literature: 24-hour helplines, primary care, Accident & Emergency (A&E) Departments and specialist mental health services, to list the main ones. A

review of treatment strategies in 1998 by Hawton et al., for suicide attempters, of relevance to primary care physicians, found that to date, "no form
of treatment has been shown to be clearly effective in reducing the risk of
repetition" (p. 668).

24-hour telephone helplines or 'hotlines' for the suicidal, have expanded
greatly both in the UK, the USA and in many other countries of the world,
since the founding of the Samaritans in London in the 1960s. These centres, it
is suggested, which are often run by lay people on a voluntary basis, provide
a good service to people in distress at any time of the day or night. The volunteers have various degrees of training and expertise. There has been some research into the effectiveness of the various helplines (Jennings, Barraclough
& Moss, 1978), and I would urge further research around this important point
of access. Future studies might look, for instance, at the effects of more solution focused training of helpline staff on the suicide rates in a particular area,
other factors being equal.

Within primary care, there have been, within the literature, various discussions about improved recognition and treatment of depression and suicidal
ideation. Some have suggested that general practitioners ought to get better
at this; others have suggested that it is the specialist mental health services
that ought to improve their practice (Macdonald & Ross, 1993 — not to be
confused with Alastair Macdonald, 1993). It is important to be aware that
during their working lives, individual general practitioners have few patients
who commit suicide, but the specialist mental health services have many.
Further ongoing professional development training, though, in the detection
of suicidal ideation amongst all patients seen in general practice can be only
beneficial.

A&E Departments of general hospitals have been another area of study.
Some of these services have excellent liaison arrangements with mental
health practitioners, who can pick up referrals very quickly and either take
them on themselves or refer them on to specialist mental health team colleagues. Other A&E Departments still have a long way to go in encouraging
attitudinal shifts in staff who might regard suicide attempters as 'a nuisance
to be ignored', while they are trying to attend to the 'real work' of dealing
with the results of DIY accidents in the home, road traffic accident victims,
or other medical emergencies. More formalised, specialist suicide prevention training amongst general nursing staff and casualty officers, in my view,
could make more of an impact on reducing suicide rates, at this point of
access.

Specialist (secondary care) mental health services continue to have an
unacceptably high rate of suicides — both within acute inpatient facilities,

outpatient departments and amongst those who have been newly discharged. It might be suggested that such high rates put into question the term 'specialist'. With regard to inpatient facilities, it has to be acknowledged that many steps have been taken in recent years to make these facilities safer: better observation procedures, collapsible curtain tracking, tighter security with razors, etc. In some services, this has led to some reductions in suicide rates.

Within formal mental health services, there are many pockets of good practice — either in individual practitioners — or within teams. This is to be applauded and encouraged. Maybe areas of 'best practice' can be identified, such that they can be more easily replicated elsewhere. The excellent contribution toward suicide prevention made by the ever-expanding sector of private counsellors and therapists should not be underestimated, either.

QUALITY OF SERVICES

Having worked within specialist mental health treatment services; visited many others; and, spoken to users of services, there are many ways in which the services provided do not meet with what service users both want and need. Many patients who have made an initial attempt on their life report more negative than positive experiences of the treatment they have received from both services as a whole, and key healthcare professionals in particular. As a result, should they suffer a relapse into depression and suicidal thinking, they may have negative expectations with regard to further help. Not unexpectedly, compliance rates are low (Diekstra, 1992), and the rate of suicide in this group is high.

For those of us within the helping agencies who are committed to working with people in distress, helping them regain both some equilibrium in life and to rediscover a better future, it is shocking to hear the reverberating statistic that over 50% of people who commit suicide have seen a care-giver or medical specialist within four weeks of their death (Barraclough, 1973; Murphy, 1975; Morgan, 1979; Michel, 1986). More recent studies show that over 40% have been in contact with a health professional in the month before their death (Vassilas & Morgan, 1993).

Hospitalisation of service users who are feeling suicidal, can create more problems and bring on an early death. It is my considered opinion that risk assessment, management and medication may have a place in a few unique cases, *but* should not be the general rule. Service users who are considering taking the last resort option — suicide — as a solution to their problems, need to talk seriously about their thoughts and feelings, while in the meantime, continuing to live their lives as fully as possible. What they can do without is being holed-up in an inpatient unit; risking future stigma; risking contamination from the 'invalidity-dependency' culture; and, spending endless periods of time waiting for something to happen. With such an experience as this, coupled with the various unwanted side effects of medication, it is no wonder that a proportion of suicidal inpatients become more suicidal as a result, and do not survive.

BETTER TRAINING

It is one thing to teach practitioners about theories of abnormal psychology or mental ill-health; it is quite another to train them in the specific knowledge and skills required to work with people who are on the boundary between life and their self-inflicted death. Not only is it necessary to train workers in the detection of suicidal thinking and behaviour, but also in the essential aspects of making meaningful contact within the crucial first 10 minutes of meeting. I agree with Reeves and Mintz (2001), who point to the need for further research both into the various approaches; and, into the role and impact of supervision, training and context, when working with this high-risk group.

In addressing this important issue of training, the UK Department of Health (1994) suggested that four questions need to be asked:

* Who needs to be trained?
* What training should they get?
* What should be the context of the training?
* What are the implications?

With regard to the first of these three questions, I believe it is time we looked at the widest possible range of staff, before looking at what needs to go into a comprehensive training programme. It is not simply about advanced training for general practitioners, psychiatrists, mental health nurses and psychologists. Mental health professionals, yes, and also other health professionals such as medical students, general nurses, health visitors, community nurses and hospital doctors. Social workers, counsellors, therapists, substance misuse workers and housing association staff could also be included in this very important training. The often under-valued and under-rated staff within 24-hour helplines and advice bureaux might benefit, too, from some of the more recent discoveries in solution focused research.

The second of these questions, if addressed fully, could provide some real pointers to further significant reductions in the suicide rate. General training in mental health and illness does not equip staff sufficiently. It is the specific 1:1 helping skills, in my view, which make a real difference to whether a person goes on to commit suicide, or not. McLaughlin (2007) highlights some of the specific skills that are required in the therapeutic relationship. These include training in noticing what is being communicated by non-verbal communication; and, the verbal responses required. Training in paraphrasing, reflecting and the use of silence are also important, he points out. Finally, appropriate questioning techniques within the therapeutic relationship are of great importance. With recent discoveries in the field of neuroscience, how we choose which words to use, how we phrase questions, how we use tone of voice and pace of speech, are all essential skills in which the practitioner should be competent. This is the stuff of basic counselling skills training, common to most helping models. Over many years of research into suicide prevention, Professor Morgan has frequently referred to practitioner competence, suggesting that further training can be helpful. In Morgan (1979), and in subsequent research papers, he has referred often to the need for greater practitioner competence, suggesting that further training can be helpful: "A suicidal individual . . . more likely to declare his problems and actively turn for help if he thinks that a positive response would be attained" (p. 76).

Another aspect of training to consider is what *is* the worker's role in suicide prevention? The role is far more than doing a good job of assessing and diagnosing before recommending a particular course of treatment. Many clients or patients become impatient with this approach. For 1:1 communication to be meaningful, practitioners must have some sort of framework to understand both their clients/patients and their motives. This issue has been well addressed by Hawton and van Heeringen (2000). In the final analysis, it does not matter too much how well the patient was assessed and the differential diagnosis reached, according to the Diagnostic and Statistical Manual of Mental Disorders, Fourth Edition (DSM-IV) (APA, 1994), if the patient takes their life anyway. What is important is that a potential suicide was prevented.

By way of a final word on training needs, the World Health Organization (WHO, 2005), stressed the need to create a sufficient and competent workforce when dealing with suicidal persons. This is a point I have made on several occasions in the book. WHO suggested 11 actions which include:

- Develop training in the recognition, prevention and treatment of mental health for all staff working within primary care;
- Plan and fund, in partnership with education institutions, programmes that address the education and training needs, of both existing and newly recruited staff;
- Create an expert workforce by designing and implementing adequate specialist mental health training for all staff working within mental health care.

A CONCENTRATION ON 'DEPRESSION?

A great deal of research has been directed at suicidal ideation and behaviour in support of the view that, not only are most people who successfully suicide depressed, but also that treating depression with medication can reduce the suicide rate overall (Diekstra, 1992). There are various figures available: Diekstra (1989) found that 15–29% of patients suffering from major depression die finally by their own hand; and, 50–60% of persons committing suicide, suffer from some sort of depressive disturbance.

It seems to me from my reading, clinical experience, discussions with colleagues, and past clients' personal testimonies, that too many practitioners become convinced that medication is the best way to treat this underlying depression. While medication has helped many, it has handicapped many more, in the form of unwanted side effects. The newer selective serotonin reuptake inhibitor (SSRI) antidepressants generally have fewer side effects, but many of their recipients would take issue with this. A big question remains: Is it wise to use medication to mask symptoms of underlying unhappiness; life difficulties; feelings of hopelessness; or, seemingly unresolvable conflicts? Are talking treatments not a better option? I believe a case can be made, too, in some cases, for both/and.

For those who get carried away by the antidepressant solution to the underlying depression, there is also the sobering fact that a high proportion of those suicidal clients who take their lives, do so by using their prescribed medication. It is my belief that generally, counselling and not medication should be the first chosen course of action. As I outlined in Chapter 3, when depression is defined as: 'the result of unexpressed emotion' or 'the result of undisclosed personal conflict', or 'the absence of hope', it makes sense to refer these sufferers to trained practitioners who have the skills to encourage their clients to express emotions and/or to talk through their undisclosed or undeclared conflicts. When this occurs, it is a personal and professional joy to see the depressive symptoms begin to fade and the client's 'depression' lift. In many cases, not one pill was swallowed.

Giving further consideration to the type of specialist suicide prevention training for practitioners, many may find it invaluable to participate in 2-day or 3-day workshops. Previous attendees have found that not only have they learned many new ideas, but also their confidence in working in this challenging area has increased significantly. Other training courses such as 'Revisiting Basic Counselling Skills + Some Advanced Skills' might also be of benefit.

NATIONAL PROGRAMMES AND TARGETS

Within both the USA and Canada, there are some impressive national programmes to reduce the suicide rate by adopting various suicide prevention strategies. Other countries are developing similar approaches. In the UK, suicide prevention targets have been set. In 1992, the Department of Health set a target to reduce the overall suicide rate by 15% up until the year 2000. This was replaced by a newer target (Department of Health, 1999), to reduce the suicide rate by one-fifth by 2010.

The question may be asked, are national strategies and targets helpful? In the case of the first UK target, although the target was not achieved, considerable progress was made towards achieving it. Rather than suicide being regarded simply as an unfortunate occurrence and an occupational hazard amongst practitioners, targets can lead to the problem of high suicide rates being taken more seriously. Both national programmes and targets can encourage inter-agency cooperation and lead to improved planning of services which can result in better mental health and mental health care. Within the UK, much good work has been achieved at the micro level concerning at-risk groups (TCRU, 2006). Noteworthy among these have been the prison population and among young men.

PROBLEM FOCUS VS. SOLUTION FOCUS

Traditionally, across many disciplines and specialties, when people are confronted with conundrums, difficulties, dilemmas, or worries, it is customary to adopt a problem-focused approach. This is done by assessing the cause of the problem, its severity, and the impact on the person and their family or social system. Once this has been achieved, it is more likely a problem diagnosis can be reached. A prognosis is often made and then treatment can follow.

For some 20 years now, a wind of change has been gathering. This has now reached significant proportions across health, education, the criminal justice system and, more recently, in the world of business and public organisations. The specialist area of suicide prevention cannot escape this trend. Is it not better to look on hope, rather than examining despair? Is it not better to ask questions about what is working, rather than what is not? And, is it not better to empower people to take steps towards building their own solutions to their difficulties, rather than trying to do things unto them? In Chapters 6 and 8, I have gone to some lengths in outlining how the solution focused approach applies to mental health problems generally, and to suicide prevention, specifically.

THE EVIDENCE-BASE

Much has been written in this book about the success of the solution focused approach to the prevention of suicide. Most of this success is practice-based evidence. My own experience over the past 10 years particularly, and my experience before that, within a UK NHS Community Mental Health team, has provided many good examples of successful outcomes. In addition, testimonies and success stories received from many past trainees on suicide prevention courses, have all built up an ever-increasing number of successful cases. It is noteworthy, as mentioned in an earlier chapter, that the majority of these cases go on to live successful and meaningful lives and do not re-present to mental health services. This is further evidence in support of the educational-preventive aspect of solution focused working. From my reading of the literature, this seems to be a different experience from many cases reviewed: which seem either to have prolonged contact with services or to return on a regular basis, each time they relapse.

In the contemporary world of social science, practice-based evidence is not sufficient: evidence-based practice is what is required.

I am of the view that there is a wealth of research possibilities in this area to demonstrate evidence-based practice. With the ever-increasing number of trained solution focused practitioners, it should now be possible in many towns and cities, to conduct double-blind trials with a rigorously designed methodology, to demonstrate the efficacy of the solution focused approach. The accumulating clinical experience amongst the growing number of practitioners and the development of a methodology in the solution focused approach, has prepared the ground well for formally controlled trials in relation to suicide prevention. Whilst acknowledging that the randomised controlled trial is the 5-star standard for the evaluation of various treatments, it is important to note that most investigations to date into the various treatment approaches to suicide have been flawed. This has been due to poor description of the content of the particular treatment; client samples being too small; and too few outcome variables. It is my hope that future research into both the efficacy and effectiveness of the solution focused approach will avoid these pitfalls.

Outcome research possibilities abound, too. As practitioners and researchers, sometimes we may think we have a monopoly on the knowledge-base of what works or what helps. Structured interviews with survivors of serious suicide attempts could throw some further light on service users' views of services and the ways in which practitioners were helpful (and maybe not so helpful) in dealing with their concerns and difficulties. The results of this research could act as useful pointers towards how training can be improved across a wide range of care-givers — both paid and voluntary.

TOWARDS A MANUALISED APPROACH TO SOLUTION FOCUSED SUICIDE PREVENTION

This book is a how-to-do book. As with most books on specialist interest areas, it is to be used in conjunction with training workshops and supervised practice. It should not be used in isolation. As I have indicated previously, the solution focused approach is simple, but it is not easy. Much practice is needed to enable the many tools and techniques to be developed into real skills such that the 1:1 encounter flows more easily.

However, that being said, we can begin to move in the direction of a manual for helping clients who are feeling suicidal. It will become a manual for solution focused procedures towards helping suicidal clients steer away from their last resort option and towards rebuilding meaningful and purposeful lives.

It is my sincere hope that this book will be regarded as an essential preparation for developing such a manualised approach to this vital area of preserving human life.

The solution focused approach is now well established in general, as mentioned above. It is now high time that its application to this specific area of preventing suicide is given more credence, across the whole range of services

FINAL THOUGHTS

Throughout my research for this book, I have been moved by the heartfelt pleas of many academics and 'suicidologists' to find better ways of treating suicidal people. The statistics of the hundreds of thousands of deaths worldwide every year speak volumes about what does not work enough, what works a little and what does not work at all.

With regard to requests to improve services, the following quotation is the most poignant:

> It is essential that pragmatic brief therapies suitable for a sizeable proportion of the suicide attempters, be developed (Hawton & van Heeringen (2000)).

SFBT is one such brief therapy.

It will never be possible to prevent all suicides. Many suicidal people do not make any contact whatsoever with helping agencies — whether helpline or face-to-face.

While I endorse fully the further promotion of solution focused approaches within mental health, I acknowledge that the risk assessment and management and medication approach will remain the dominant model for a while longer yet.

Another great attraction of SFBT is that it can work alongside other models and approaches. Indeed, I have worked with many clients, over many years, doing just that. The secret, I have found, is to work with the other models rather than against them, in order to maximise the chances of clients achieving their goals. One can work alongside antidepressant prescribing, as one can work alongside a 12-step programme. In both cases, one can maintain a solution focused orientation in the therapeutic work, while at the same time, acknowledging the effects and the influences of the other approach. What I think is essential, is that many of the points I have put forward (especially those in Chapter 7), should be applied immediately by all models of helping, especially as applied to the suicidal.

I would like to conclude with a quote from Sharry, Darmody & Madden (2002):

> Traditionally, professional responses to suicidal and self-harming clients have consisted of risk assessment and management, followed by treatment interventions such as medication or problem-focused psychotherapy. In recent times, there has been a growing interest in exploring more collaborative and strengths-based approaches to working with this client group . . . to reorient the therapy away from an exclusive focus on the problem and to help clients envision a positive future where suicide is not an option. (p. 398)

Appendix 1   Flow Diagram for an Episode of Treatment

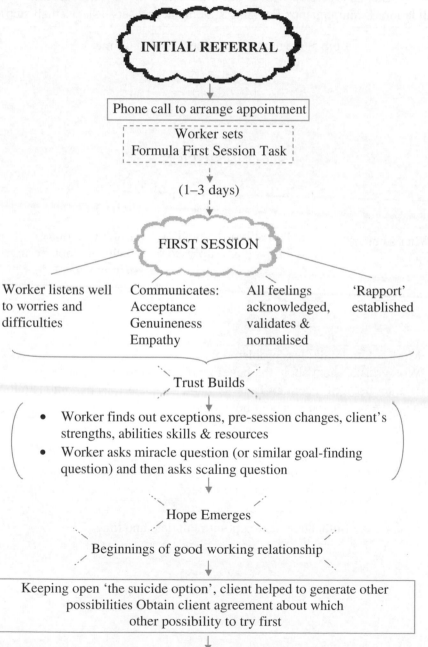

INITIAL REFERRAL

Phone call to arrange appointment

Worker sets
Formula First Session Task

(1–3 days)

FIRST SESSION

| Worker listens well to worries and difficulties | Communicates: Acceptance Genuineness Empathy | All feelings acknowledged, validates & normalised | 'Rapport' established |

Trust Builds

- Worker finds out exceptions, pre-session changes, client's strengths, abilities skills & resources
- Worker asks miracle question (or similar goal-finding question) and then asks scaling question

Hope Emerges

Beginnings of good working relationship

Keeping open 'the suicide option', client helped to generate other possibilities Obtain client agreement about which other possibility to try first

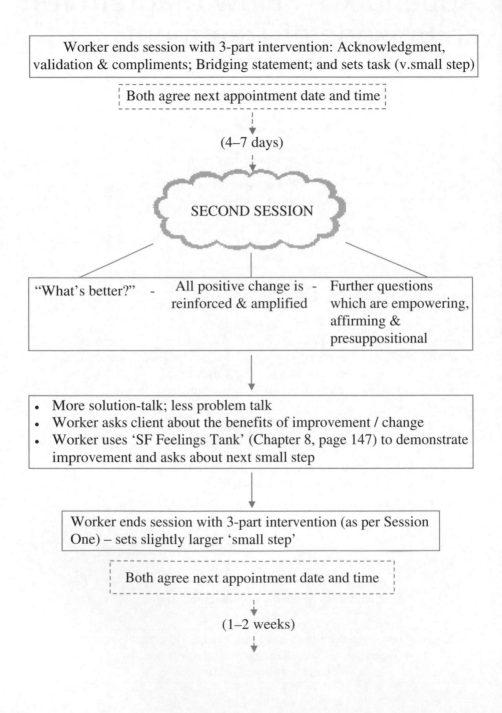

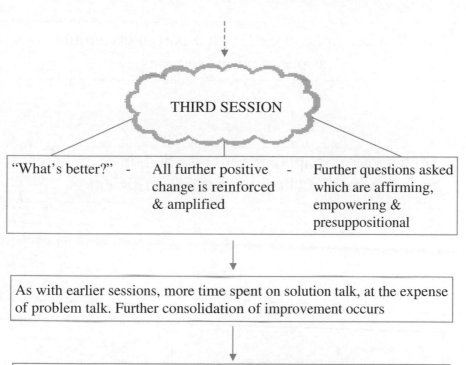

THIRD SESSION

"What's better?" - All further positive - Further questions asked
change is reinforced   which are affirming,
& amplified   empowering &
presuppositional

As with earlier sessions, more time spent on solution talk, at the expense
of problem talk. Further consolidation of improvement occurs

- A further picture is now painted of what the client's life will look
  like, as he / she moves further away from the problem
- Client asked about other thoughts or ideas they are having as a
  result of changes made
- Future, preventative & early intervention strategies are discussed
  with the client

Client further empowered to take larger steps

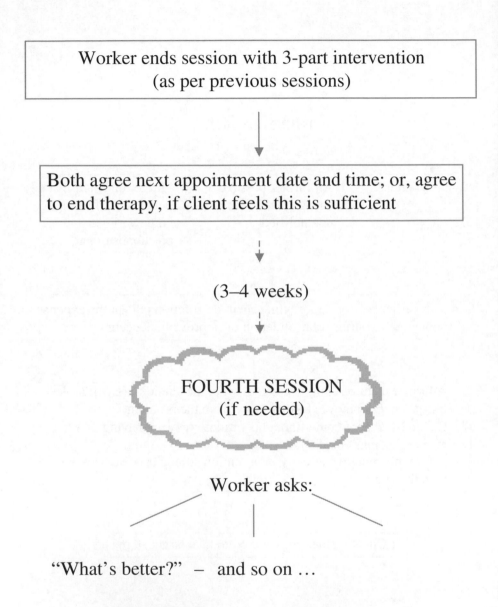

Worker ends session with 3-part intervention
(as per previous sessions)

Both agree next appointment date and time; or, agree
to end therapy, if client feels this is sufficient

(3–4 weeks)

FOURTH SESSION
(if needed)

Worker asks:

"What's better?" – and so on …

Appendix 2   Training Workshops

For information on 2-day and 3-day training workshops worldwide, on: 'Preventing Suicide Using a Solution Focused Approach', please email as follows: info@johnhendenconsultancy.co.uk

These workshops enable participants to apply the basic solution focused tools & techniques to working with the suicidal and to develop expertise in applying the specialised tools & techniques outlined in this book.

What some past workshop participants have said:

"All workers who deal with the severely depressed and/or the suicidal need to attend these workshops."

Ulla Johansson, Stockholm, Sweden

"John Henden has a unique way of communicating both hope and optimism for this important work. Having completed the workshop, I feel I can pass these qualities on to my clients."

Jemma Hudson, Leeds

"I have always felt fearful of working with this client group. This workshop has given me the skills to use and has increased my confidence no end."

Tony Lopresti, London

References

Abramson, L. Y., Metalsky, G. I. & Alloy, C. B. (1989). Hopelessness depression: A theory-based sub-type of depression. *Psychological Review*. **96**, 358–372.

Adams, J. F., Piercy, F. P. & Jurich, J. A. (1991). Effects of solution focused therapy's 'formula first session task' on compliance and outcome in family therapy. *Journal of Marital & Family Therapy*, **17**, 277–290.

Aldridge, D. (1998). *Suicide: the tragedy of hopelessness*. London: Jessica Kingsley.

Aldridge, D. & Rossiter, J. (1983). A strategic approach to suicidal behaviour. *Journal of Systemic & Strategic Therapy*, **24**, 49–62.

Aldridge, D. (1992). Suicidal behaviour: A continuing cause for concern. *British Journal of General Practice,* **42**, 482–485.

American Psychiatric Association (1994). *Diagnostic and Statistical Manual of Mental Disorders* (4th edn, Text Revision). Washington, DC: American Psychiatric Association.

American Psychiatric Association (APA) (1994). *Diagnostic and Statistical Manual of Mental Disorders* (DSM-IV) (4th edn). Washington, DC: American Psychiatric Association.

Appleby, L. (1992). Suicide in psychiatric patients: Risk and prevention. *Arch. General Psychiatry*, **161**, 749–758.

Appleby, L. (2000). Prevention of Suicide in Psychiatric Patients. In K. Hawton & K. van Heeringen (Eds), *The International Handbook of Suicide and Attempted Suicide*. Chichester: John Wiley & Sons.

Appleby, L., Amos, T., Doyle, U., Tommenson, B. & Woodman, M. (1996). General practitioners and young suicides. *British Journal of Psychiatry*, **168**, 330–333.

Appleby, L. et al. (1999). Suicide within 12 months of contact with mental health services: National Clinical Survey. *British Medical Journal,* **318**, 1235–1239.

ASIST (Applied Suicide Intervention Skills Training) (2005). Living Works Education Inc., Canada.

Bagley, C. (1968). The evaluation of a suicide prevention scheme by an ecological method. *Soc. Sci. Med.*, **2**, 1–14.

Battegay, C. & Baldessarini, R. J. (2003). *Cyclothymia, a circular mood disorder. Classic text 55 by Ewald Hecker* (translation). *J. History Psychiatry*, **14**, 391–399.

Baldessarini, R. J., Tondo, L. & Hennen, J. (1990). Effects of lithium treatment and its discontinuation on suicidal behaviour in bipolar manic depressive disorders. *Journal of Clinical Psychiatry*, **60** (suppl. 2), 57–62.

Barraclough, B. (1973). Differences between national suicide rates. *Brit. Journal Psychiatry*, **122**, 95–96.

Barraclough, B., Bunch, J., Nelson B. & Sainsbury P. (1974). A hundred cases of suicide: clinical aspects. *Brit. J. Psychiatry*, **125**, 355–373.

Basuttil, A. & Obafunwa, J. O. (1993). Suicide. *Lancet*, 342–744.

Battegay, R. (1990). Suicide notes: predictive clues and patterns (Review of suicide notes). *Crisis*, **11**, 74–75.

Beck, A. T. (1963). Thinking and depression: idiosyncratic content and cognitive distortions. *Archives of General Psychiatry*, **9**, 324–333.

Beck, A. T. (1967). *Depression: Clinical, experimental & theoretical aspects*. New York: Harper & Row.

Beck, A. T. (1976). *Cognitive therapy and emotional disorders*. New York: International Universities Press.

Beck, A. T. (1993). *B D I: Beck Depression Inventory*. San Antonio, TX: The Psychological Corporation.

Beck, A. T. & Steer, R. A. (1989). *Manual for the Beck Hopelessness Scale*. San Antonio, TX: The Psychological Corporation.

Beck, A. T., Beck, R. & Kovacs, M. (1975). Classification of Suicidal Behaviours: 1. Quantifying Intent and Medical Lethality. *American Journal of Psychiatry*, **132**, 285–287.

Beck, A. T., Brown, G. K. & Steer, R. A. (1989). Prediction of eventual suicide in psychiatric inpatients by clinical rating of hopelessness. *Journal of Consulting & Clinical Psychology*, **57**, 309–310.

Beck, A. T., Kovacs, M. & Weissman, A. (1979). Assessment of suicidal intention: The scale for suicidal ideation. *Journal of Consulting & Clinical Psychology*, **47**, 343–352.

Beck, A. T., Schyler, D. & Herman, J. (1974). Development of suicidal intent scales. In A. J. Beck, H. L. P. Resnik & D. J. Lettiere (Eds), *The prediction of suicide*, pp. 45–56. Philadelphia, PA: Charles Press.

Beck, A. T., Steer, R. A. & Brown, G. K. (1996). *Beck depression inventory* (2nd edn). San Antonio, TX: The Psychological Corporation.

Beck, A. T., Rush, A. J., Shaw, B. F., & Emery, G. (1979). *Cognitive therapy of depression*. New York: Guilford Press.

Beck, A. T., Weissman, A., Lester, D. & Trexler, L. (1974). The measurement of pessimism: The hopelessness scale. *Journal of Consulting & Clinical Psychology*, **42**, 861–865.

Beck, J. S. (1995). *Cognitive Therapy: Basics and Beyond*. New York: Guilford Press.

Berg, I. K. (1991). *Family Preservation — A brief therapy workbook*. London: Brief Therapy Press.

Berg, I. K. (2003). *Correspondence by email on solution focused list server*: http://home.ease.lsoft.com/archives/solutions-L.html

Berg, I. K. & de Jong, P. (1998). Interviewing for Solutions. Videotape. Brief Family Therapy Centre, Milwaukee, Wisconsin, USA.

Berg, I. K. & Miller, S. D. (1992). *Working with the problem drinker*. New York: Norton.

Berman, A. L. & Jobes, D. A. (1995). Suicide prevention in adolescence (age 12–18). *Suicide & Life Threatening Behavior*, **25**, 1, 143–154.

Berne, E. (1964). *Games People Play: The psychology of human relationships*. Harmondsworth: Penguin.

Blauner, S. R. (2002). *How I stayed alive when my brain was trying to kill me: One person's guide to suicide prevention*. New York: HarperCollins.

Bongar, B., Lomax, J. & Harmatz, M. (1992). Training and supervisory issues in the assessment and management of the suicidal patient. In B. Bongar (Ed.), *Suicide: Guidelines for assessment, management, and treatment* (pp. 253–267). New York: Oxford University Press.

Bonner, R. & Rich, A. (1987). Toward a predictive model of suicidal ideation and behaviour: Some preliminary data in college students. *Suicide and Life-Threatening Behavior*, **17**, 50–63.

Bostock, T. & Williams, C. L. (1974). Attempted suicide as an operant behaviour. *Archives of General Psychiatry*, **31**, 482–486.

Brent, D. A. (1993). Depression and Suicide in Children and Adolescents. *Pediatric Rev*, **14**(10), 380–388.

Bridges, K. & Goldberg, D. (1987). Somatic presentation of depressive illness in primary care. In P. Freeling, L. J. Downey & T. C. Malkin (Eds), *The presentation of depression: current approaches*. London: Royal College of General Practitioners.

Brief Therapy Family Centre (1995). *"I'd hear laughter": Finding solutions for the family*. Insoo Kim Berg Brief. Family Therapy Centre videotape. New York: Norton.

Brief Therapy Family Centre (1998). *"Over the Hump": Interviewing for Solutions*. New York: Norton.

Brown, G. K., Beck, A. T. & Steer, R. A. (2000). *BDI — fast screen for medical patients manual*. San Antonio, TX: The Psychological Corporation.

Brown, G. K., Beck. A. T., Steer, R. A. & Grisham, J. R. (2000). Risk factors for suicide in psychiatric outpatients: A 20-year prospective study. *Journal of Consulting & Clinical Psychology*, **68**, 371–377.

Brown, G. K., Have, T. T., Henriques, G. R., Xye, S. X., Hollander, J. E. & Beck, A. T. (2005). Cognitive therapy for the prevention of suicide attempts: A randomised controlled trial. *Journal of the American Medical Association*, **294**, 563–570.

Burns, D. D. & Auerbach, A. (1996). *Therapeutic empathy in cognitive-behavioural therapy: Does it really make a difference?* (pp. 135–164). New York: Guilford Press.

Burns, K. (2005). *Focus on solution: A health professional's guide*. London: Whurr.

Bushman, B. J., Baumeister R. F. & Stack, A. D. (1999). Catharsis, aggression and persuasive influence: Self-fulfilling of self-defeating prophecies? *Journal of Personality & Social Psychology*, **76**, 367–376.

Buzan, R. & Weissberg, M. P. (1992). Suicide: risk factors and prevention in medical practice. *Annu. Rev. Med.*, **43**, 37–46.

Callcott, A. & Mackenzie, J. (2001). *Solution focused approach with people who have self harmed*. Paper presented to CPNA Conference, March.

Callcott, A. (2003). Solution-focused assessment and interventions with suicidal or self-harming patients. *Journal of Primary Care Mental Health*, **7**, 75–77.

Callcott, A. (2003). *Correspondence by email on solution focused list server*: http://home.ease .lsoft.com/archives/solutions-L.html

Camus, A. (1942) (edition 2006). *The myth of Sisyphus*. Harmondsworth: Penguin.

Camus, A. (1955). *The myth of Sisyphus and other essays* (Justin O'Brien, trans.). New York: Random House. (Original work published 1942).

Canadian Task Force on the periodic health examination (1990). Update 2. Early detection of depression and prevention of suicide. *Canadian Medical Association Journal*, **142**(11), 1233–1238.

Carkhuff, R. R. (1969). *Helping and human relations* (Vols 1 & 2). New York: Holt, Rinehart & Winston.

Carson, A. J., Best, S., Warlow, C. & Sharpe, M. (2000). Suicidal ideation among outpatients at several neurology clinics: Prospective study. *BMJ*, **320**, 1311–1312.

Chiles, J. A. & Strosahl, K. (1995). *The suicidal patient: Principles of assessment, treatment and case management.* Washington, DC: American Psychiatric Press.

Conwell, Y. (1994). Suicide in elderly patients. In L. S. Schneiden, C. F. Reynolds III, B. D. Lebowitz & A. T. Friedhoff (Eds), *Diagnosis of depression in later life* (pp. 397–418). Washington, DC: American Psychiatric Press.

Crumbaugh, J. C. & Maholick, L. T. (1963). The case for Frankl's 'will to meaning'! *Journal of Existential Psychiatry*, **4**, 43–48.

Crumbaugh, J. C. (1968). Cross validation of purpose-in-life test, based on Frankl's concepts. *Journal of Individual Psychology*, xxiv, 74–81.

Dahlsgaard, K. K., Beck, A. T. & Brown, G. K. (1998). Inadequate response to therapy as a predictor of suicide. *Suicide & Life Threatening Behavior*, **28**, 197–204.

Davis (1968). Lithium Treatment (***)

de Shazer, S. (1985). *Keys to solutions in brief therapy.* New York: Norton.

de Shazer, S. (1988). *Clues: investigating solutions in brief therapy.* New York: Norton.

de Shazer, S. (1991). *Putting difference to work.* New York: Norton.

de Shazer, S. (1994). *Words were originally magic.* New York: Norton.

de Shazer, S. & Berg, I. K. (1997). 'What works?': Remarks on research aspects of solution focused brief therapy. *Journal of Family Therapy*, **19**, 121–124.

de Shazer, S. & Gingerich, W. J. (1987). Using pre-treatment change to construct a therapeutic solution: an exploratory study. *Journal of Marital & Family Therapy*, **13**, 359–363.

de Shazer, S. et al. (1986). Brief therapy: focused solution development. *Family Process*, **25**, 207–221.

Department for Education and Skills (2003). *Focusing on solutions: a practical approach to managing behaviour.* London: HMSO. (www.dfes.gov.uk/; http://www.standards.dfes .gov.uk/primary/pdf/ba_focus_solns_tnotes075903.pdf?version=1)

Department of Health (1999). *Saving Lives: Our Healthier Nation.* Cmd 4386. London: The Stationery Office.

Department of Health (2002). *National suicide prevention strategy for England.* London: Department of Health.

Department of Health (2003). *National suicide prevention strategy for England – Consultation response.* London: Department of Health.

Department of Health (2004). *National standard, local action: Health & Social Care Standards & Planning Frameworks.* London: Department of Health.

Department of Health (2004). *National suicide prevention strategy for England: Annual report on progress 2004.* London: Department of Health.

Department of Health (2005). *National suicide prevention strategy annual progress report 2004 – Update on goals and actions.* Leeds: NIMHE.

Department of Health (2005). *Press release.* 10 March 2005.

Department of Health (2006). *National suicide prevention strategy: 3rd annual report.* London: Department of Health.

Diekstra, R. F. (1988). Towards a comprehensive strategy for the prevention of suicidal behaviour: a summary of recommendations for national task forces. *Crisis*, **9**(2), 119.

Diekstra, R. F. (1989). Suicidal behaviour in adolescents and young adults: the international picture. *Crisis*, **10**, 16–35.

Diekstra, R. F. (1989). Suicide and attempted suicide: An international perspective. *Acta Psychiatrica Scandinavica*, **80** (Suppl. 354), 1–24.

Diekstra, R. F. (1992). The prevention of suicidal behavior — evidence for the efficacy of clinical and community-based programs. *International Journal of Mental Health*, **21**, 3, 69–87.

Diekstra, R. F. (1993). The epidemiology of suicide and para-suicide. *Acta Psychiactrica Scand.*, **371** (Suppl.), 9–20.

Diekstra, R. F., Engels, G. I. & Methorst, G. J. (1988). Cognitive theory of depression: a means of crisis intervention. *Crisis*, **9**, 32–44.

Dolan, Y. (1991). *Resolving sexual abuse: solution focused therapy & Ericksonian hypnosis for adult survivors*. New York: Norton.

Dolan, Y. (1998). *Beyond survival: living well is the best revenge*. London: B T Press.

Domino, G. & Swain, B. J. (1986). Recognition of suicide lethality and attitudes towards suicide in mental health professionals. *OMEGA*, **16**, 301–308.

Dukas, H. E. & Hoffman, B. (Eds) (1997). *Albert Einstein on: Prayer; Purpose in Nature; Meaning of Life; the Soul; a Personal God*. Princeton, NJ: Princeton University Press.

Durkheim, E. (1897). *Le Suicide*. Translated as 'Suicide: a study in sociology', by J. Spalding & G. Simpson. London: Routledge & Kegan Paul (1952).

Dyck, R., Joyce, A. & Azim, H. (1984). Treatment Compliance as a Function of Therapist Attributes and Social Support. *Canadian Journal of Psychiatry*, **29**, 212–216.

Egan, G. (1998). *The Skilled Helper*. Pacific Grove, CA: Brooks/Cole Publishing.

Ellis, A. (1973). *Humanistic psychotherapy: The rational emotive approach*. New York: Julian Press.

Ellis, A. (1989). Using rational-emotive therapy (RET) as crisis intervention: A single session with a suicidal client. *Journal of Adlerian Theory, Research, and Practice*, **45**, 75–81.

Ellis, T. E. (2006). *Cognition & Suicide: A Theory, Research & Therapy*. American Psychological Association.

Ellis, T. E. & Newman, C. F. (1996). *Choosing to live: How to defeat suicide through cognitive therapy*. Oakland, CA: New Harbinger.

Ellis, T. E. & Ratliff, K. (1986). Cognitive characteristics of suicidal and nonsuicidal psychiatric inpatients. *Cognitive Therapy and Research*, **10**, 625–634.

Encarta 1998 (1993–1997) CD Rom.

Encyclopaedia Britannica (1994–1997). Chicago, IL.

Erickson, M. H. In Haley, J. (1973). *Uncommon therapy: the psychiatric techniques of Milton H. Erickson* (1st edn). New York: Norton.

European Brief Therapy Association. www.ebta.nu

Farrelly, F. & Brandsma, J. (1974). *Provocative therapy*. Cupertino, California: Meta Publications Inc.

Fawcett, J. (1969). Suicide: Clues from interpersonal communication. *Archives of general psychiatry*, **21**, 129–137.

Felner, R. D., Jason, L. A., Moritsugu, J. N. & Farber, S. S. (Eds) (1983). *Preventive psychology: theory, research and practice*. NY: Pergamon Press.

Fiske, H. (2006). *Hope in action: Solution focused conversation about suicide*. New York: Haworth.

Fiske, H. & Taylor, L. (2005). Tapping into hope. Canadian Brief Therapy Network Annual Conference: Toronto, Canada.

Fowler, H. W. & Fowler, F. G. (Eds) (1964). The Concise Oxford English Dictionary, (5th edn rev.). Oxford: Clarendon Press.

Frankl, V. E. (1960). Paradoxical Intention: a logotherapeutic approach. *American Journal of Psychotherapy*, **14**, 520–535.

Frankl, V. E. (1963). Experience with the Logotherapeutic Technique of Paradoxical Intention in the Treatment of Phobic and Obsessive-Compulsive Patients. (Paper read at the Symposium of Logotherapy at the 6th International Congress of Psychotherapy, London, UK, August 1964.) *American Journal of Psychiatry*, **CXX 111**, No. 5 (Nov. 1966), 548–553.

Frankl, V. E. (1964). *Man's search for meaning: An introduction to logotherapy*. London: Hodder & Stoughton.

Frankl, V. E. (1973). *The Doctor and the Soul: from Psychotherapy to Logotherapy*. Harmondsworth: Pelican Books.

Frankl, V. E. (1976). *Psychotherapy & existentialism*: *Selected papers on logotherapy*. Harmondsworth: Pelican Books.

Frankl, V. E. (1978). *The unheard cry for meaning*. London: Hodder & Stoughton.

Frankl, V. E. (1959). *From death-camp to existentialism*: Boston: Beacon Press.

Freeling, P., Rao, B. M., Paykel, E. S., Sineting, C. I. & Burton, R. H. (1985). Unrecognised depression in general practice. *BMJ*, **290**, 1880–1883.

Freeman, A. & Reinecke, M. (1993). *Cognitive therapy of suicidal behaviour*. New York: Springer.

Freud, S. (1901b). *The psychopathology of everyday life*. Standard edition. Volume 5. Harmondsworth: Penguin Freud Library.

Furman, B. (1997). It's Never Too Late to Have a Happy Childhood. B. T. Press.

Garfield, S. & Bergin, A. (Eds) (1994). *Handbook of psychotherapy & behaviour change* (4th edn). New York: John Wiley & Sons.

Garland, A. & Zigler, E. (1993). Adolescent suicide prevention — current research and social policy implications. *American Psychologist*, **48**, 2, 169–182.

Gaston, L., Thompson, L., Gallagher, D., Cournoyer, L. G. & Gagon, R. (1998). Alliance, technique, and their interactions in predicting outcome of behavioural, cognitive, and brief dynamic therapy. *Psychotherapy Research*, **8**, 190–209.

George, E., Iveson, C. & Ratner, H. (1990). *Problem to Solution: Brief Therapy with Individuals and Families*. London: B T Press.

Goffman, E. (1961). *Asylums*. New York: Anchor Books, Doubleday & Co.

Goffman, E. (1963). *Stigma*. New Jersey: Prentice-Hall, Inc.

Gresham, F. M. (1998). Social skills training with children. In T. S. Watson & F. M. Gresham (Eds), *Handbook of child behaviour therapy* (pp. 475–497). New York: Plenum Press.

Gunnell, D. (1994). *The potential for preventing suicide: A review of the literature on the effectiveness of interventions aimed at preventing suicide*: Bristol: Health Care Evaluation Unit, University of Bristol.

Haley, J. (1973). *Uncommon therapy: the psychiatric techniques of Milton H. Erickson* (1st edn). New York: Norton.

Hamelinck, L. (1990). Client-centred therapy and psychiatric crisis intervention following suicide attempts. In G. Lietaer, J. Rombauts & R. van Balen (Eds), *Client-centred and experiential psychotherapy in the nineties* (pp. 579–597). Leuven, Belgium: Leuven University Press.

Hawton, K. & van Heeringen, K. (Eds) (2000). *The international handbook of suicide and attempted suicide*. Chichester: John Wiley & Sons.

Hawton, K. (1987). Assessment of suicide risk. *Brit. Journal. Psychiatry*, **150**, 145–153.

Hawton, K. et al. (1998). Deliberate Self-Harm: Systematic review of efficiency of psychosocial and pharmacological treatments in preventing reputation. *British Medical Journal*, **317**, 441–447.

Hawton, K., Simkin, S., Malmberg, A., F., Fagg, J. & Harriss, L. (1998). *Suicide and stress in farmers* (DoH funded research). London: The Stationery Office.

HealthCare Evaluation Unit (HCEU), University of Bristol (1994). *The potential for preventing suicide*. (See Gunnell, D., 1994)

Healthopedia (2006). Suicide — Treatment and monitoring treatment. www.healthopedia.com

Heard, H. L. (2000). Psychotherapeutic approaches to suicidal behaviour. In Hawton & van Heeringen (Eds), *The International Handbook of Suicide and Attempted Suicide*. Chichester: John Wiley & Sons.

Henden, J. (1991). The changing language of mental health. In D. R. Trent (Ed.), *The Promotion of Mental Health*, Vol. **1**. Avebury: Ashgate.

Henden, J. (2005). Preventing suicide using a solution focused approach. *Journal of Primary Care Mental Health*, **8**, No. 3, 81–88.

HM Stationery Office (HMSO) (1992). *The Health of the Nation: A strategy for health in England*. (Cm. 1986.) London: HMSO.

Hurding, R. F. (1985). *Roots and shoots: A guide to counselling and psychotherapy*. London: Hodder & Stoughton.

Isebaert, L. (2005). A Solution-Focused Protocol for Anxiety Disorders and Depression. Workshop presentation at the 2005 European Brief Therapy Association Conference, Salamanca, Spain, September 2005.

Isometsa, E. T. (2000). Suicide. *Current Opinion in Psychiatry*, **13**, 143–147.

Isometsa, E. T., Henricksson, M. M., Aro, H. M., Heikkinen, M. E., Kuoppasalmi, K. I., & Lonnqvist, J. K. (1994). Suicide in major depression. *Am. J. Psychiatry*, **151**, 530–536.

Isometsa, E. T. et al. (1995). Mental disorders in young and middle-aged men who commit suicide. *British Medical Journal*, **310**, 1366–1367.

Israeli (1997)

Jackson, P. Z. & McKergow, M (2002). *The Solutions Focus: the simple way to positive change* (pp. 13–14). London: Nicholas Brealey.

Jacob, F. (2001). *Solution focused recovery from eating distress*. London: B T Press.

Jansson, L. (1984). Social skills training for unipolar depression. *Scandinavian Journal of Behavior Therapy*, **13**, 237–241.

Jenkins, R., Griffiths, S., Wylie, I., Hawton, K., Morgan, G. & Tylee, A. (1994). *The prevention of suicide*. London: HMSO (Dept. of Health).

Jennings, C., Barraclough, B, M. & Moss, J. R. (1978). Have the Samaritans lowered the suicide rate? A controlled study. *Psychological Medicine*, **8**, 413–422.

Jobes, D. A. (2006). *Managing Suicidal Risk: A collaborative approach*. New York: Guilford Press.

Kalafat, J. (2002). Crisis intervention and counselling by telephone. In D. Lester (Ed.), *Crisis intervention and counselling by telephone* (pp. 64–82). Springfield, IL: Charles C. Thomas.

Karasu, T. B. (1986). The specificity versus non-specificity dilemma: toward identifying therapeutic change agents. *American Journal of Psychiatry*, **143**, 867–695.

Kelly, G. A. (1955). *The Psychology of Personal Constructs*. New York: Norton.

Kelly, G. A. (1963). *The Theory of Personal Constructs*. New York: Norton.

Kim, J. (2006). *Examining the effectiveness of solution-focused brief therapy: a meta-analysis using random effects modelling*. SFBTA Conference, Denver. (University of Michigan Dissertation Database).

Kohlenberg, R. J., & Tsai, M. (2000). Radical behavioural help for Katrina. *Cognitive and Behavioural Practice*, **7**, 500–505.

Lambert, M. J. (2004). *Bergin & Garfield's Handbook of Psychotherapy and Behavior Change* (5th edn). New York: John Wiley & Sons.

Leenaars, A. A. (2004). *Psychotherapy with suicidal people: a person-centred approach*. Chichester: John Wiley & Sons.

Leenaars, A. A. (Ed.) (1991). *Life span perspectives of suicide*. NY: Plenum.

Linehan, M. M. (1981). A social-behavioural analysis of suicide and parasuicide: Implications for clinical assessment and treatment. In H. G. Glazer & J. F. Clarkin (Eds), *Depression: Behavioural and directive intervention strategies* (pp. 229–294), New York: Garland.

Linehan, M. M. (1986). Suicidal people: One population or two? In J. J. Mann & M. Stanley (Eds), *Annals of the New York Academy of Sciences,* **487**, 16–33.

Linehan, M. M. (1993). *Cognitive-Behavioural treatment of borderline personality disorder.* New York: Guilford Press.

Linehan, M. M., Armstrong, H. E., Suarez, A., Allmore, D. & Heard, H. L. (1991), Cognitive behavioural treatment of chronically suicidal parasuicidal borderline patients. *Archive of General Psychiatry,* **48**, 1060–1064.

Linehan, M. M. et al. (2005). *Two year randomized trial and follow-up of dialectical behaviour therapy vs. treatment-by-experts for suicidal behaviours and borderline personality disorder.* Manuscript submitted for publication.

Lipchik, E. & de Shazer, S. (1986). The purposeful interview. *Journal of Strategy & Family Therapies*, 5 (1), 88–9.

Litman, R. E. (1967). Sigmund Freud on suicide. In E. S. Schneidman (Ed.), *Essay in self-destruction* (pp. 324–344). New York: Science House.

Luborski, L., McLellan, A., Woody, G., O'Brien, C. & Auerbach, A. (1985). Therapist Success and its Determinants. *Archives of General Psychiatry,* **42**, 602–611.

Lueger, G. & Korn, H-P. (Eds) (2006). *Solution Focused Management.* (Proceedings of 5th International Conference on Solution Focused Practice in Organisations, Vienna, 2006.) Munchen und Mering: Rainer, Hampp Verlag.

Macdonald, Alastair (1993). The myth of suicide prevention by general practitioners. *The British Journal of Psychiatry*, **163**, 260.

Macdonald, A. J. (2007). *Solution-focused therapy: Theory, research and practice.* London: Sage.

Macdonald, A. J. & Ross, J. (2003). Solution-focused brief therapy in general practice. *The Journal of Primary Care Mental Health*, **7**, 68–69.

Maltsberger, J. T. & Goldblatt, M. J. (1996). *Essential papers on suicide.* New York: New York University Press.

Maris, R. & Silverman, M. (1995). Postscript: Summary and synthesis. *Suicide & Life Threatening Behavior* **25**, 1, 205–209.

Maris, R. (1995). Suicide prevention in adults (age 30–65). *Suicide & Life Threatening Behavior*, **25**, 1, 171–179.

Maris, R. W. et al. (1973). Education and training in suicidology for the seventies. In H. L. P. Resnik & B. C. Hathorne (Eds), *Suicide prevention in the seventies*. Washington, DC: USGPO, DHEW Publication No. (HSM) 72–9054.

Marx, E. M., Williams, J. M. G. & Claridge, G. C. (1992). Depression and social problem solving. *Journal of Abnormal Psychology,* **101**, 78–86.

McGaughey, J., Long, A. & Harrison, S. (1995). Suicide and parasuicide: A selected review of the literature. *Journal of Psychiatric and Mental Health Nursing*, **2**, 199–206.

McLaughlin, C. (1994). Casualty nurses' attitudes and attempted suicide. *Journal of Advanced Nursing*, **20**(6), 1111–1118.

McLaughlin, C. (2007). *Suicide related behaviour: Understanding, caring and therapeutic responses.* Chichester: John Wiley & Sons.

Mehrabian, A. (1981). *Silent messages: Implicit communication of emotion and attitude* (2nd edn). Belmont, CA: Wadsworth.

Michel, K. (1986). Suizide and suizidversuche: Konnte der arzt mehr tun. *Schweizerische Medizinische Wochenschrift*, **116**, 770–774.

Michel, K. (2000). Suicide prevention and primary care. In K. Hawton & K. van Heeringen (Eds), *The International Handbook of Suicide and Attempted Suicide,* pp. 661–674. Chichester: John Wiley & Sons.

Michel, K. & Dalach, L. (1997). Suicide as goal-directive behaviour. *Archives of Suicide Research, 3*, 213–221.

Miller, A. L., Rathus, J. H. & Linehan, M. M. (2007). *Dialectical Behaviour Therapy with Suicidal Adolescents.* New York: Guilford Press.

Milner, J. & Myers, S. (2007). *Working with violence: policies and practices in risk assessment and management.* Basingstoke: Palgrave/Macmillan.

Milner J. & O'Byrne, P. (1998). *Assessment in Social Work.* Basingstoke: Palgrave/Macmillan.

Milton, J. (2001). Psychoanalysis and cognitive behavioural therapy — rival paradigms or common ground? *International Journal of Psychoanalysis*, **82**, 431–446.

Milton, M. & Crompton, J. (2001). Recent research on suicide: Issues for British Counselling Psychologists. *Counselling Psychology Review*, **16**, 3, 28–33.

Minkoff, K., Bergman, E., Beck, A. T. & Beck, R. (1973). Hopelessness, depression, and attempted suicide. *American Journal of Psychiatry*, **130**, 455–459.

Modestin, J. & Schwarzenbach, F. (1992). Effect of psychopharmacotherapy on suicide risk in discharged psychiatric patients. *Acta Psychiatrica Scandinavica*, **85**, 173–175.

Morgan, H. (1979). *Death Wishes? The understanding and management of deliberate self harm.* Chichester: John Wiley & Sons.

Morgan, H. G. & Priest, P. (1991). Suicide and other unexpected deaths among psychiatric inpatients: The Bristol Confidential Inquiry. *British Journal of Psychiatry*, **158**, 368–374.

Morgan, H. G. (1992). Suicide prevention: hazards in the fast lane of community care. *British Journal of Psychiatry, 160*, 149–153.

Morgan, H. G. (1993). Long term risks of attempted suicide. *BMJ*, **306**, 1626–1627.

Morgan, H. G. & Vassilas, C. A. (1993). General Practitioners' contact with victims of suicide. *BMJ*, **307**, 300–301.

Murphy, G. E. (1975). The physician's responsibility for suicide. II. Errors of omission. *Annals of Internal Medicine*, **82**, 305–309.

National Electronic Library for Health (NeLMH) (2006). Mental health Internet site: www.cebmh.warne.ox.ac.uk/cebmh/elmh/nelmh/suicide/

National Institute for Mental Health in England (NIMHE) (2003). *Toolkit for local services to measure progress for the national confidential inquiry into suicide and homicide by people with mental illness — safer services.* London: The Stationery Office.

Norman, H. (2000). *Upward spiral effect of practitioners' optimism and client progress resulting in increased client change and further practitioner optimism.* Private conversation.

Nunnally, E., de Shazer, S., Lipchik, E. & Berg I. K. (1986). Study of Change: Therapeutic Theory and Process. In D. E. Effron (Ed.), *Journeys: Expansion of the Strategic-Systemic Therapies.* NY: Brunner/Mazel.

O'Connell, B. (1998). *Solution Focused Therapy.* London: Sage Publications.

O'Connell, B. (2005). *Solution Focused Therapy* (2nd edn). London: Sage Publications.

O'Farrell, T. J., Goodenough, D. D. & Cutter, H. S. G. (1981). Behavioural contracting for repeated suicide attempts. *Behaviour Modification, 5*, 255–272.

O'Hanlon, W. H. (1993). Possibility therapy. Two-day training workshop hosted by Brief Therapy Practice, London.

O'Hanlon, W. H. (2000). *Do one thing different: Ten simple steps to change your life*. New York: HarperCollins.

O'Hanlon, W. H. & Beadle, S. (1996). *A Field Guide to Possibility-Land*. London: B T Press.

O'Hanlon, W. H. & Weiner-Davis, M. (1989). *In Search of Solutions: A new direction in psychotherapy*. New York: Norton.

O'Hara, M. W., Stuart, S., Gorman, L. L. & Wentzel, A. (2000). Efficacy of interpersonal psychotherapy for post-partum depression. *Archives of General Psychiatry*, **57**, 11, 1039–1045.

Oliver, C. & Storey, P. (2006). *Evaluation of mental health promotion pilots to reduce suicide amongst young men. Final Report*. University of London: Thomas Coram Research Unit.

Orton, J. D. (1974). A transactional approach to suicide prevention. *Clinical Social Work Journal*, **2**, 57–63.

Palazzoli, M. S. (1986). Hypothesizing — Circularity — Neutrality. *Family Process*, **19**, 3–12.

Patterson, P., Whittingham, R. & Bogg, J. (2007). Testing the effectiveness of an educational intervention aimed at changing attitudes to self harm. *Journal of Psychiatric and Mental Health Nursing*, **14**(1), 100–105.

Paykel, E., Myers, J., Underthal, J. & Tanner, J. (1974). Suicidal feelings in the general population: 8–9% of general population had similar feelings within last year. A prevalence study. *British Journal of Psychiatry*, **124**, 460–469.

Peacock, F. (2001). *Water the flowers, not the weeds*. Montreal, Canada: Open Heart Publishing.

Pease, A. (1984). *Body Language: How to Read Others' Thoughts by Their Gestures*. London: Sheldon Press.

Pescosolido, B. A. & Joseph, P. (1996). Americans' View of Mental Health and Illness at Century's End: Continuity and Change. Indiana Consortium of Mental Health Services Research, Columbia University.

Petrie, K., Chamberlain, K. & Clarke, D. (1988). Psychological predictors of future suicidal behaviour in hospitalised suicide attempters. *British Journal of Clinical Psychology*, **3**, 247–257.

Phillips, M. (2006). *Londonistan: How Britain is developing a terror state within*. London: Gibson Square.

Pirkis, J. & Burgess, P. (1998). Suicide and recency of health care contacts: A systematic review. *British Journal of Psychiatry*, **173**, 462–474.

Procter, H. G. & Walker, G. H. (1988). Brief Therapy. In E. Street & W. Dryden (Eds), *Family Therapy in Britain*, p. 133. Milton Keynes: Open University Press.

Quinnett, P.G. (1992). *Suicide: The Forever Decision*. New York: Crossroads.

Rajwal, M. & Gash, A. (2006). Risk assessment in self-harm. *Psychiatric Bulletin*, **30**, 436.

Reeves, A. & Mintz, R. (2001). Counsellors' experiences of working with suicidal clients: an exploratory study. *Counselling and Psychotherapy Research*, **1**, (3), 172–176.

Reinecke, M. (2000). Suicide and depression. In F. Dattilio & A. Freeman (Eds), *Cognitive-behavioural strategies in crisis intervention* (2nd edn), pp. 84–125. New York: Guilford Press.

Repper, J. (1999). A review of the literature on the prevention of suicide through interventions in Accident and Emergency Departments. *Journal of Clinical Nursing*, **8**, Issue 1, p. 3.

Rich, C. L., Warsadt, G. N., Neimorff, R. A., Fowler, R. C. & Young, D. (1991). Suicide, stressors and lifecycle. *American Journal of Psychiatry*, **148**, 524–527.

Richards, B. M. (2000). Impact upon therapy and therapist when working with suicidal patients: Some transference and counter transference aspects. *British Journal of Guidance & Counselling*. **8**, 3, 325–337.

Richman, J. & Eyman, J. R. (1990). Psychotherapy of suicide: individual, group and family approaches. In D. Lester (Ed), *Understanding suicide: the state of the* (date unknown).

Rihmer, Z. (1996). Strategies of suicide prevention: Focus on healthcare. *Journal of Affective Disorders,* **39**, 2, 83–91.

Rogers, C. R. (1951). *Client-Centred Therapy: Its current practice, implications and theory.* Boston: Houghton Mifflin.

Rogers, C. R. (1959). *A theory of therapy, personality, and interpersonal relationships, as developed in the client-centred framework.* In S. Koch (Ed.), *Psychology: A study of a science Vol. 3,* (pp. 184–256), New York: McGraw-Hill.

Rogers, C. R. (1967). *On becoming a person. A therapist's view of psychotherapy.* London: Constable.

Rosenthal, H. (1986). The learned helplessness syndrome. *Emotional First Aid,* **3** (2), 5–8.

Rossi, E. L. (Ed.) (1980). *Innovative Hypnotherapy by Milton H. Erickson. The collected papers of Milton H. Erickson on Hypnosis, Vol. IV,* p. 504. New York: Irvington Publishers.

Rubino, A., Roskell, N., Tennis, P., Mines, D. & Welch, S. & Andrews, E. (2006). The risk of suicide during treatment with Venlafaxine, Citalopram, Fluoxetine and Dothiepin: Retrospective cohort study. *BMJ,* **334**, 242.

Rudd, M., Joiner, T. & Rajab, M. (2001). *Treating suicidal behaviour.* New York: Guilford Press.

Rutz, W., von Knorring, L. & Walider, J. (1989) Frequency of suicide on Gotland after systematic postgraduate education of general practitioners. *Acta Psychiatrica Scandinavica,* **80,** 151–154.

Rutz, W., von Knorring, L. & Walider, J. (1992). Long-term effects of an educational programme for general practitioners given by the Swedish Committee for the Prevention and Treatment of Depression. *Acta Psychiatrica Scandinavica,* **85,** 83–88.

Schmidtke, A. et al. (1996). Attempted suicide in Europe. Rates, trends and socio-demographic characteristics of suicide attempters during the period 1989–1992. Results of the WHO EURO multicentre study on parasuicide. *Acta Psychiatrica Scandinavica,* **93**, 5, 327–338.

Scott, V. & Armson, S. Volunteers and Suicide Prevention. In K. Hawton & K. van Heeringen (Eds), *The International Handbook of Suicide and Attempted Suicide.* Chichester: John Wiley & Sons.

Seligman, M. (1978). Comment and integration. *Journal of Abnormal Psychology,* **87**, 165–179.

Sharry, J., Darmody, M. & Madden, B. (2002). A solution focused approach to working with clients who are suicidal. *British Journal of Guidance & Counselling,* **30**, No. 4.

Sharry, J., Madden, B. & Darmody, M. (2001). *Becoming a Solution Detective.* London: B T Press.

Schneidman, E. (1981). Psychotherapy with suicidal patients. *Suicide & Life Threatening Behavior,* **11** (4), 341–348.

Schneidman, E. (1984). Aphorisms of suicide and some implications for psychotherapy. *American Journal of Psychotherapy,* **38** (3), 319–328.

Schneidman, E. S., (1993). Suicide as a psychache. *Journal of Nervous & Mental Disease,* **181** (3), 145–147.

Schneidman, E. S. (1999a). Psychotherapy with Suicidal Patients. In A. Lennaars (Ed.), *Lives and Deaths: Selections from the work of Edwin S. Schneidman* (pp. 363–371). Philadelphia: Brunner/Mazel.

Schneidman, E. S. (1999b). Aphorisms of Suicide and Some Implications for Psychotherapy. In A. Lennaars (Ed.), *Lives and Deaths: Selections from the work of Edwin S. Schneidman* (pp. 372–381).

Schneidman, E. (2001). Anodyne Therapy: Relieving the Patient's Psychache. In H. Rosenthal (Ed.), *Favourite Counselling and Therapy Homework Assignments*, pp. 180–183. Philadelphia: Taylor & Francis.

Siegler , M., Osmond, H. & Mann, H. (1972). Laing's models of madness. In R. Boyers & R. Orrill (Eds), *Laing and Anti-Psychiatry*. Harmondsworth: Penguin

Silverman, M. & Felner, R. D. (1995). The place of suicide prevention in the spectrum of intervention: Definitions of critical terms and constructs. *Suicide & Life Threatening Behavior*, **25**, 1, 70–81.

Silverman, M. & Maris, R. W. (1995). The prevention of suicidal behaviours: An overview. *Suicide & Life Threatening Behavior*, **25**, 1, 10–21.

Simon, R. I. (1988). *Concise guide to clinical psychiatry and the law*. Washington, DC: American Psychiatric Publishing.

Simon, R. I. (2002). Suicide risk assessment: what is the standard of care? *Journal of the American Academy of Psychiatry and the Law,* **30**, 340–342.

Simon, R. I. & Hales, R. (Eds) (2006). *Textbook of suicide assessment and management*. Washington, DC: American Psychiatric Publishing.

Snyder, C. R. (Ed) (2000). *Handbook of hope: Theory, measures and applications*. San Diego, CA: Academic Press.

Snyder, C. R., Michael, S. J. & Cheavens, J. (1999). Hope as a psychotherapeutic foundation of common factors, placebos, and experiences. In M. A. Hubble, B. Duncan & S. Miller (Eds), *Heart and soul of change* (pp. 179–200). Washington, DC: American Psychological Association.

Spirito, A. (1997). Individual therapy techniques with adolescent suicide attempters. *Crisis*, **18**, 62–64.

Spirito, A. (2001)

Steinberg and Steinberg (1987)

Steinberg, J. A. & Silverman, M. M. (1997). *Preventing mental disorders: a research perspective* (DHSS publication no: ADM. 87–1492) Rockville, MD: US Department of Health & Human Services.

Stenger, E. & Jensen, K. (1994). Attempted suicide and contact with the primary care authorities. *Acta Psychiatrica Scandinavica*, **90**, 109–113.

STORM (Risk assessment training)

Street, E. & Dryden, W. (Eds) (1988). Family Therapy in Britain. In H. Proctor & G. Walker, Chapter 6: *Brief Therapy,* p. 133. Milton Keynes: Open University Press.

Szasz, T. S. (1971). The ethics of suicide. *The Antioch Review*, **31**, 7–17.

Szasz, T. S. (1986). The case against suicide prevention. *American Psychologist*, **41**, 1, 806–812.

Tabatchnik, N. (1970). Most suicidal persons want to live. *Californian Medicine*, **112**, 1–8.

Tanny, B. (1995). Suicide prevention in Canada: A national's perspective highlighting progress and problems. *Suicide & Life Threatening Behavior,* **1**, 105–122.

Taylor, S., Rider, I., Turkington, D., Mackenzie, J. & Garside, M. (2006). Does a specialist team impact upon repetition rates and discharge outcomes following the first episode of self-harm? *Journal of Mental Health Practice*, **9** (7), 30–32.

Thase, M. E. & Jindal, R. D. (2004). Combining psychotherapy and psychopharmacology for treatment of mental disorders. In M. J. Lambert (Ed,), *Bergin & Garfields's Handbook of Psychotherapy and Behaviour Change* (5th edn). New York: John Wiley & Sons.

Truax, C. B. & Carkhuff, R. R. (1967). *Toward effective counselling and psychotherapy: Training and practice*. Chicago: Aldine.

Trimble, L., Jackson, K. & Harvey, D. (2000). Client suicidal behaviour: Impact, interventions and implications for psychologist. *Australian Psychologist, 35*, 3, 227–32.

Vassilas, C. A. & Morgan, H. G. (1993). General practitioners' contact with victims of suicide. *BMJ*, **307**, 300–301.

Verkes, R. J. & Cowan, P. J. (2000). Pharmacotherapy of Suicidal Ideation and Behaviour. In K. Hawton & K. van Heeringen (Eds), *The International Handbook of Suicide and Attempted Suicide*. Chichester: John Wiley & Sons.

Verkes, R. J., Van der Mast, R. C., Hengeveld, M. W., Tuyl, J. P., Zwinderman, A. H. & van Kempen, G. M. J. (1998). Reduction by paroxetine of suicidal behaviour in patients with repeated suicide attempts but not major depression. *American Journal of Psychiatry,* **155**, 543–547.

Watzlawick, P. (1978). *The language of change: elements of therapeutic communication*. New York: Basic Books.

Watzlawick, P., Weakland, J. H. & Fisch, R. (1974). *Change: principles of problem formation and problem resolution*. New York: Norton.

Weakland, J., Fisch, R., Watzlawick, P. & Bodin, A. (1974). Brief Therapy: Focused Problem Resolution. *Family Process*, **13**, 141–168.

Weiner-Davis, M., de Shazer, S. & Gingerich, W. (1987). Building on pre-treatment change to construct the therapeutic solution. *Journal of Marital Family Therapy*, **13**, 4, 359–363.

Whitaker, C. (1973). My Philosophy of Psychotherapy. *Journal of Contemporary Psychotherapy*, **6**, 49–52.

Whitfield, W. & Southern, D. (1996). The prevention of suicide: some practical steps. *Journal of the Royal Society for the Promotion of Health*, **116**, 5, 295–298.

Wikipedia (2008). www.wikipedia.org/wiki/Hope

Williams, D. (2007). Suicide Assessment; Suicide Treatment. From Internet site: www.peaceandhealing.com/suicide_treatment

Wilstrand, C, Lindgren, B. M., Gilje, F. & Olufsson, B. (2007). Being burdened and balancing boundaries: A qualitative study of nurses' experiences caring for patients who self-harm. *Journal of Psychiatric and Mental Health Nursing, 14* (1), 72–78.

Woollams, S., Brown, M. & Huige, K. (1977). What transactional analysts want their clients to know. In G. Barnes (Ed.), *Transactional analysis after Eric Berne* (pp. 487–525). New York: Harper's College Press.

World Health Organization (WHO) (1989). *World health statistics annual (1998)*. Geneva: WHO.

World Health Organization (WHO) (1996). *World health statistics annual (1995)*. Geneva: WHO.

World Health Organization (WHO) (2000). Suicide. www.who.int/health_topics/suicide/en/

World Health Organization (WHO) (2005). World Health Organization — European Ministerial Conference on Mental Health. www.euro.who.nt/mentalhealth/topics

Yufit, R. I. & Lester, D. (2005). *Assessment, treatment and prevention of suicidal behaviour*. New York: John Wiley & Sons.

Zunin, L. (1972). *Contact: The First Four Minutes*. London: Talmy Franklin.

Author Index

Abrahamson, L. Y. 56
Adams, J. F. 110
Aldridge, D. 5, 18, 34, 38
Allmore, D. 57
Alloy, C. B. 56
American Psychiatric Association (APA) 193
Andrews, E. 42
APA (American Psychiatric Association) 193
Appleby, L. 15, 19, 35
Applied Suicide Intervention Skills Training (ASIST) 124, 141
Armson, S. 12, 24
Armstrong, H. E. 57
Aro, H. M. 21, 25, 37
ASIST (Applied Suicide Intervention Skills Training) 124, 141
Auerbach, A. 49, 114
Azim, H. 49

Baldessarini, R. J. 41
Barraclough, B. 18

Barraclough, B. M. 190, 191
Battegay, C. 41
Baumeister, R. F. 108
Beadle, S. 98, 99, 187
Beck, A. T. 51, 52, 53, 56, 58
Beck, J. S. 52
Beck, R. 51, 58
Berg, I. K. 14, 67, 72, 90, 96, 104
Bergman, E. 58
Berne, E. 61, 63
Blauner, S. R. 2
Bodin, A. 38
Bongar, B. 19
Bonner, R. 51
Bostock, T. 54
Brandsma, J. 54
Brent, D. A. 20
Bridges, K. 20
Brief Therapy Family Centre 90, 96
Brown, G. K. 52, 56
Brown, M. 61
Bunch, J. 18
Burgess, P. 18

Burns, D. D. 114
Bums, K. 14, 68, 188
Burton, R. H. 20
Bushman, B. J. 108
Buzan, R. 36

Camus, A. 5
Carkhuff, R. R. 10
Chamberlain, K. 52
Cheavens, J. 138, 140
Chiles, J. A. 24
Claridge, G. C. 53
Clarke, D. 52
Conwell, Y. 19
Cowan, P. J. 36, 40
Crompton, J. 24
Crumbaugh, J. C. 65, 66
Cutter, H. S. G. 54

Dahlsgaard, K. K. 52
Darmody, M. 31, 188, 198
Davis 23
de Jong, P. 104
de Shazer, S. 67, 68, 69, 71, 72, 73, 75,
    79, 104, 108
Department of Education and Skills 13,
    14
Department of Health 14, 19, 32, 37,
    192, 195
Diekstra, R. F. 16, 17, 19, 26, 40, 58,
    191, 194
Dolan. Y. 14, 68, 143, 145, 163
Domino, G. 20, 37
Dukas, H. E. 64
Durkheim, E. 23
Dyck, R. 49

Egan, G. 50, 51
Einstein, A, 64
Ellis, A. 58
Ellis, T. E. 57, 58
Encarta 23
Encyclopaedia Britannica 23

Engels, G. I. 58
Erickson, M. H. 34, 89, 98, 99
European Brief Therapy Association 13

Fagg, J. 190
Farber, S. S. 25
Farrelly, F. 54
Felner, R. D. 25
Fisch, R. 38, 67
Fiske, H. 139, 140
Fowler, F. G. 25
Fowler, H. W. 25
Frankl, V. E. 34, 54, 64, 65, 66
Freeling, P. 20
Freeman, A. 51
Freud, S. 59, 64
Furman, B. 171

Garside, M. 33
George, E. 187
Gilje, F. 20
Gingerich, W. 67, 69
Goldberg, D. 20
Goodenough, D. D. 54
Gresham, F. M. 54
Griffiths, S. 37, 39, 121
Grisham, J. R. 52, 56
Gunnell, D. 11, 12, 18

Haley, J. 34
Hamelinck, L. 48
Harmatz, M. 19
Harrison, S. 20
Harvey, D. 8, 37
Hawton, K. 11, 24, 35, 36, 37, 39, 121,
    190, 193, 198
HealthCare Evaluation Unit
    (HCEU) 42
Healthopedia 32
Heard, H. L. 11, 13, 57
Heikkinen, M. E. 21, 25, 37
Henden, J. 14, 16, 124, 136
Hengeveld, M. W. 42

Henricksson, M. M. 21, 25, 37
Herman, J. 51
HM Stationary Office (HMSO) 32
Hoffman, B. 64
Huige, K. 61
Hurding, R. F. 10

Isebaert, L. 55
Isometsa, E. T. 21, 25, 36, 37
Israeli 29
Iveson, C. 187

Jackson, K. 8, 37
Jacob, F. 14, 68, 187
Jansson, L. 54
Jason, L. A. 25
Jenkins, R. 37, 39, 121
Jennings, C. 190
Jensen, K. 18
Jobes, D. A. 35, 53
Joiner, T. 51, 115, 117, 118
Joseph, P. 45
Joyce, A. 49
Jung, C. G. 64
Jurich, J. A. 110

Kalafat, J. 48
Karasu, T. B. 48
Kelly, G. A. 55
Kim, J. 107
Kohlenberg, R. J. 54
Korn, H-P. 14
Kovacs, M. 51, 52
Kratochvil 65
Kuoppasalmi, K. I. 21, 25, 37

Laing, R. D. 42
Leenaars, A. A. 24, 48, 49, 50
Lester, D. 29, 55, 60
Lindgren, B. M. 20
Linehan, M. M. 55, 56, 57, 109
Lipchik, E. 71, 72
Litman, R. E. 60

Lomax, J. 19
Long, A. 20
Lonnqvist, J. K. 21, 25, 37
Luborski, L. 49
Lueger, G. 14

Macdonald, A. J. 68, 74,
    188, 190
Macdonald, Alastair, 12, 190
Mackenzie, J. 33
Madden, B. 31, 188, 198
Maholick, L, T. 65
Malmberg, A. F. 190
Mann, H. 42
Mans, R. W. 12, 19, 25,
    26, 189
Marx. E. M. 53
McGaughey, J. 20
McLaughlin, C. 24, 193
McLellan, A. 49
Mehrabian, A. 1ll, 126
Meninger, K. 59
Metalsky, G. I. 56
Methorst, G. J. 58
Michael, S. J. 138, 140
Michel, K. 11, 18, 24,
    36, 191
Miller, A. L. 57
Miller, S. D. 14
Milner, J. 14
Milton, J. 9, 24
Milton, M. 24
Mines, D. 42
Minkoff, K. 58
Mintz, R. 9, 192
Modestin, J. 42
Morgan, H. G. 18, 19, 20, 37, 39, 191,
    193
Moritsugu, J. N. 25
Moss, J. R. 190
Murphy, G. E. 18, 37, 191
Murray, H. A. 59
Myers, S. 14

National Electronic Library for Health
(NeLMH) 38, 41
Nelson, B. 18
Newman, C. F. 58
Norman, H. 71
Nunnally, E. 72

O'Brien, C. 49
O'Byrne, P. 14
O'Connell, B. 68, 188
O'Farrell, T. J. 54
O'Hanlon, W. H. 67, 69, 70, 79, 98, 99,
187
Olufsson, B. 20
Orton, J. D, 62
Osmond, H. 42

Palazzoli, M. S. 38
Paykel, E. S. 20
Peacock, F. 87, 97, 104
Pease, A. 111
Pescosolido, B. A. 45
Petrie, K. 52
Phillips, M. 30
Piercy, F. P. 110
Pirkis, J. 18
Planova 65
Priest, P. 20, 37
Procter, H. G. 68

Quinnett, P. G. 2

Rajab, M. 51, 115, 117, 118
Rao, B. M. 20
Ratcliff, K. 58
Rathus, J. H. 57
Ratner, H. 187
Reeves, A. 9, 192
Reich 52
Reinecke, M. 25, 51
Repper, J. 19
Rich, A. 51
Richards, B. M. 8

Rider, I. 33
Rogers, C. R. 9, 48, 49, 50, 113, 122
Rosenthal, H. 54, 55
Roskell, N. 42
Ross, J. 74, 190
Rossi, E. L. 34
Rossiter, J. 34, 38
Rubino, A. 42
Rudd, M. 51, 115, 117, 118
Rutz, W. 12

Schneidman, E. S. 24, 49, 56, 115
Schwarzenbach, F. 42
Schyler, D. 51
Scott, V. 12, 24
Seligman, M. 25
Sharry, J. 31, 188, 198
Siegler, M. 42
Silverman, M. 12, 25, 26, 189
Simkin, S. 190
Simon, R. I. 6, 115
Sineting, C. I. 20
Snyder, C. R. 138, 140
Southern, D. 20, 25, 33, 34
Stack, A. D. 108
Steer, R. A. 52, 56
Stenger, E. 18
Strosahl, K. 24
Suarez, A. 57
Swain, B. J. 20, 37

Tabatclmik, N. 18
Taylor, L. 139, 140
Taylor, S. 33
TCRU (Thomas Coram Research Unit)
195
Tennis, P. 42
Thomas Coram Research Unit (TCRU)
195
Trimble, L. 8, 37
Truax, C. B. 10
Tsai, M. 54
Turkington, D. 33

Tuyl, J. P. 42
Tylee, A. 37, 39, 121

Van der Mast, R. C. 42
van Heeringen, K. 11, 24, 35, 36, 193, 198
Vassilas, C. A. 19, 191
Verkes, R. J. 36, 40, 42
von Knotting, L. 12

Walider, J. 12
Walker, G. H. 68
Watzlawick, P. 38, 67
Weakland, J. 38, 67
Weiner-Davis, M. 67, 69
Weissberg, M. P. 36
Weissman, A. 51, 52
Welch, S. 42
Whitaker, C. 34

Whitfield, W. 20, 25, 33, 34
WHO (World Health Organization) 16, 17, 193
Wikipedia 138
Williams, C. L. 54
Williams, D. 32, 38
Williams, J. M. G. 53
Wilstrand, C. 20
Woody, G. 49
Woollams, S. 61
World Health Organization (WHO) 16, 17, 193
Wylie, I. 37, 39, 121

Yufit, R. I. 29, 55, 60

Zilboorg, G. 59
Zunin, L. 109, 111
Zwinderman, A. H. 42

Subject Index

Note: SFBT = solution focused brief therapy

A&E Departments 19–20, 189–90
ABC model 58–9
abuse survivors 7, 14, 27–8
    see also trauma survivors
acceptance
    dialectical behaviour therapy 56, 57
    therapeutic relationship 10, 113
access points to services 26, 189–91
Accident & Emergency Departments
        19–20, 189–90
acknowledgment 91, 92, 98, 100–1,
        108, 117
addiction 73
adolescents
    dialectical behaviour therapy 57–8
    wise old you question 143
affirming questions 71, 73, 97, 137–8
aggression 55
alcohol abuse 14, 17, 81, 145
Alex, case study 180–2
anger 54–5, 146, 147–8
antidepressants 36, 40–2, 194–5
anxiety, practitioners' 9
assertiveness skills 55

assessment of suicide risk 20–1, 31–7,
        123–30, 198
attempted suicide
    definition 24
    intervention effectiveness 11–12, 190
    lessons to be learned from 18, 52
    mental health policy 15
    World Health Organization 16
awfulisation 58

baby (small) steps, SFBT 88–9,
        148–9
Barry, case study 178–9
Beck Hopelessness Scale (BHS)
        51–2
behaviour therapy *see* cognitive behav-
        ioural therapy
biological model, depression 25, 64–5
    see also medical model
blinkered thinking 49, 56, 118, 132
bridging statements 101–2
brief therapy 67–8
    solution focused *see* solution focused
        brief therapy

care-givers *see* practitioners
care plans, Culverhay CMHC 39–40
case studies 151–88
cat and mouse game 145
catastrophisation 58
catharsis 108
change
    dialectical behaviour therapy 56, 57
    solution focused theory of 68–71
child abuse survivors 7, 27–8
child neglect
    author's experience 7
    case study of Reg 151–76
client-centred therapy *see* person-
        centred counselling
clients
    case studies 151–88
    collaboration in therapy 39, 50–1
    encounters with practitioners *see*
        therapeutic encounters
    lead in SFBT 103, 104, 106
    'radar' 9, 10, 110–11, 112
    relationship with practitioner *see*
        therapeutic relationship
    SFBT *see* solution focused brief
        therapy
clinicians *see* practitioners
clues, SFBT 96–7, 102–3, 130–8
cognitive behavioural therapy (CBT)
        51–5
    dialectical behaviour therapy 55–8
    rational emotive behaviour therapy
        58–9
cognitive constriction 49, 56
cognitive restructuring 53
collaboration, clinician–client 39, 50–1
    see also therapeutic relationship
communication 6–7
    dialectical behaviour therapy 57
    of hope 139–40
    non-verbal 6–7, 111–12, 113, 123–4,
        126–8
    suicidal intent 123–8
    training 193
    transactional analysis 62–3

community institutionalisation 46
Community Mental Health Centres
        (CMHCs) 39–40
competence, practitioners' 8–9, 193
compliments 90–1, 100
confidence
    communication of 118–19
    scaling 88
congruence, suicide intent 123–8,
        129–30
contracts, therapy 54
control
    loss of 128, 138
    self-harm and 27
conversational flow 107, 187
coping questions 84
cost effectiveness, suicide prevention
        12–14, 175
counselling, person-centred *see* person-
        centred counselling
counselling skills training 193
counsellors *see* practitioners
crematorium scenario question 144–5,
        181–2
crisis interventionists 21
crisis interventions
    access points 26, 189–91
    cognitive behavioural 53–4
    rational emotive behaviour therapy 58
    SFBT 122–3
crucial first ten minutes 109–19, 122–3,
        213
cutting (self-harm) 27

deathbed scenario (DBS) 145–6
deep empathy 113–14, 122–3
degrimming 99–100, 183
deliberate self-harm 27–8
depression 194–5
    antidepressants 36, 40–2, 194–5
    cognitive behavioural therapy 51–2,
        56, 58
    definition 25
    dialectical behaviour therapy 56
    endogenous 64–5

rational emotive behaviour therapy 58
research evidence for interventions
    12, 41
suicide risk assessment 20, 21, 31,
    35, 36, 123–30
trough of 127
World Health Organization 16, 17
despair, practitioners' 140
    see also hopelessness
dialectical behaviour therapy (DBT)
    55–8
distress
    defining suicide 23, 24
    practitioners' 9
doctors *see* general practitioners
double blind trials 14, 196–7
drug abuse 73, 145
drug therapy 40–2, 194–5
    self-poisoning with 18, 40, 194
    suicide risk assessment 36
dual awareness exercise 156

eating disorders 14
ego states 61–3
emotional abuse 7
emotional dysregulation 56
    see also pain, psychological
empathy 10, 113–14, 122–3
empowering questions, SFBT 71, 73,
    97, 137–8
empowerment 99, 140–1, 170, 175
endogenous depression 64–5
evidence-based practice *see* research
    evidence
exceptions to problems, SFBT 84–5
existential logotherapy 64–6
eye contact 126

facial expressions 128
fast-forwarding the video technique 82,
    83
feelings tank 146–8
financial costs, suicide prevention
    12–14, 175
5 o'clock rule 80

flashbacks 70–1, 156–7
formula first session task (FFST) 69,
    76–7, 97, 110
free association 59
functional analytic therapy 54

game playing 63, 145
general practitioners (GPs)
    research evidence 12
    suicide after contact with 18, 19, 20
    suicide risk assessment 20, 37
    training 190
genuineness, practitioners' 9–10, 113
goal development, SFBT 81–2, 138–9
going with the client 98, 153, 175
Gotland Study 12
government policy, mental health
    14–16, 195
graveside scenario question 144–5,
    181–2
guaranteeing against suicide principle
    130–1
guilt 59, 65

healing letters exercise 163–7, 172
health professionals *see* practitioners
healthier nation policy 14–16
helpers *see* practitioners
helping model 50–1
helplessness
    learned 54
    practitioners' 8–9
helplines 189–90, 192–3
homework *see* tasks
hope
    cognitive behavioural therapy 52–3,
        55, 57, 64
    practitioners' 8–9, 139–40
    SFBT 117, 138–40
hope kits 53
hopelessness
    cognitive behavioural therapy 51–3,
        56, 57, 58
    practitioners' 140
    SFBT 117, 118, 140

hospital admissions 38–9, 190–2
humour, degrimming 99–100, 183

incongruence, suicide intent 123–8, 129–30
interpretation, psychoanalysis 60
interventions *see* preventive interventions

Josephine, case study 182–5
joyfulness, superficial 126–7

keys, SFBT 96–7, 102–3, 130–8

learned helplessness 54
lethality, risk assessment 20–1, 32, 51
life, meaning in 64–6
logotherapy 64–6

magic wand technique 82–3
manualised approaches 197
meaning in life 64–6
medical model 42–6, 198
medication 18, 36, 40–2, 194–5
mental health policy 14–16, 195
mental health practitioners *see* practitioners
mental health services *see* service provision
mental ill-health, medical model 43–6
metaphors, SFBT 94–5
mindfulness 55
miracle question (MQ) technique 80–1, 82, 83, 84–5, 87, 141–3, 154, 184–5
motivation, scaling 87–8
multi-modal therapies 48–9, 56, 198

national prevention targets 16, 195
National Service Frameworks 15, 16
negative beliefs, measurement 51–2
negative thinking 118
    see also hopelessness
non-possessive warmth 10

non-verbal communication 6–7
    crucial first ten minutes 111–12, 113
    of hope 139
    suicidal intent 123–4, 126–8
noögenic neurosis 64, 65
normalisation, SFBT 92, 108, 117, 136–7, 138

optimism 118, 138
outcomes, evidence base *see* research evidence
overdoses, prescribed drugs 18, 40, 194

pain, psychological
    causal pathways 56
    definition of suicide 23, 24
    existential logotherapy 65
    person-centred therapy 49–50
paradox, small steps 88–9
paradoxical intention 34–5, 54, 65, 92–3
paraphrasing client's language 95–6, 193
patients *see* clients
person-centred counselling 48–51
    therapeutic relationship 9–10, 48, 49–50
personal hygiene 127
personality disorders 57
pessimism 118
Peter, case study 179–80
political suicides 28–9, 30
possibility generation, SFBT 98–9
postural clues, suicidal intent 126
practitioners
    competence 8–9, 193
    encounters with clients *see* therapeutic encounters
    qualities 9–10
    relationship with clients *see* therapeutic relationship
    skills 15, 50–1, 193
    training 190, 192–4, 195
        in empathy 114
        mental health policy 15

SFBT 107, 220
suicide risk assessment 37
therapeutic relationship 18–19, 119
use of book 1–2
pre-session change, SFBT 69, 73, 134–5
presuppositional language 71, 89–90,
97, 110, 130–2, 137–9, 143–4
prevention, definition 25–7
preventive interventions 37–40
pharmacological *see* medication
psychotherapeutic *see* psychotherapy
research evidence 11–12, 38, 41,
196–7
secondary prevention 26
World Health Organization 16–17
primary care
access points 26, 189–90
mental health policy 15, 16
suicide after contact with 18, 19, 20,
21, 191
suicide risk assessment 20, 21, 36, 37
see also general practitioners
primary prevention, definition 26
problem focused therapy 67, 103, 177,
195–6, 198
solution focused alternative *see*
solution focused brief therapy
(SFBT)
problem-free talk (PFT) 75, 77–9, 112
problem land 79–80
problem solving
CBT technique 53
dialectical behaviour therapy 57
SFBT compared 104
psychache 24, 56
see also pain, psychological
psychiatrists 18, 20–1, 37
psychoanalytic therapy 59–61
see also transactional analysis
psychotherapy 47–68
cognitive behavioural 51–9
dialectical behaviour 55–8
existential logotherapy 64–6
person-centred 48–51

psychoanalytic 59–61
rational emotive behaviour 58–9
research evidence 11–12, 196–7
solution focused *see* solution focused
brief therapy (SFBT)
transactional analysis 61–3
psychotropic medication 40, 41
purpose in life (P-I-L) 65, 66

'radar', clients' 9, 10, 110–11, 112
randomised controlled trials 11
rapport building 9–10, 113, 114, 115,
122–3, 213
rational emotive behaviour therapy
(REBT) 58–9
Reg, case study 151–76
research evidence 11–12, 38, 41, 196–7
resources
cost of suicide prevention 12–14, 175
identification of personal 53
risk assessment 20–1, 31–7, 123–30,
198
risk factors 35–6
risk management 37–40, 198

Samaritans 24, 190
Saving Lives: Our Healthier Nation
14–16
scaling tool, SFBT 85–8, 133–5, 154–5
secondary care 189–92
mental health policy 15, 16
risk assessment 20–1, 36–7
risk management 38
suicide after contact with 18, 19–21,
191
secondary prevention, definition 26–7
self-harm, definition 27–8
self-punishment 59
service provision 31–46
access points 26, 189–91
medical model 42–6, 198
medication 40–2
mental health policy 16, 195
prevention targets 16, 195

service provision (*continued*)
  quality 191–2
  risk assessment 31–7
  risk factors 35–6
  risk management 37–40, 198
service users *see* clients
sexual abuse survivors 14, 27–8
silence, use of 83
Simon, case study 185–7
skills
  clients' 53, 54, 75, 97, 140
  practitioners' 15, 50–1, 192–3
small steps, SFBT 88–9, 148–9
social skills training 54
solution focused brief therapy (SFBT)
        67–108, 195–8
  case studies 151–88
  catharsis 108
  clients' feelings 108, 146–8
  conversational flow 107, 187
  cost effectiveness 13–14, 175
  crucial first ten minutes 109–19,
        122–3, 213
  evidence base 196–7
  focus on the positives 105–6
  guiding principles 72–5
  key points 149–50
  manualised approach 197
  myths about 102–8
  number of episodes of 104–5
  origins 67–8
  pre-session change 69, 73, 134–5
  starting the first session 112–14,
        122–3
  sticking plaster criticism 102–3,
        106–7
  theory of change 68–71
  tools and techniques 76–102, 107,
        122–49, 213–19
    acknowledgment 91, 92, 98,
        100–1, 108, 117
    assessing suicidal intent 123–30
    bridging statements 101–2
    clues 96–7, 102–3, 130–8

compliments 90–1, 100
deathbed scenario 145–6
degrimming 99–100, 183
eliciting suicidal ideation 128–30,
        182–3, 186–7
end of session tasks 101–2, 148–9
exceptions to the problem 84–5
fast-forwarding the video 82, 83
feelings tank 146–8
formula first session task 69, 76–7,
        97, 110
goal development 81–2, 138–9
hearing out the problem 79–80,
        105
keys 96–7, 102–3, 130–8
magic wand 82–3
metaphors 94–5
miracle question 80–1, 82, 83,
        84–5, 87, 141–3, 154, 184–5
normalisation 92, 108, 117, 136–7,
        138
paradoxical intention 92–3
possibility generation 98–9
presuppositional language 71,
        89–90, 97, 110, 130–2, 137–9,
        143–4
problem-free talk 75, 77–9, 112
question examples 128–49
rapport building 122–3, 213
scaling 85–8, 133–5, 154–5
session ending 100–2
small steps 88–9, 148–9
stories 93–4
using the client's language 95–6
validation 91–2, 101, 108, 117
wise old you question 143–4
worst case scenario 144–5, 181–2
training 107, 220
solution forced therapy 103
solution land 79–80
specialist mental health services *see*
        secondary care
stigma 45
'Stop!' technique 70

stories, SFBT 93–4
stress, practitioners' 9
substance abuse 16, 17, 81, 145
suffering, existential logotherapy 65
suicidal ideation
    continuum of 33–4
    questions to elicit 128–30, 182–3,
        186–7
    scale of 51
    see also suicidal intent, assessment
suicidal intent, assessment 20–1, 31–7,
        123–30, 198
suicidality, use of term 24
suicide, definition 23–5
suicide attempters *see* attempted suicide
suicide bombers 29–30
suicide encounters *see* therapeutic
        encounters
Suicide Intent Scale (SIS) 51
suicide mode 52
suicide option 7–8, 24, 28, 52, 53, 129,
        136–7, 170
suicide prevention, definition 25–7
suicide rates
    UK mental health policy 15, 16, 195
    World Health Organization 16–17
suicide risk *see* risk assessment; risk
        management
suicidology 2, 24

task forces 16, 17
tasks, SFBT 69, 76–7, 97, 101–2, 110,
        148–9
telephone helplines 189–90, 192–3
terrorism, suicide bombers 29–30
tertiary prevention, definition 26
therapeutic alliance 114–15
therapeutic conversations, flow 107, 187
therapeutic empathy 114
therapeutic encounters
    crucial first ten minutes 6–7, 8, 9, 10,
        109–19, 122–3, 213
    practitioners' feelings 8–9
    risk assessment 20–1, 36–7, 123–30

suicide committed after 17–21, 119,
        191
    see also psychotherapy; solution
        focused brief therapy (SFBT);
        therapeutic relationship
therapeutic relationship
    building 9–10, 113, 114–19, 122–3,
        213
    importance 114–15
    person-centred counselling 9–10, 48,
        49–50
    research evidence 11
    training for 18–19, 119, 193
therapists *see* practitioners
therapy contracts 54
training 190, 192–4, 195
    in empathy 114
    mental health policy 15
    SFBT 107, 220
    suicide risk assessment 37
    therapeutic relationship 18–19,
        119
transactional analysis (TA) 61–3
transference 60
trauma survivors, solution focused
        therapy 14, 70–1
    see also abuse survivors; Reg, case
        study
treatment, definition 25–7
    pharmacological *see* medication
    psychotherapeutic *see*
        psychotherapy
    see also preventive interventions
trust, development 115–16, 213
24-hour helplines 189–90, 192–3

unconditional positive regard 10, 113
unconscious, the 59, 60, 61

validation
    SFBT 91–2, 101, 108, 117
    strategies 55
very, very small steps 148–9
video fast-forwarding technique 82, 83

warmth, practitioners' 10
will to meaning 64, 65
wise old you (WOY) question
    143–4
workers *see* practitioners
working relationship *see* therapeutic
    relationship

World Health Organization (WHO)
    16–17, 193–4
worst case scenario question 99, 144–5,
    181–2

youth suicide 17
    see also adolescents